USAGI ™
YOJIMBO
Book Three

USAGI ^{T.M.}

YOJIMBO

Book Three

By STAN SAKAI

FANTAGRAPHICS BOOKS

Seattle, Washington

To Tsuyoshi and Agnes Ota,
whose daughter married
a cartoonist.

FANTAGRAPHICS BOOKS
7563 Lake City Way N.E.
Seattle, WA 98115

Design and Production by Mark Thompson
Edited by Kim Thompson
Production assistance by Roberta Gregory and Loren Trayes

The stories in this volume originally appeared in *Usagi Yojimbo* #7-12 and *Turtle Soup.*

First Fantagraphics Books Edition, July, 1989
Second Fantagraphics Books Edition: June, 1995
Third Fantagraphics Books Edition: April, 1999

ISBN (hardcover edition): 1-56097-147-9
ISBN (softcover edition): 1-56097-146-0

Printed in Canada by Ronald's/Quebecor

CONTENTS

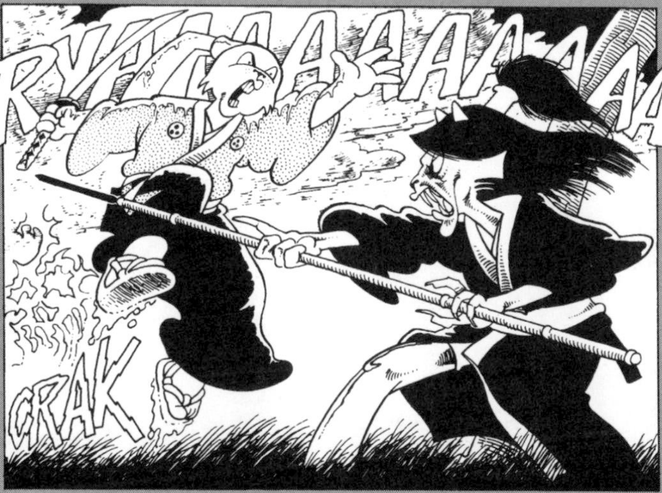
RYAAAAAAAAAAAAA
CRAK

INTRODUCTION

For me, one of the greatest things about having some of my work adapted into graphic form was that it gave me, being basically a novelist, a perfectly legitimate reason to associate and converse with many professionals in a field which has always fascinated me. . .to wit, comics and graphics.

Such it was as Valentino and I drove up and down Southern California a few years back on a promotional tour for the *MythAdventures* comic. Aside from the usual comparing of business notes on pay scales and contract terms that all creatives indulge in when their paths cross, I was intensely curious about his views on graphic storytelling. . .a subject I had barely scratched the surface of.

One question I recall specifically asking him was: "why funny animals?" I mean, why was there this apparent obsession with using talking, humanized animals for one's characters instead of using "regular people" as focal points for the story. Though we kicked it around at length, returning to the topic several times during the tour, to my recollection we never *did* come up with a satisfactory answer.

It wasn't until several months later, in fact, that something struck me. . .I mean, *all* the classic cartoon characters are animals! Whether we're looking at Mickey and Donald or Bugs and Daffy, Foghorn, Scrooge McDuck, the whole pack, we're looking at "animals." What many of the cartoonists of today are trying to do is follow in the footsteps of the greats who have gone before! To me, however, the interesting thing is that throughout my study of the field and my conversations with Val, I didn't (and still don't) think of Bugs or Foghorn as *animals*! They're *characters*. . .and therein lies the telling difference.

All too often, the "wannabe" artists fall back on funny-animals as an easy out to avoid character development. I mean, the fact that an armadillo can talk and wear pajamas should be enough to amaze and amuse the reader. . . right? [NOTE: If there is a comic or strip out there which uses an armadillo, I didn't know about it and as such this comment should not be taken as a slur or critique of that specific work. I specifically tried to cite an animal not currently "in use" so I could make my point without singling any one artist or project out for condemnation or ridicule.] Unfortunately, today's reader is far too sophisticated to make that statement true. To avoid the pitfall of anonymity, the graphic artist must be as much a storyteller as an artist to hope to catch and hold the attention of even the smallest slice of the audience.

All of which brings us to Stan Sakai.

When I first met Stan at the San Diego Comic Con in 1988 and tried to compliment him on his work, he modestly down-played it, insisting that "all [he was] doing [was] retelling some of the old samurai adages and ghost stories in comic form."

Uh huh. That's *all*, eh?

"Re-telling" a story is a deceptive task. (In fact, on the rare occasions I work with young writers, one of the assignments I give is to have them re-tell "Cinderella" *their* way.) To catch the essence of *any* familiar story, much less ones with as subtle and complex philosophies and lessons as the tales Stan targets, is a challenge. It's only when it's done well that it looks easy. In his novel *Shogun*, James Clavell gave Westerners an insight and understanding of Japanese history and philosophies. It also took him over a thousand pages of fine print text to do it. . .using a Western viewpoint character at that. Stan does the same thing in 28-page segments. His characters are characters first, with clear and well-defined personalities and foibles, and their images grow naturally from those concepts. That is, Stan doesn't simply use a lion-figure as a lazy means of telling the reader the character is noble, Katsuichi *is* noble. . .both in character and bearing. Throughout the series, Stan's considerable artistic talents are simply a means by which his stories, characters, and concepts are communicated to the reader. . .rather than his stories and characters being the excuse to showcase his art.

Just as Usagi has learned that swordsmanship is more than fighting, Stan has obviously learned that art is more than just drawing. The entire field would be richer if more artists embraced this lesson.

—**ROBERT L. ASPRIN**
1989

CHAPTER ONE

"The Tower"

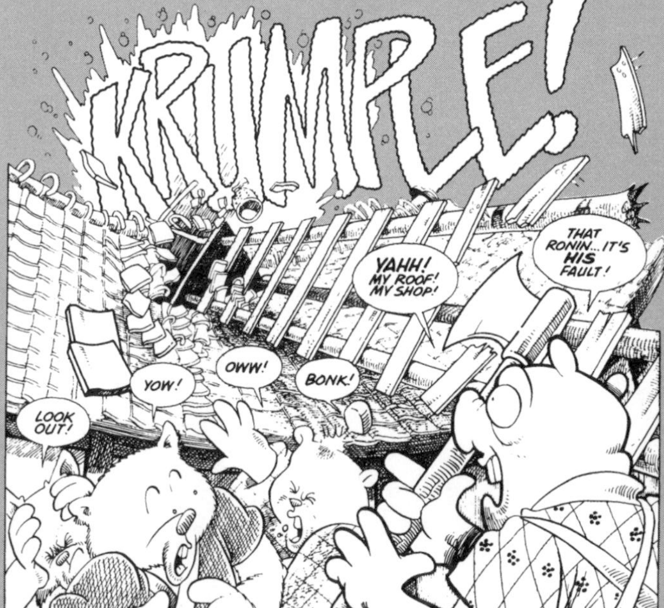
KRUMPLE!
THAT RONIN... IT'S HIS FAULT!
YAHH! MY ROOF! MY SHOP!
BONK!
OWW!
YOW!
LOOK OUT!

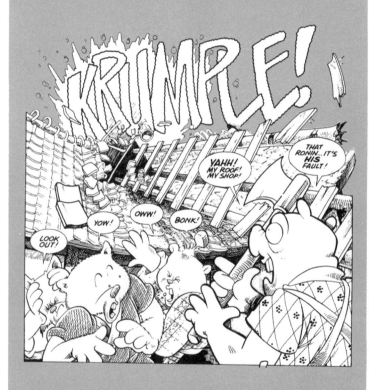

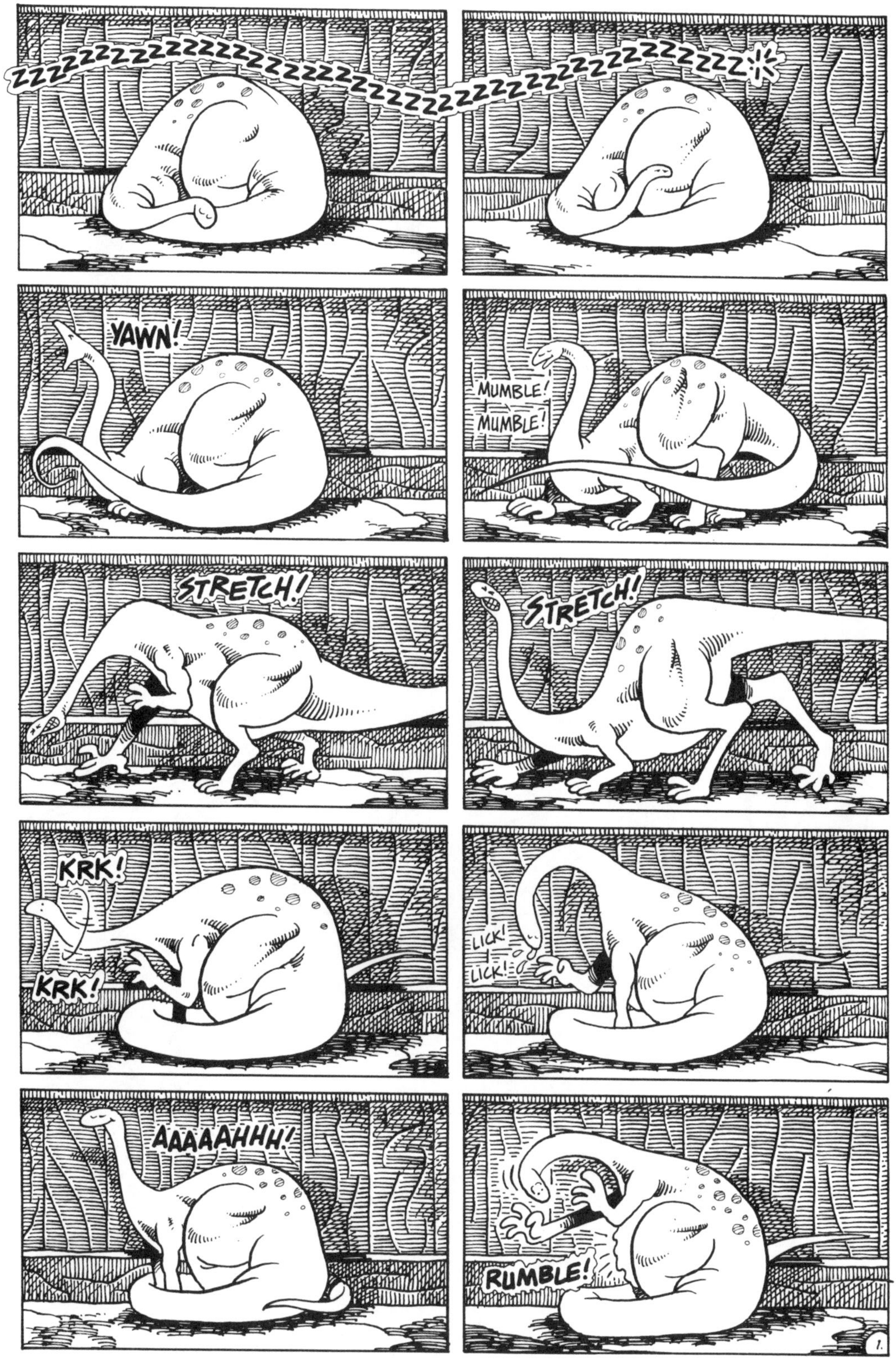
ZZZZZZZZZZZZZZZZZZZZZZZZZZZZZZZZZZZZZZZZZZZZZZZ
YAWN!
MUMBLE!
MUMBLE!
STRETCH!
STRETCH!
KRK!
KRK!
LICK!
LICK!
AAAAAHHH!
RUMBLE!
1.

4

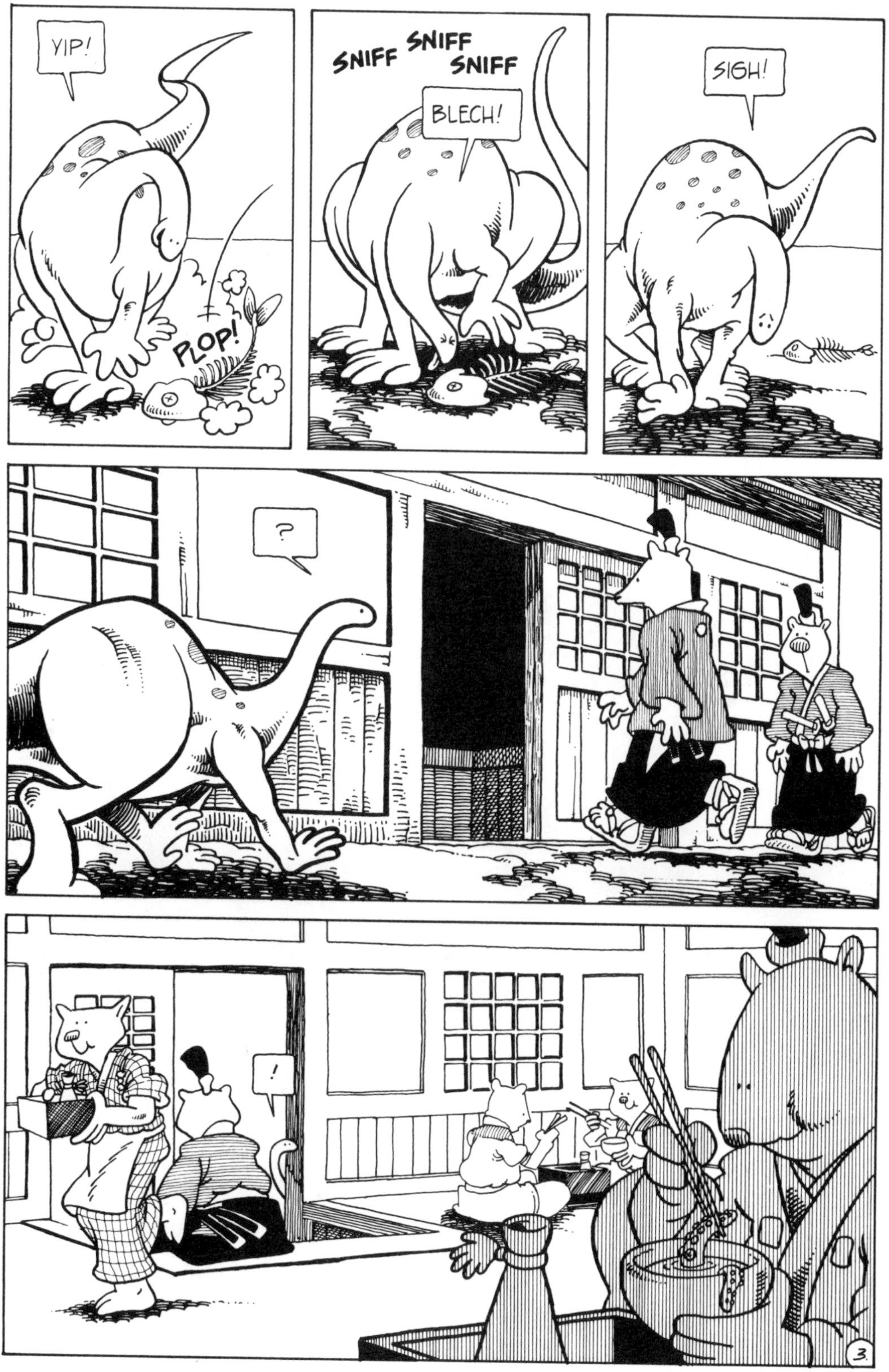
YIP!
PLOP!
SNIFF SNIFF SNIFF
BLECH!
SIGH!
?
!
3.

EEP?
HEY!
!
YIPE!
SO YOU AGAIN, EH? ALWAYS COMING IN AND STEALING MY CUSTOMERS' FOOD!
WELL, THIS IS THE LAST TIME IT'S GOING TO HAPPEN!
?
ULP!
I'M GOING TO GET RID OF YOU IF IT'S THE LAST THING I DO!
COME BACK HERE, YOU!
EEK!
4

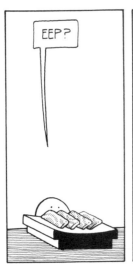

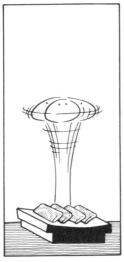

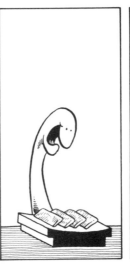

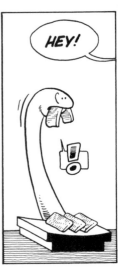

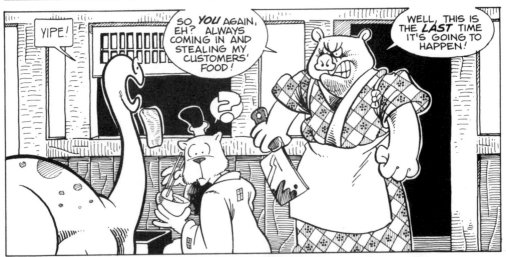

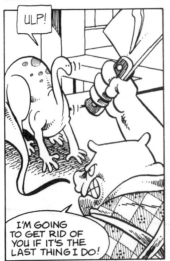

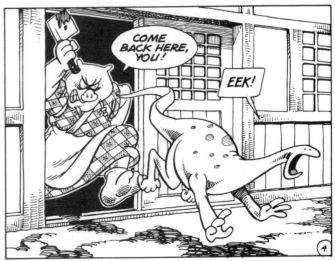

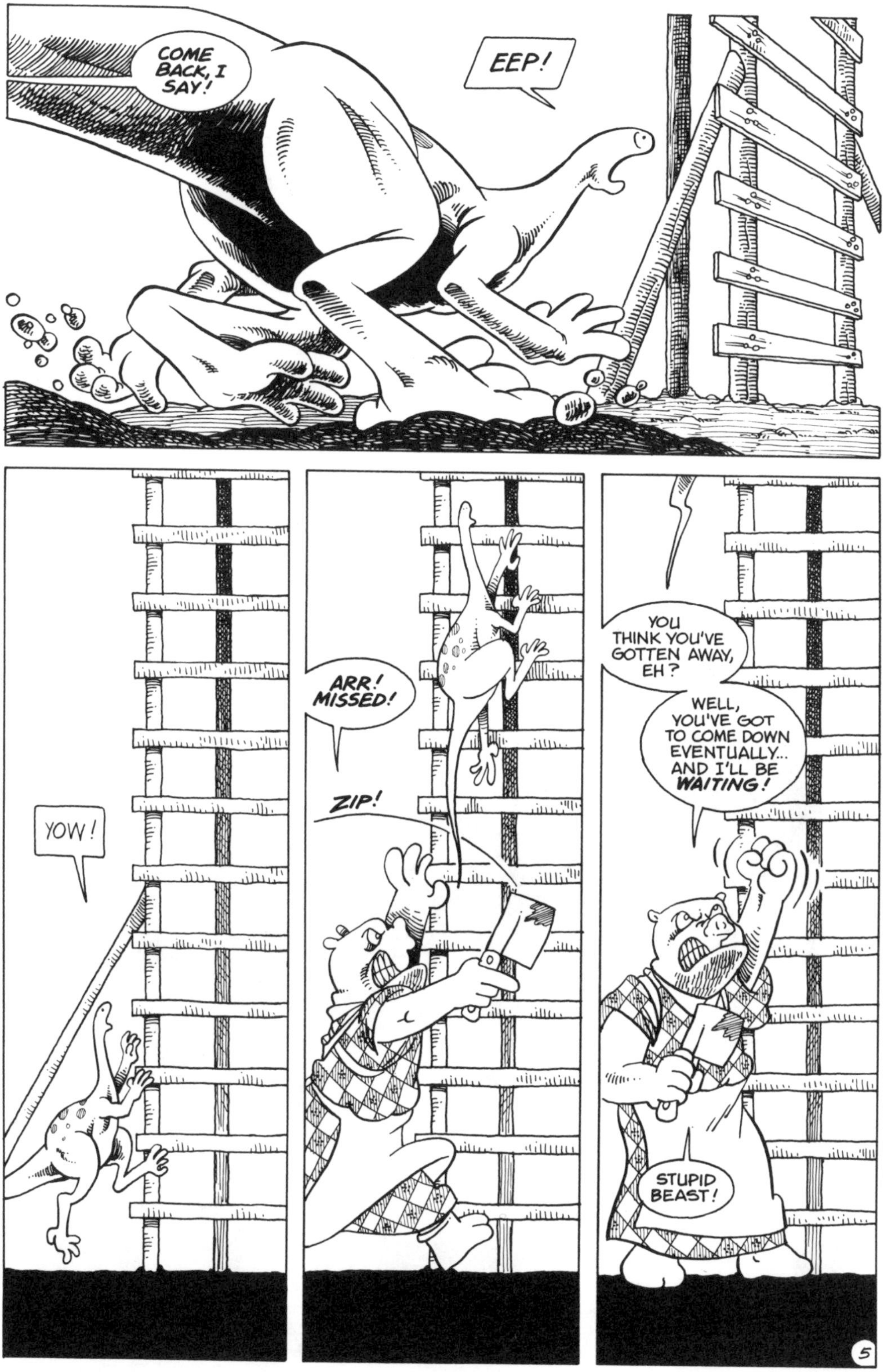
COME BACK, I SAY!
EEP!
YOW!
ARR! MISSED!
ZIP!
YOU THINK YOU'VE GOTTEN AWAY, EH?
WELL, YOU'VE GOT TO COME DOWN EVENTUALLY... AND I'LL BE **WAITING**!
STUPID BEAST!
5

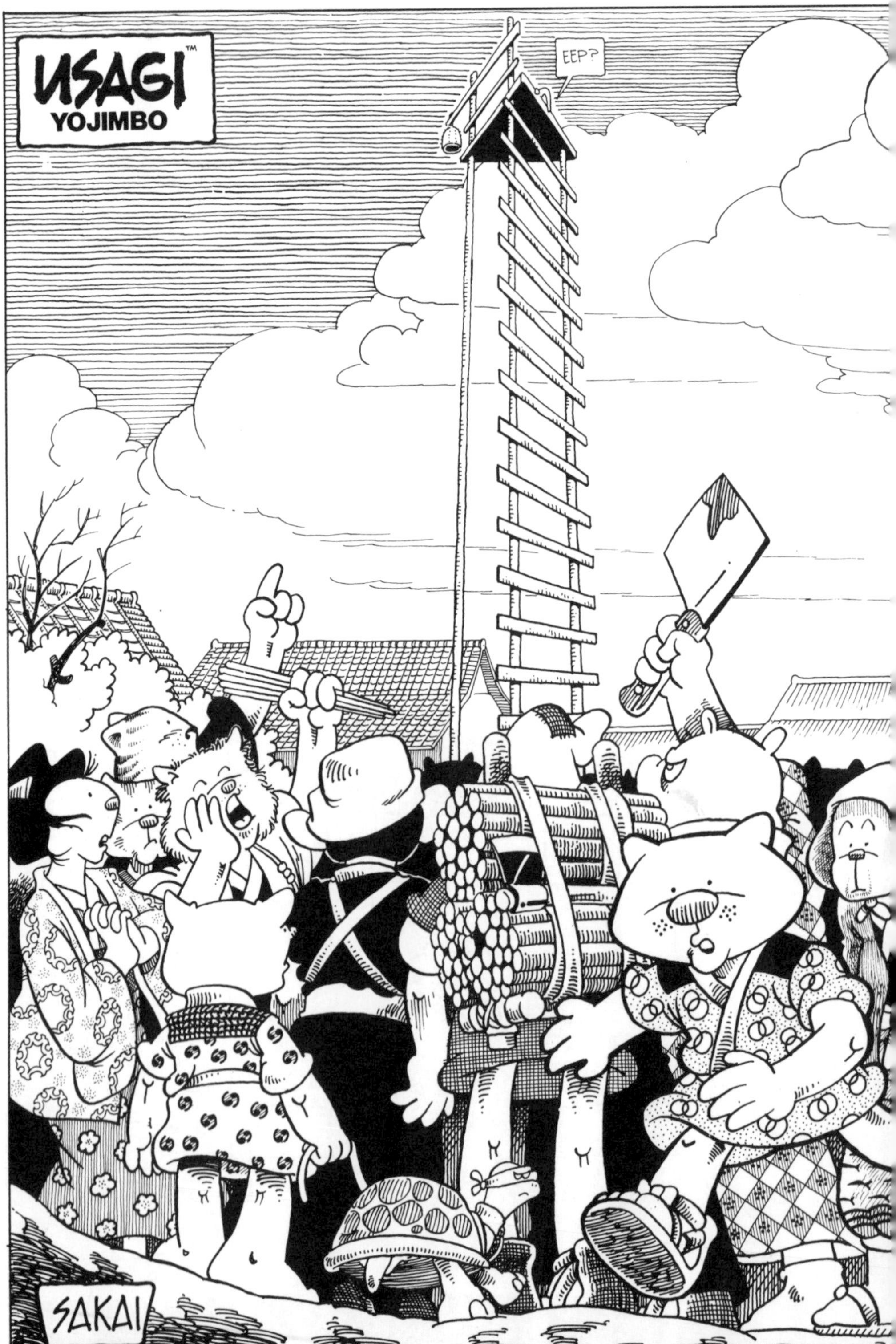
USAGI™
YOJIMBO
EEP?
SAKAI

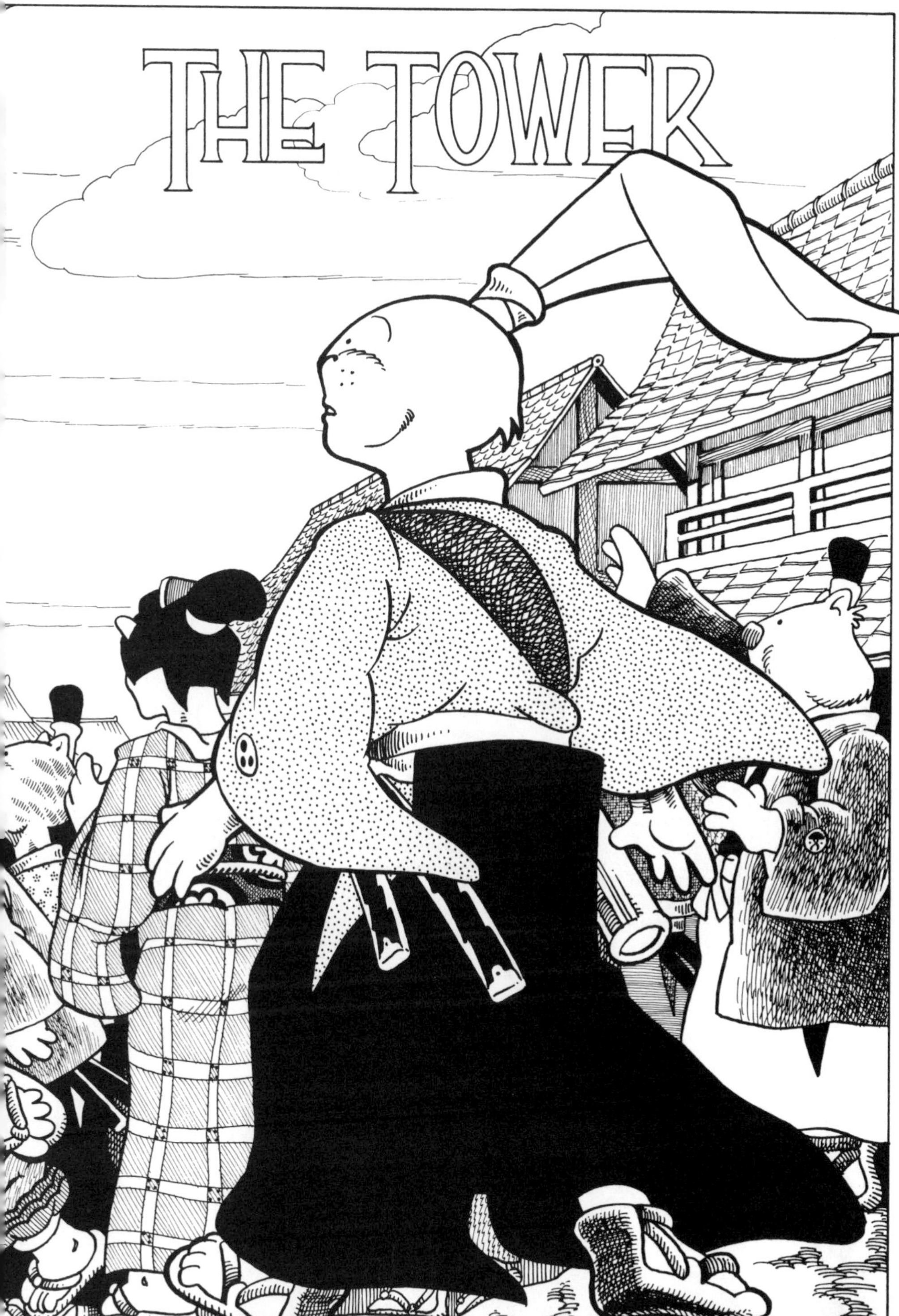
THE TOWER

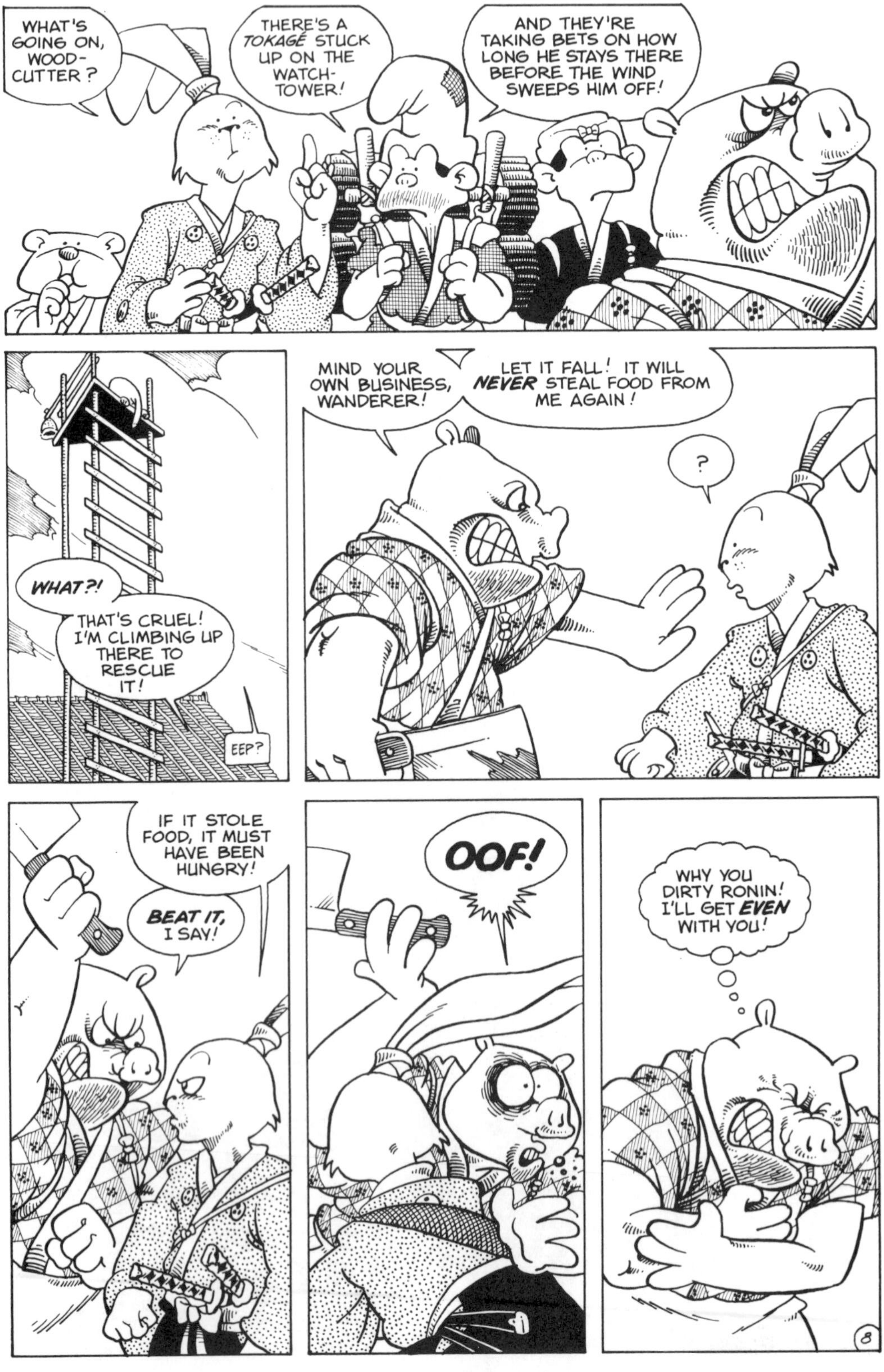

WHAT'S GOING ON, WOOD-CUTTER?
THERE'S A *TOKAGÉ* STUCK UP ON THE WATCH-TOWER!
AND THEY'RE TAKING BETS ON HOW LONG HE STAYS THERE BEFORE THE WIND SWEEPS HIM OFF!
WHAT?!
THAT'S CRUEL! I'M CLIMBING UP THERE TO RESCUE IT!
EEP?
MIND YOUR OWN BUSINESS, WANDERER!
LET IT FALL! IT WILL ***NEVER*** STEAL FOOD FROM ME AGAIN!
?
IF IT STOLE FOOD, IT MUST HAVE BEEN HUNGRY!
BEAT IT, I SAY!
OOF!
WHY YOU DIRTY RONIN! I'LL GET ***EVEN*** WITH YOU!
8

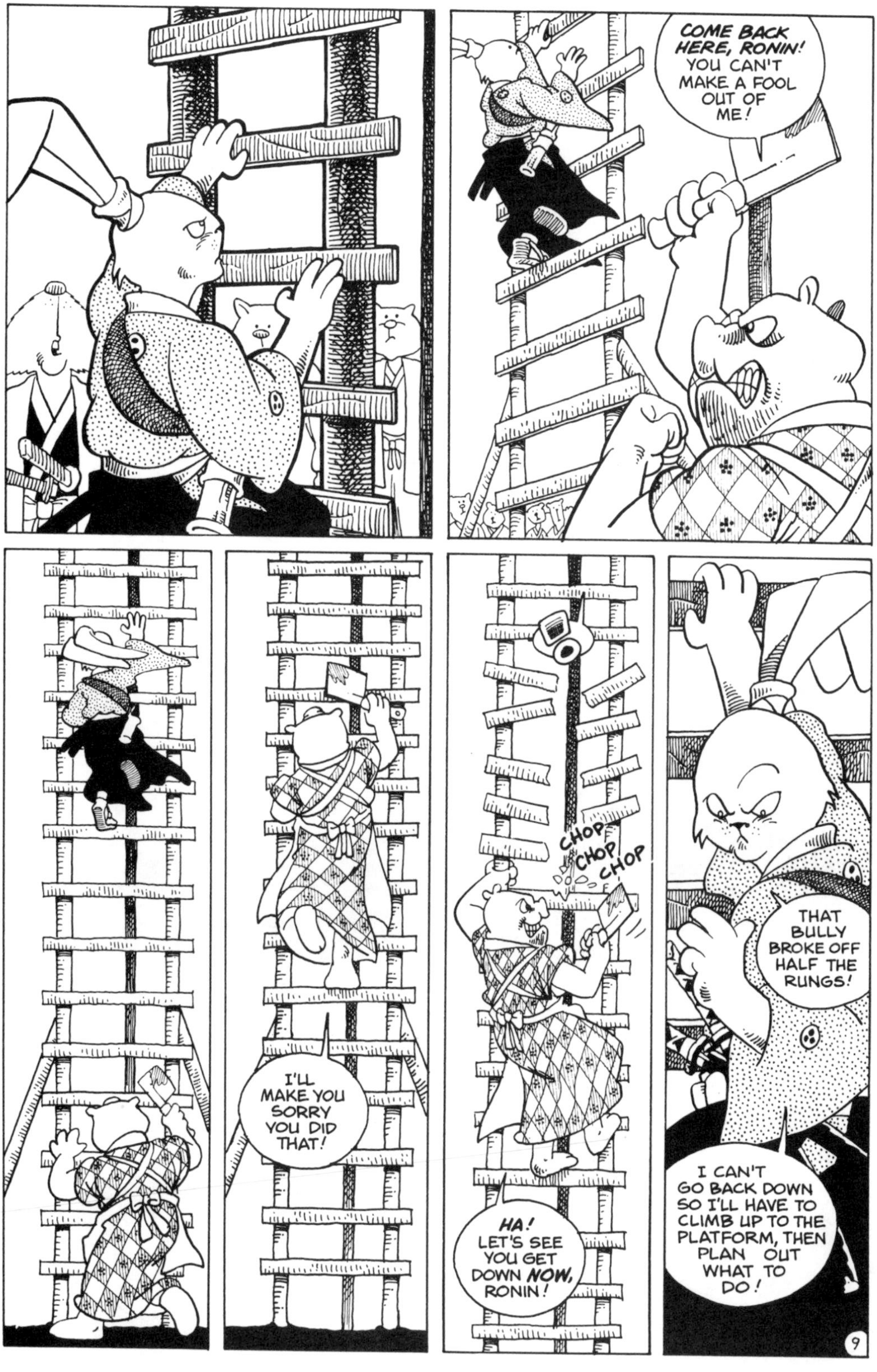
COME BACK HERE, RONIN! YOU CAN'T MAKE A FOOL OUT OF ME!
I'LL MAKE YOU SORRY YOU DID THAT!
CHOP CHOP CHOP
HA! LET'S SEE YOU GET DOWN NOW, RONIN!
THAT BULLY BROKE OFF HALF THE RUNGS!
I CAN'T GO BACK DOWN SO I'LL HAVE TO CLIMB UP TO THE PLATFORM, THEN PLAN OUT WHAT TO DO!
9

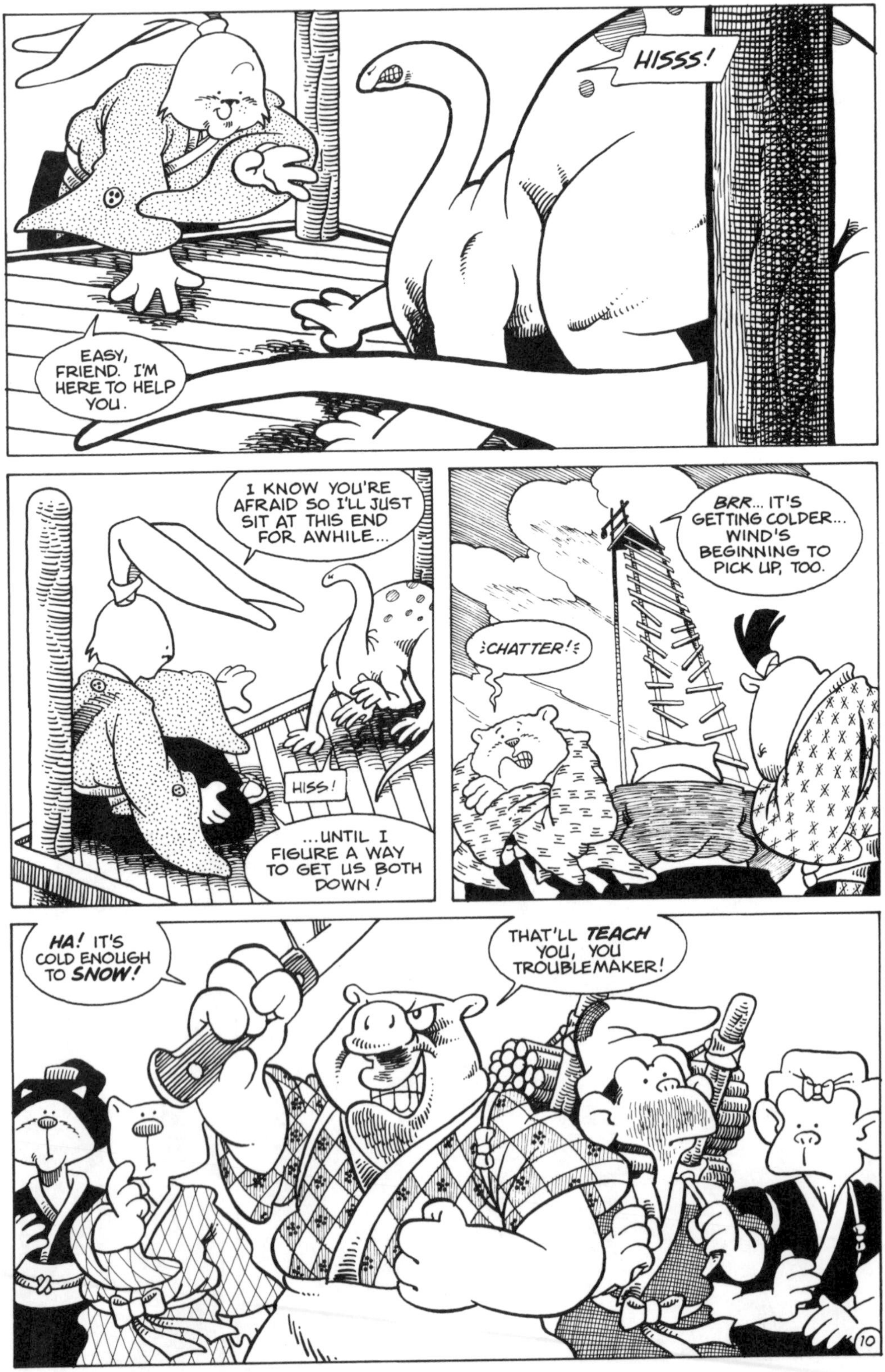
HISSS!
EASY, FRIEND. I'M HERE TO HELP YOU.
I KNOW YOU'RE AFRAID SO I'LL JUST SIT AT THIS END FOR AWHILE...
HISS!
...UNTIL I FIGURE A WAY TO GET US BOTH DOWN!
BRR... IT'S GETTING COLDER... WIND'S BEGINNING TO PICK UP, TOO.
CHATTER!
HA! IT'S COLD ENOUGH TO SNOW!
THAT'LL TEACH YOU, YOU TROUBLEMAKER!
10

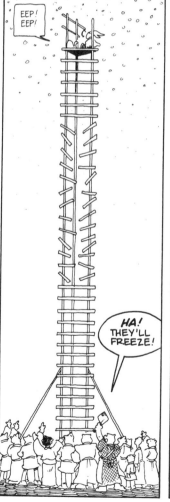

11

13

MUNCH! MUNCH

LATER...

WE'D BETTER BRUSH SOME OF THIS SNOW OFF THE PLATFORM BEFORE WE SLIP OFF!

EEP?

FROOMP!

HAHA GRRRR! HAHAHAHA

YOU DID THAT ON PURPOSE, RONIN!

OH NO! HERE COMES THE WIND!

ULP!

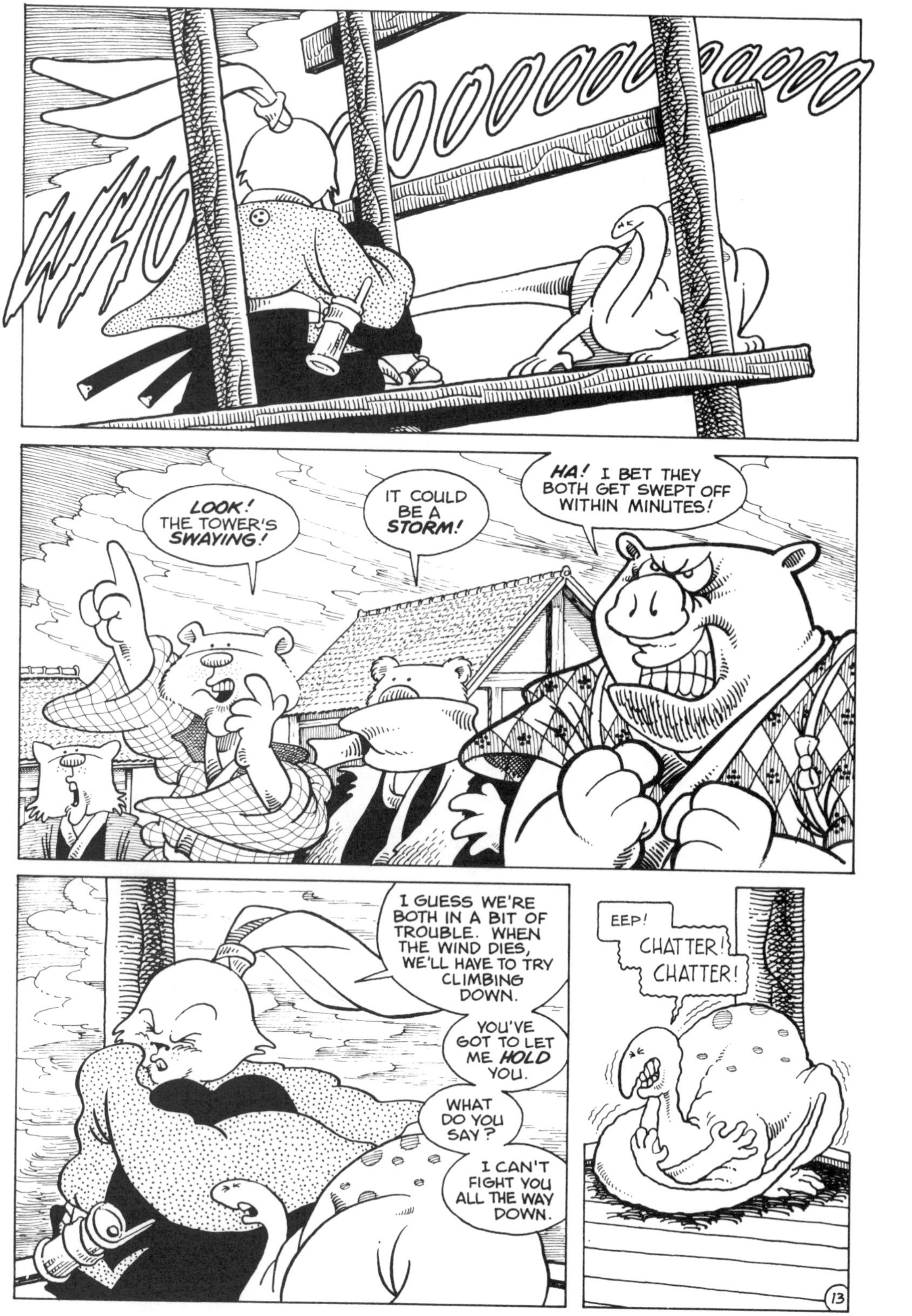
WHOOOOOOOOOOOOOOOO
LOOK! THE TOWER'S SWAYING!
IT COULD BE A STORM!
HA! I BET THEY BOTH GET SWEPT OFF WITHIN MINUTES!
I GUESS WE'RE BOTH IN A BIT OF TROUBLE. WHEN THE WIND DIES, WE'LL HAVE TO TRY CLIMBING DOWN.
YOU'VE GOT TO LET ME HOLD YOU.
WHAT DO YOU SAY?
I CAN'T FIGHT YOU ALL THE WAY DOWN.
EEP!
CHATTER! CHATTER!
13

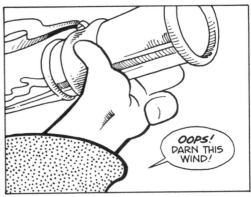

I'VE GOT SOME TEA IN MY BAMBOO FILLER... MAYBE THAT WILL HELP TO WARM YOU.

OOPS! DARN THIS WIND!

GOT IT!

NO, IT SLIPPED AWAY!

SPLASH!

THAT DOES IT!

YOU'RE DEAD, RONIN!

YOU AND THAT PEST UP THERE!

KONK!

OWK!

14

16

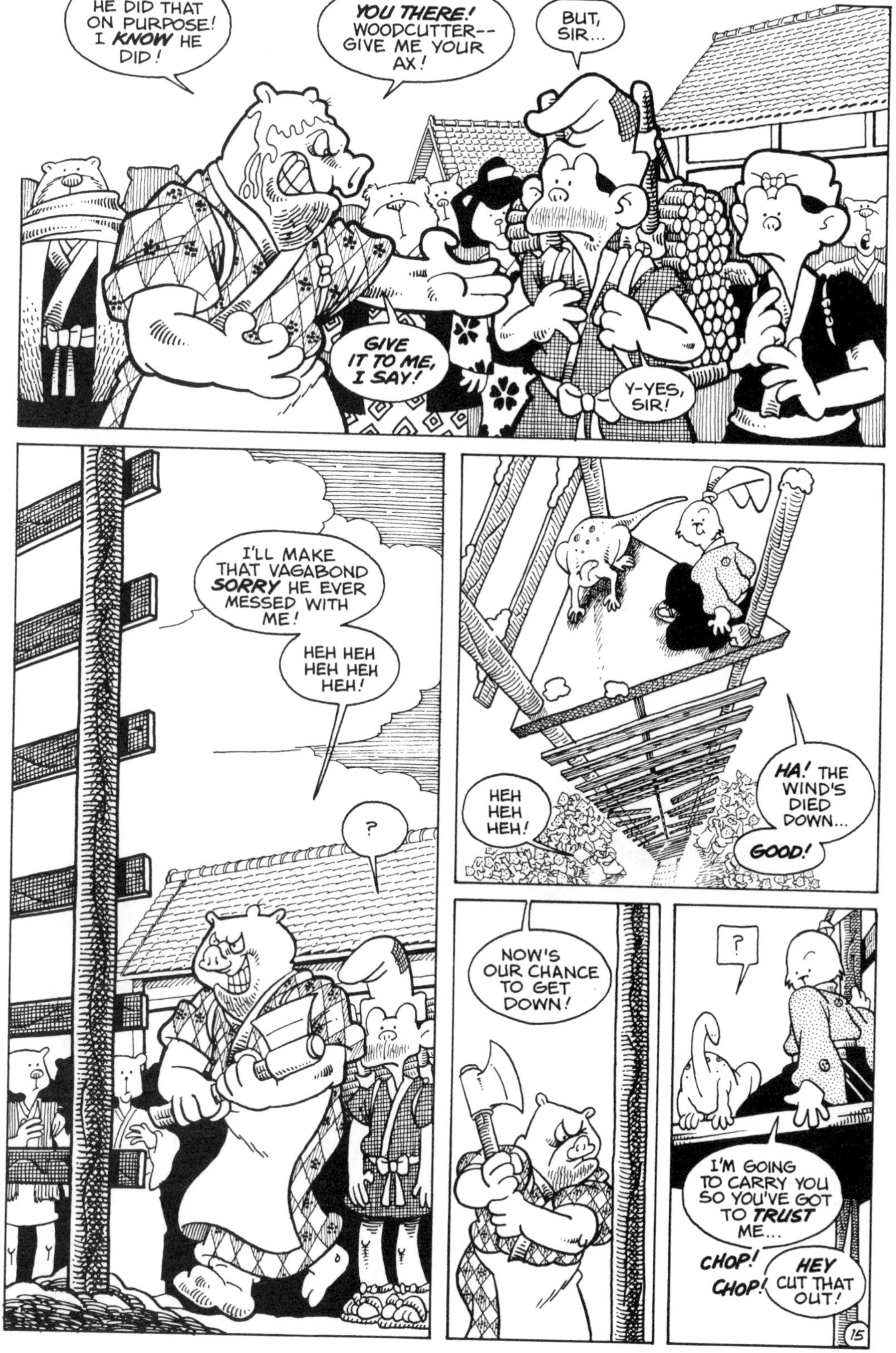
HE DID THAT ON PURPOSE! I KNOW HE DID!
YOU THERE! WOODCUTTER-- GIVE ME YOUR AX!
BUT, SIR...
GIVE IT TO ME, I SAY!
Y-YES, SIR!
I'LL MAKE THAT VAGABOND SORRY HE EVER MESSED WITH ME!
HEH HEH HEH HEH HEH!
?
HEH HEH HEH!
HA! THE WIND'S DIED DOWN...
GOOD!
NOW'S OUR CHANCE TO GET DOWN!
?
I'M GOING TO CARRY YOU SO YOU'VE GOT TO TRUST ME...
CHOP! CHOP!
HEY CUT THAT OUT!
15

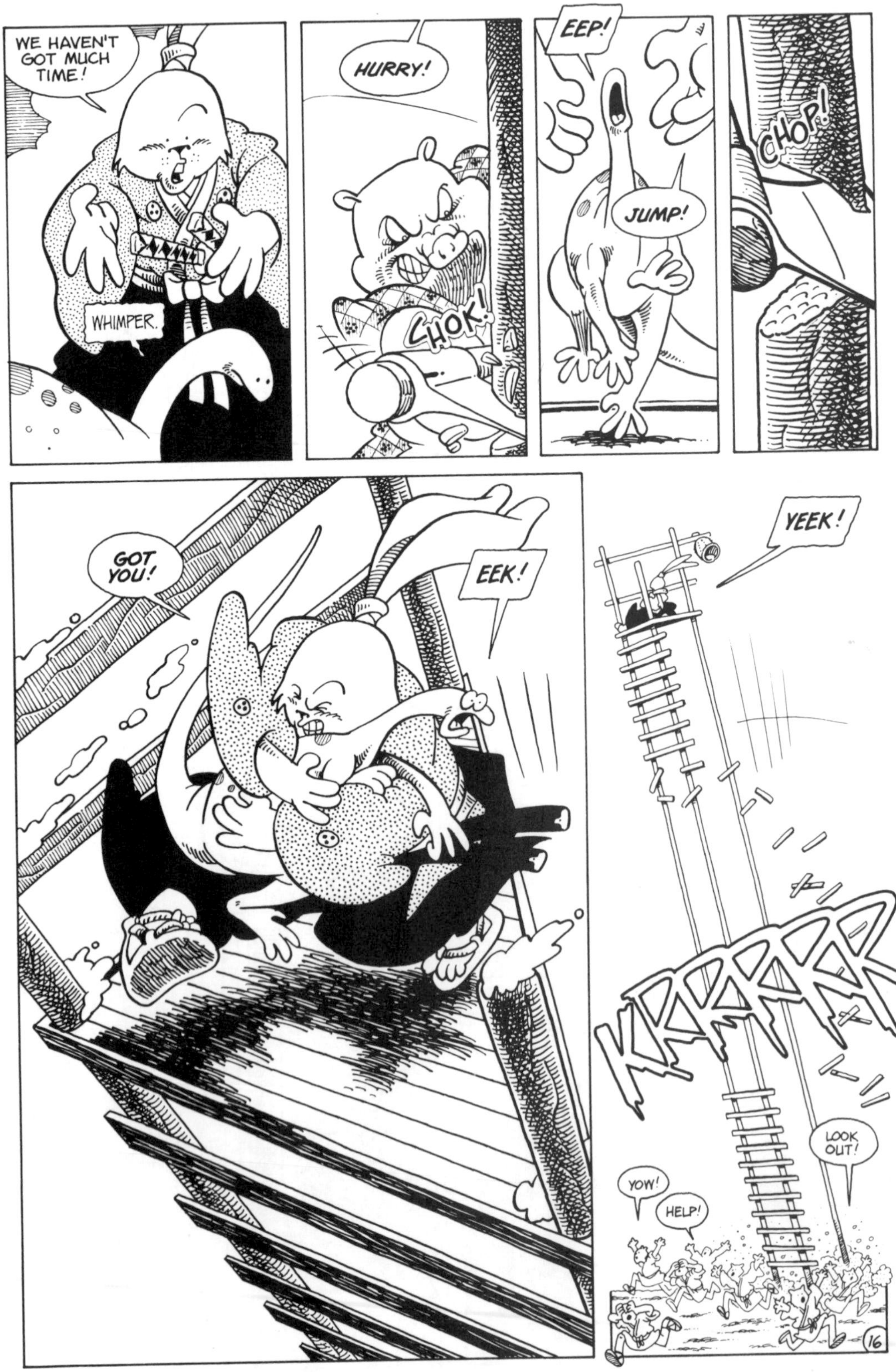
WE HAVEN'T GOT MUCH TIME!
WHIMPER.
HURRY!
CHOK!
EEP!
JUMP!
CHOP!
GOT YOU!
EEK!
YEEK!
KRRRRRR
LOOK OUT!
YOW!
HELP!
16

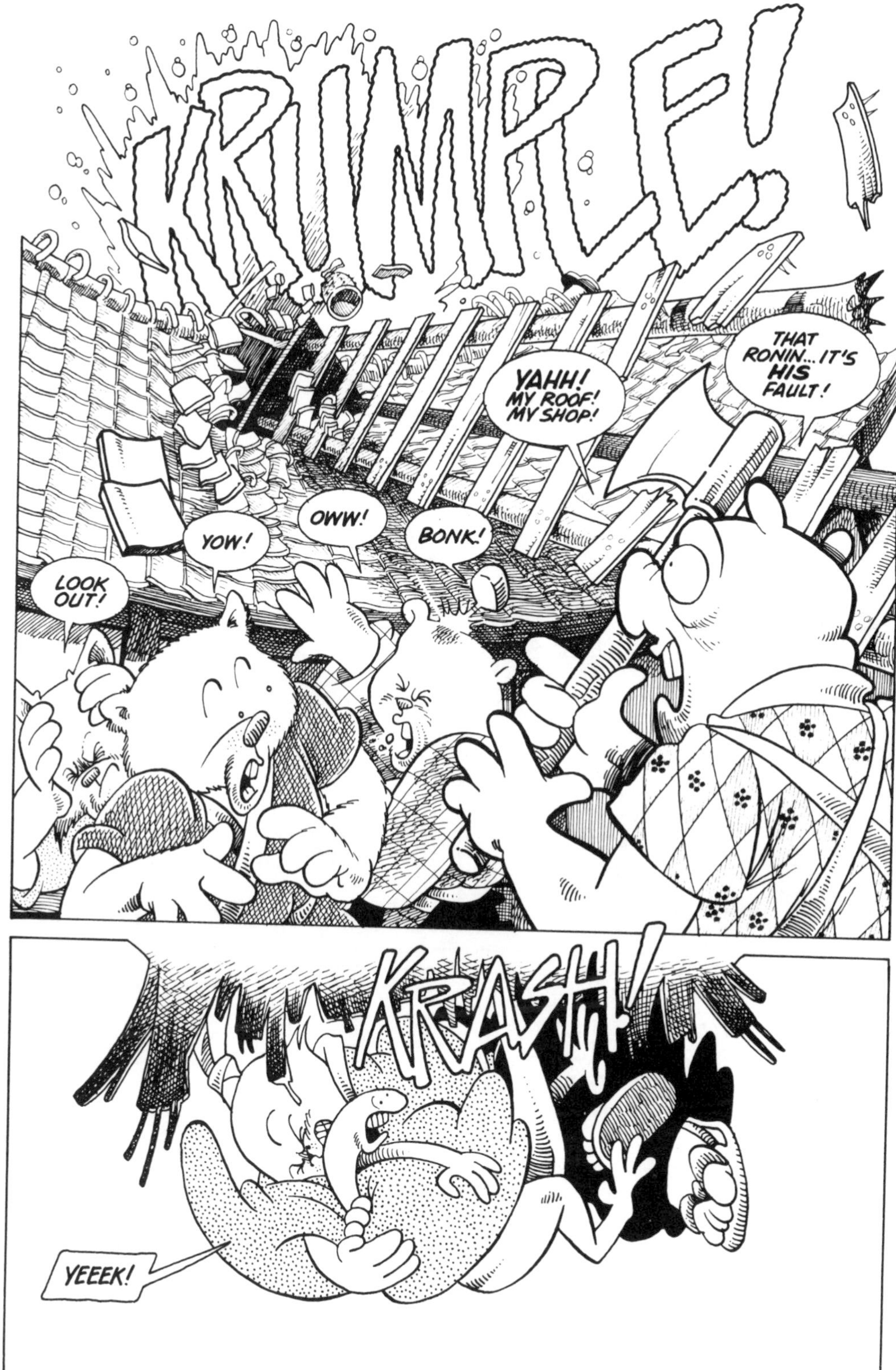
KRUMPLE!
THAT RONIN... IT'S HIS FAULT!
YAHH! MY ROOF! MY SHOP!
BONK!
OWW!
YOW!
LOOK OUT!
KRASH!
YEEEK!
17

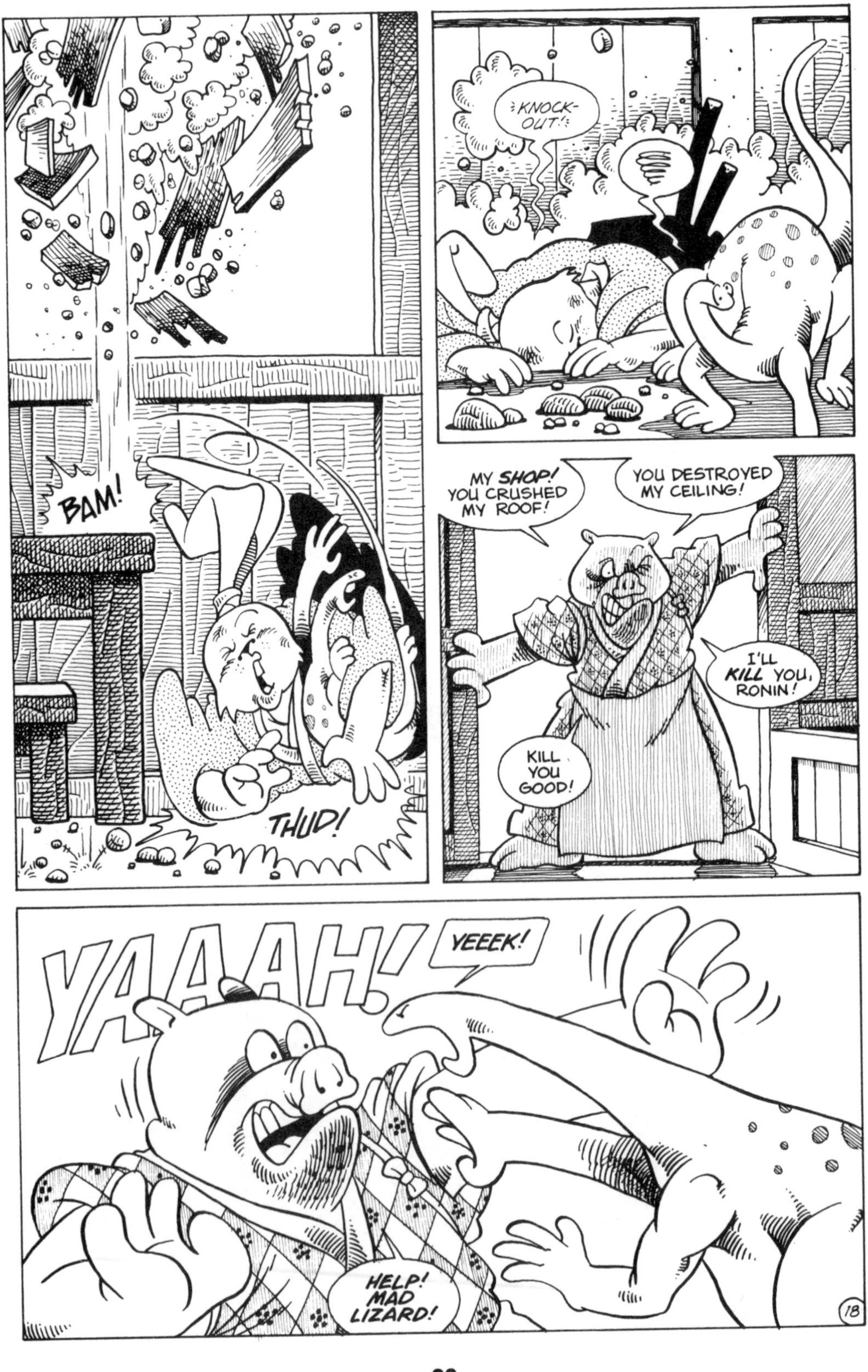
BAM!
THUD!
KNOCK-OUT
MY SHOP! YOU CRUSHED MY ROOF!
YOU DESTROYED MY CEILING!
I'LL KILL YOU, RONIN!
KILL YOU GOOD!
YAAAH!
YEEEK!
HELP! MAD LIZARD!
18

COFF! COFF!

OOoOHH! MY HEAD! IT FEELS LIKE I'VE BEEN POUNDED BY MALLETS!

I THINK I'VE TWISTED MY ARM AND...

YAAGH! GET IT OFF! GET IT OFF!

GRR!

THAT'S ENOUGH.

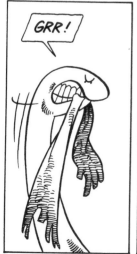

GRR!

OOOOOH.

EEP!

IT SEEMS I'VE GOT A COMPANION.

19

21

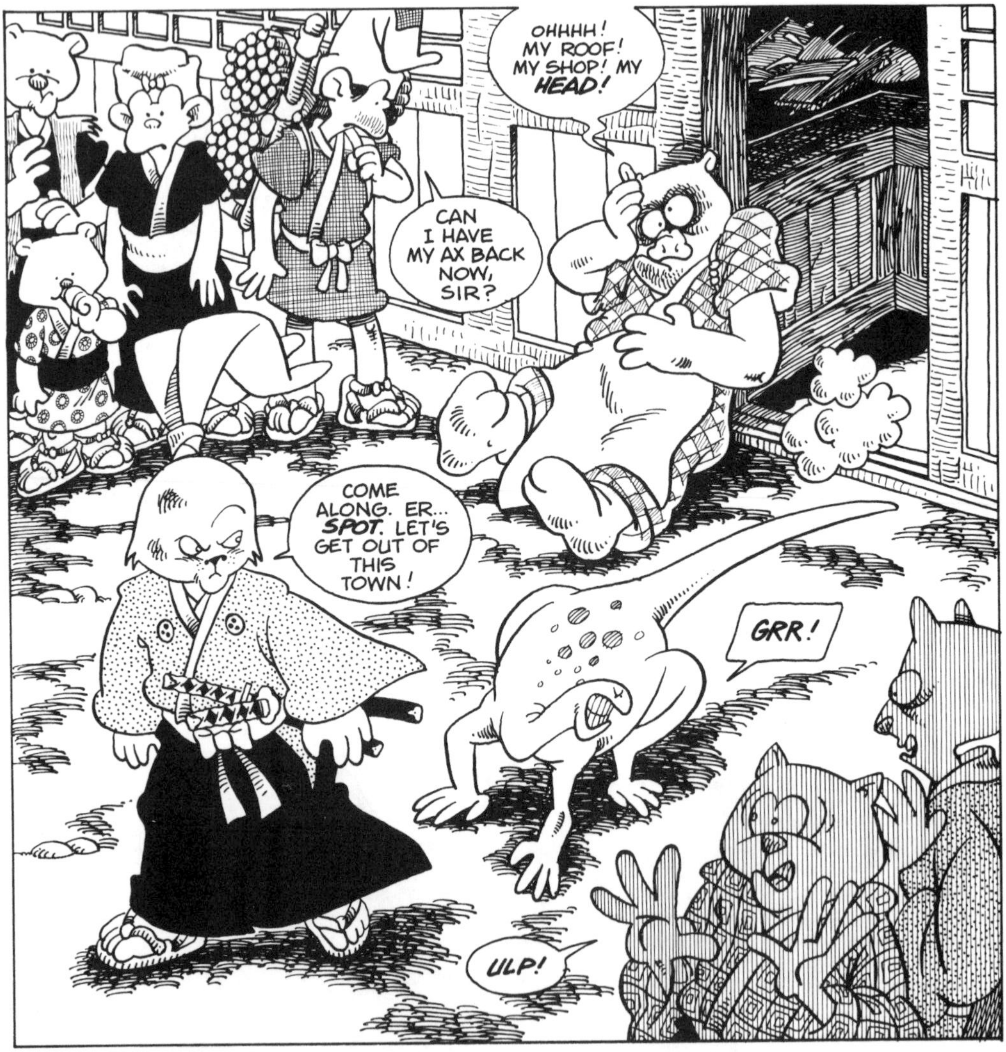
OHHHH! MY ROOF! MY SHOP! MY **HEAD!**
CAN I HAVE MY AX BACK NOW, SIR?
COME ALONG. ER... **SPOT.** LET'S GET OUT OF THIS TOWN!
GRR!
ULP!

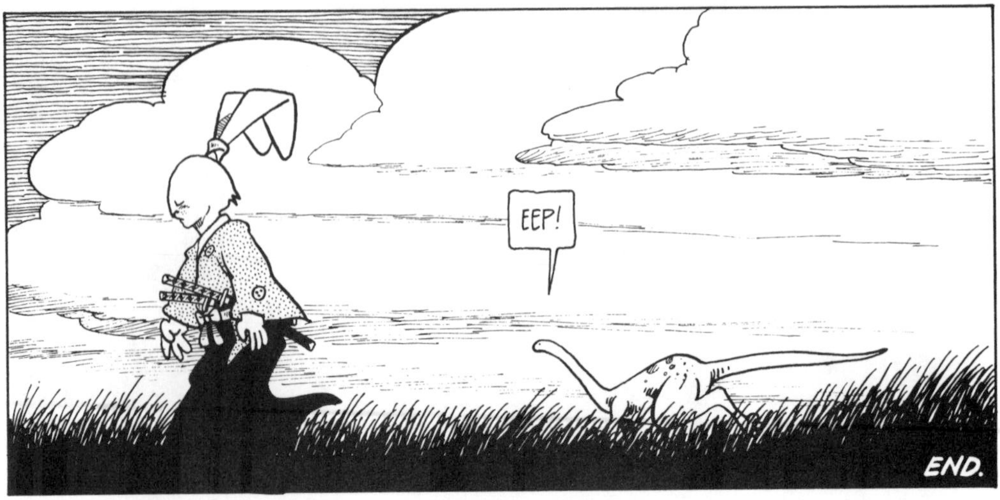
EEP!
END.

CHAPTER TWO

"A Mother's Love"

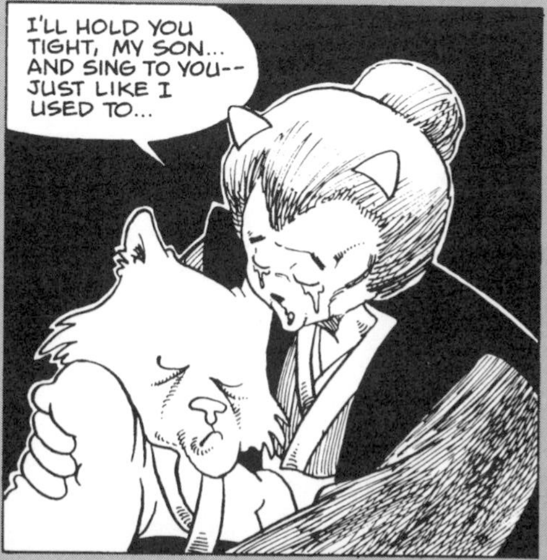
I'LL HOLD YOU TIGHT, MY SON... AND SING TO YOU-- JUST LIKE I USED TO...

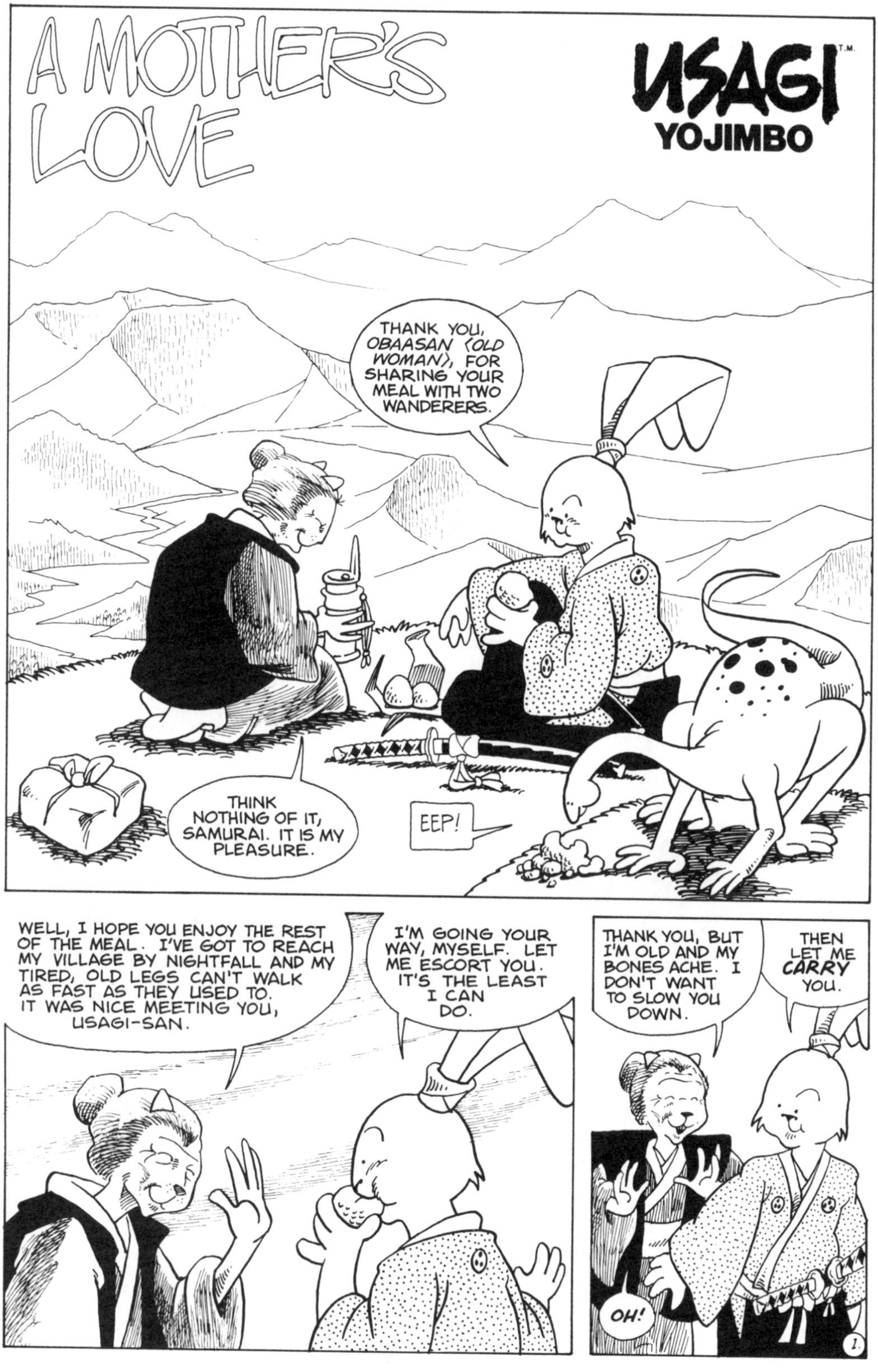
A MOTHER'S LOVE
USAGI YOJIMBO T.M.
THANK YOU, OBAASAN ⟨OLD WOMAN⟩, FOR SHARING YOUR MEAL WITH TWO WANDERERS.
THINK NOTHING OF IT, SAMURAI. IT IS MY PLEASURE.
EEP!
WELL, I HOPE YOU ENJOY THE REST OF THE MEAL. I'VE GOT TO REACH MY VILLAGE BY NIGHTFALL AND MY TIRED, OLD LEGS CAN'T WALK AS FAST AS THEY USED TO. IT WAS NICE MEETING YOU, USAGI-SAN.
I'M GOING YOUR WAY, MYSELF. LET ME ESCORT YOU. IT'S THE LEAST I CAN DO.
THANK YOU, BUT I'M OLD AND MY BONES ACHE. I DON'T WANT TO SLOW YOU DOWN.
THEN LET ME CARRY YOU.
OH!
1.

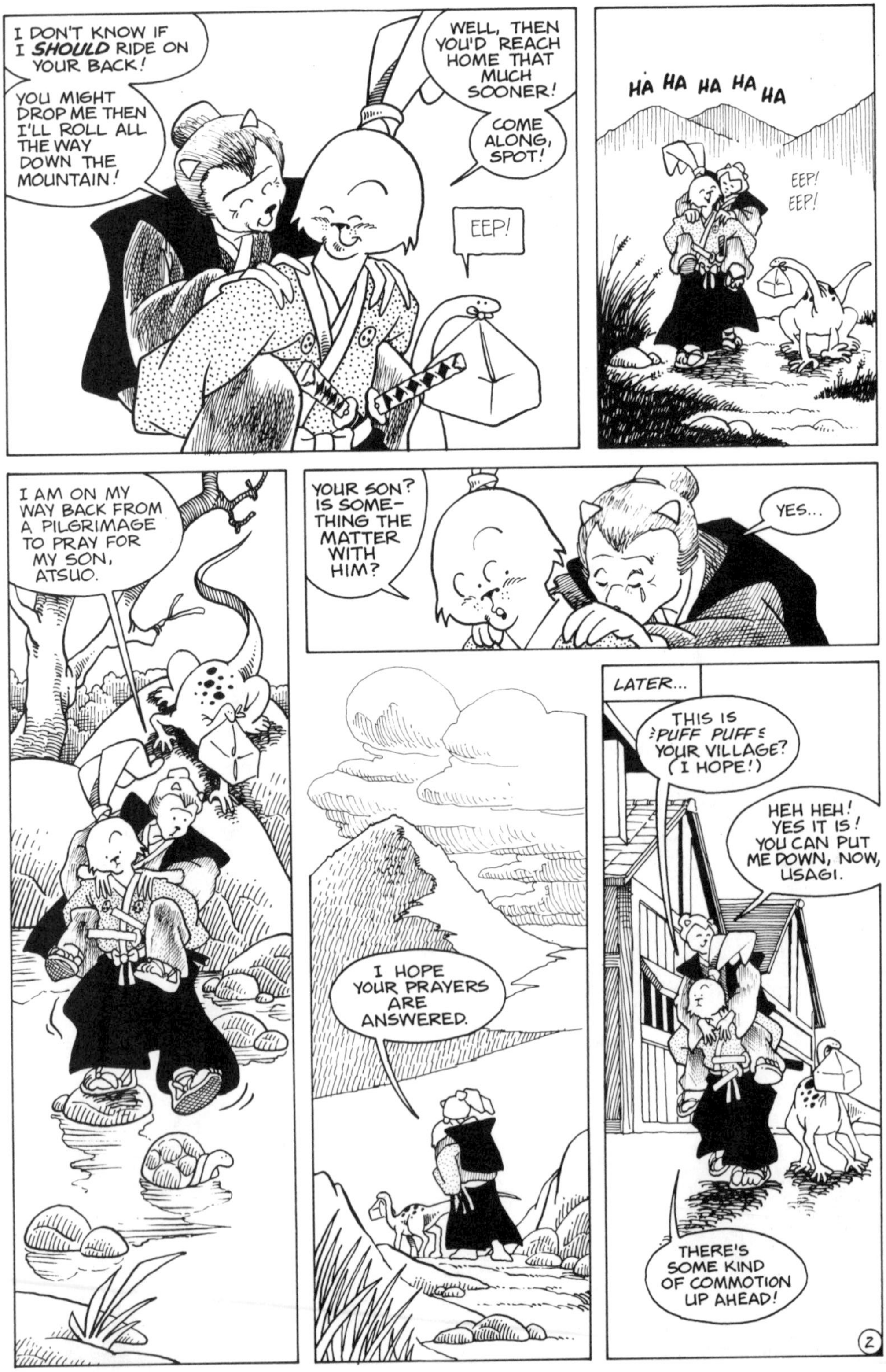

I DON'T KNOW IF I SHOULD RIDE ON YOUR BACK!
YOU MIGHT DROP ME THEN I'LL ROLL ALL THE WAY DOWN THE MOUNTAIN!
WELL, THEN YOU'D REACH HOME THAT MUCH SOONER!
COME ALONG, SPOT!
EEP!
HA HA HA HA HA
EEP! EEP!
I AM ON MY WAY BACK FROM A PILGRIMAGE TO PRAY FOR MY SON, ATSUO.
YOUR SON? IS SOMETHING THE MATTER WITH HIM?
YES...
I HOPE YOUR PRAYERS ARE ANSWERED.
LATER...
THIS IS *PUFF PUFF* YOUR VILLAGE? (I HOPE!)
HEH HEH! YES IT IS! YOU CAN PUT ME DOWN, NOW, USAGI.
THERE'S SOME KIND OF COMMOTION UP AHEAD!
2

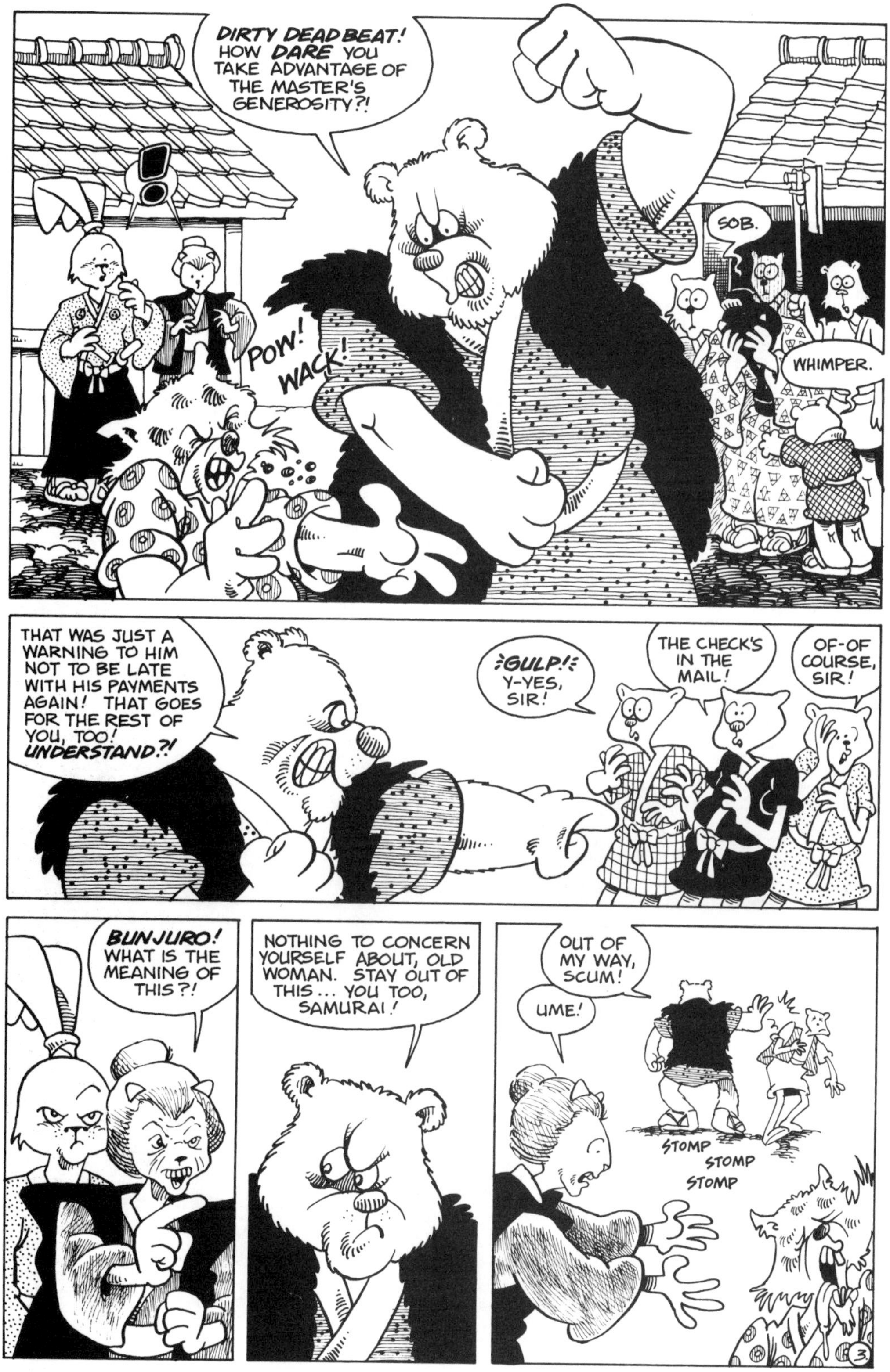
DIRTY DEADBEAT! HOW DARE YOU TAKE ADVANTAGE OF THE MASTER'S GENEROSITY?!
POW!
WACK!
SOB.
WHIMPER.
THAT WAS JUST A WARNING TO HIM NOT TO BE LATE WITH HIS PAYMENTS AGAIN! THAT GOES FOR THE REST OF YOU, TOO! UNDERSTAND?!
GULP! Y-YES, SIR!
THE CHECK'S IN THE MAIL!
OF-OF COURSE, SIR!
BUNJURO! WHAT IS THE MEANING OF THIS?!
NOTHING TO CONCERN YOURSELF ABOUT, OLD WOMAN. STAY OUT OF THIS... YOU TOO, SAMURAI!
OUT OF MY WAY, SCUM!
UME!
STOMP
STOMP
STOMP
3

28

I'M IMPRESSED, USAGI-SAN! YOU REALLY ARE QUICK WITH THE SWORD, AREN'T YOU?

WELL, A RONIN HAS TO KEEP HIS SKILLS HONED TO STAY ALIVE.

MOTHER! WHAT'S GOING ON IN HERE? ONE OF MY MEN CLAIMS HE WAS ASSAULTED!

SLAM

WHO IS THIS?!

ATSUO, THIS IS MIYAMOTO USAGI. HE WAS KIND ENOUGH TO ESCORT ME BACK TO TOWN AFTER MY VISIT TO THE TEMPLES.

GLAD TO MEET YOU.

EEP!

THIS IS MY FRIEND, SPOT.

WE CAN'T CATER TO EVERY TWO-BIT RONIN YOU BRING HOME! GET HIM OUT OF HERE... HIM AND THAT DIRTY ANIMAL!

BUT HE HELPED ME! THE LEAST WE CAN DO IS SHOW THEM SOME KINDNESS!

HOW DARE YOU CONTRADICT ME!

OH!

SLAP!

THIS IS A **FAMILY** MATTER, RONIN!

STAY OUT OF IT!

YEAH! PUT YOUR SWORD AWAY!

SOB.

ONLY A **CUR** WOULD STRIKE HIS OWN MOTHER!

HA! HA! HA! I'M THE **BOSS** OF THIS TOWN AND I DON'T **CARE** WHAT YOU OR ANYBODY ELSE THINK OF ME, RONIN.

I HEARD OF HOW YOU INTERFERED WITH ONE OF MY MEN AS HE WAS DOING HIS JOB, MOTHER!

DO IT AGAIN AND YOU'LL BE BEATEN!

HOW DARE YOU SPEAK TO HER LIKE THAT! APOLOGIZE AT ONCE!

HA! YOU CAN'T BE SERIOUS, RONIN!

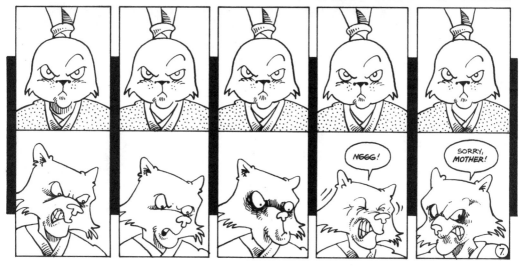

NGGG!

SORRY, MOTHER!

⑦

31

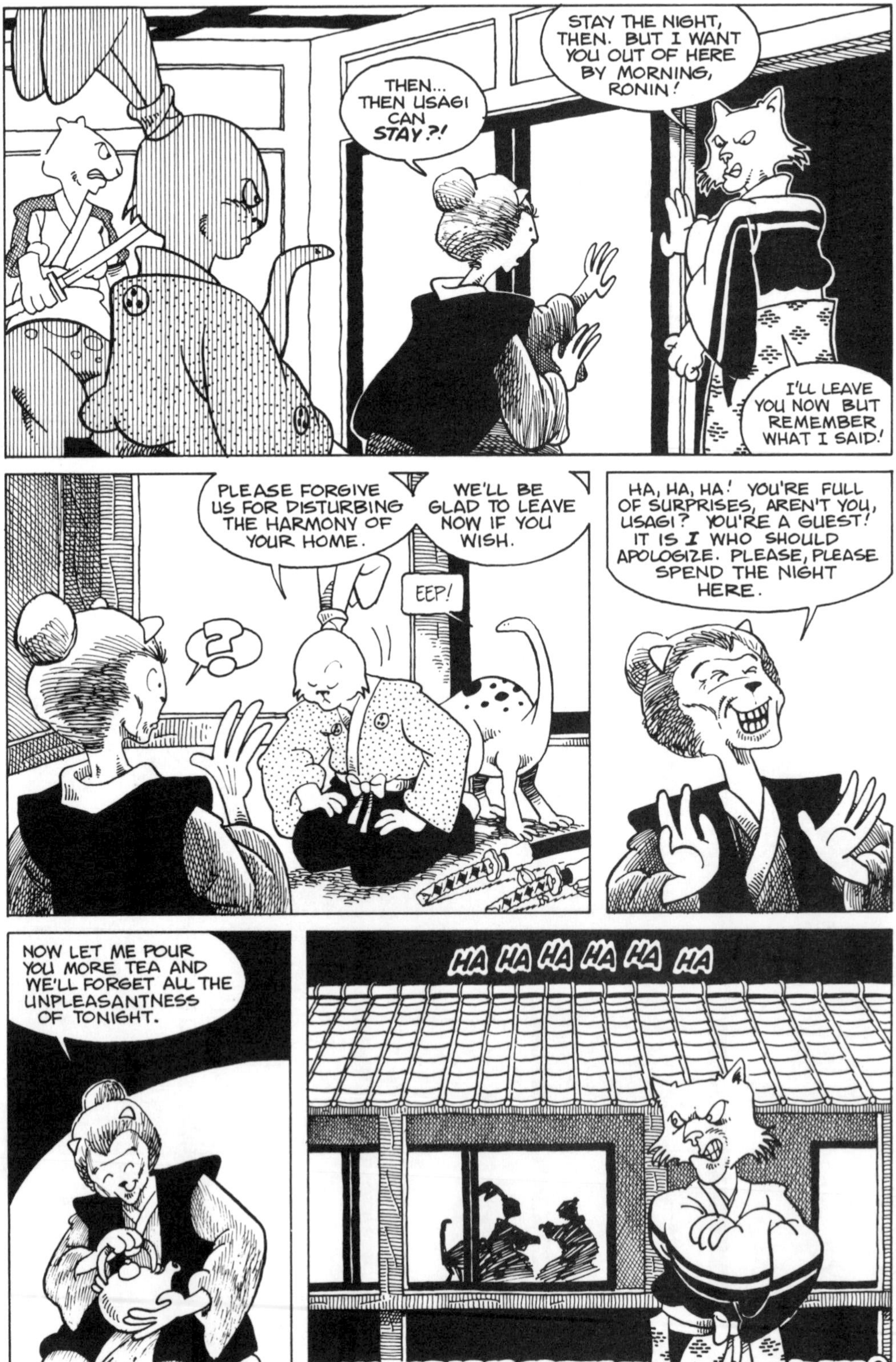
THEN... THEN USAGI CAN STAY?!
STAY THE NIGHT, THEN. BUT I WANT YOU OUT OF HERE BY MORNING, RONIN!
I'LL LEAVE YOU NOW BUT REMEMBER WHAT I SAID!
PLEASE FORGIVE US FOR DISTURBING THE HARMONY OF YOUR HOME.
WE'LL BE GLAD TO LEAVE NOW IF YOU WISH.
?
EEP!
HA, HA, HA! YOU'RE FULL OF SURPRISES, AREN'T YOU, USAGI? YOU'RE A GUEST! IT IS I WHO SHOULD APOLOGIZE. PLEASE, PLEASE SPEND THE NIGHT HERE.
NOW LET ME POUR YOU MORE TEA AND WE'LL FORGET ALL THE UNPLEASANTNESS OF TONIGHT.
HA HA HA HA HA HA
8

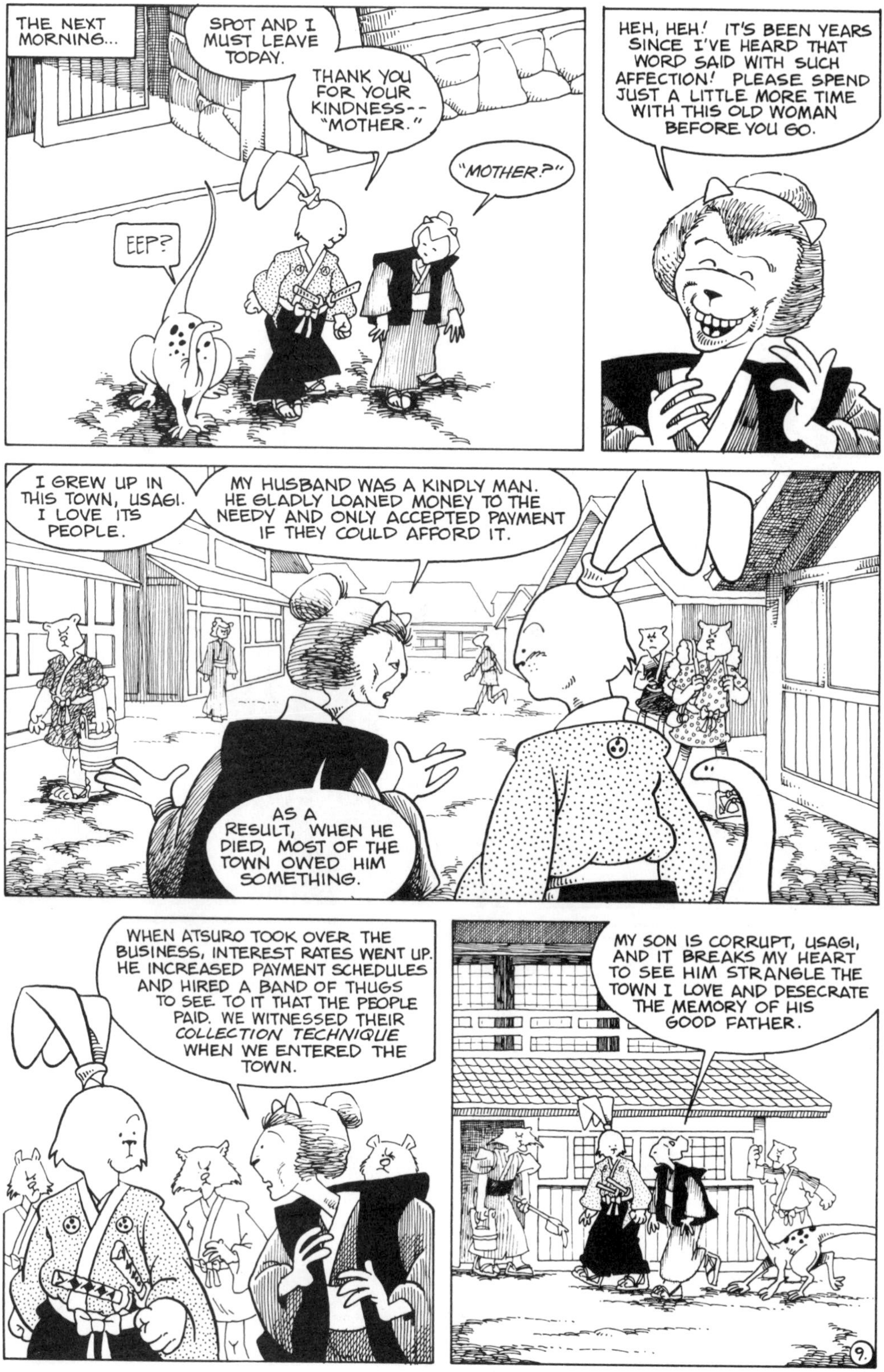
THE NEXT MORNING...
SPOT AND I MUST LEAVE TODAY.
THANK YOU FOR YOUR KINDNESS-- "MOTHER."
"MOTHER?"
EEP?
HEH, HEH! IT'S BEEN YEARS SINCE I'VE HEARD THAT WORD SAID WITH SUCH AFFECTION! PLEASE SPEND JUST A LITTLE MORE TIME WITH THIS OLD WOMAN BEFORE YOU GO.
I GREW UP IN THIS TOWN, USAGI. I LOVE ITS PEOPLE.
MY HUSBAND WAS A KINDLY MAN. HE GLADLY LOANED MONEY TO THE NEEDY AND ONLY ACCEPTED PAYMENT IF THEY COULD AFFORD IT.
AS A RESULT, WHEN HE DIED, MOST OF THE TOWN OWED HIM SOMETHING.
WHEN ATSURO TOOK OVER THE BUSINESS, INTEREST RATES WENT UP. HE INCREASED PAYMENT SCHEDULES AND HIRED A BAND OF THUGS TO SEE TO IT THAT THE PEOPLE PAID. WE WITNESSED THEIR *COLLECTION TECHNIQUE* WHEN WE ENTERED THE TOWN.
MY SON IS CORRUPT, USAGI, AND IT BREAKS MY HEART TO SEE HIM STRANGLE THE TOWN I LOVE AND DESECRATE THE MEMORY OF HIS GOOD FATHER.
9.

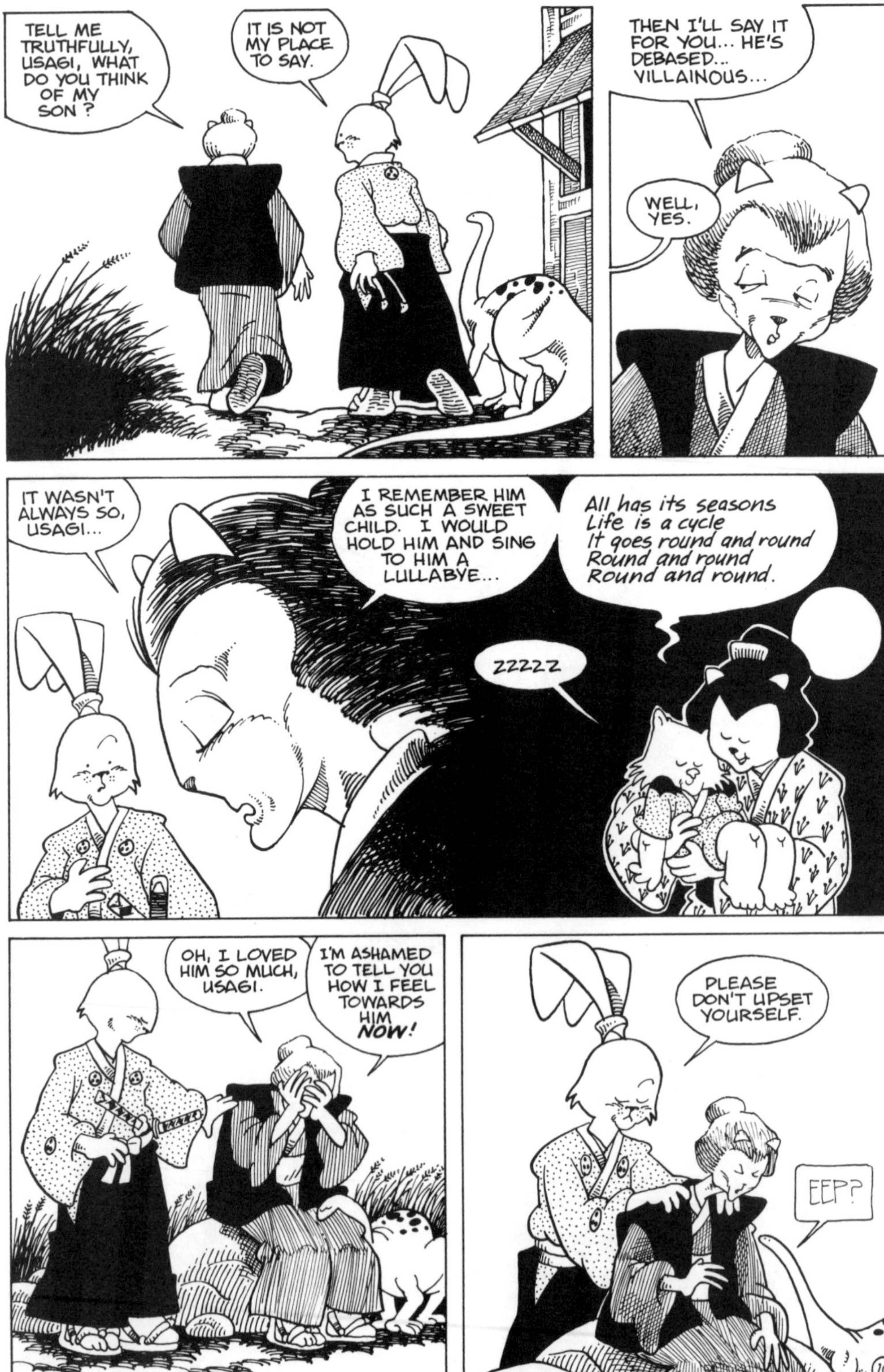
TELL ME TRUTHFULLY, USAGI, WHAT DO YOU THINK OF MY SON ?
IT IS NOT MY PLACE TO SAY.
THEN I'LL SAY IT FOR YOU... HE'S DEBASED... VILLAINOUS...
WELL, YES.
IT WASN'T ALWAYS SO, USAGI...
I REMEMBER HIM AS SUCH A SWEET CHILD. I WOULD HOLD HIM AND SING TO HIM A LULLABYE...
All has its seasons
Life is a cycle
It goes round and round
Round and round
Round and round.
ZZZZZ
OH, I LOVED HIM SO MUCH, USAGI.
I'M ASHAMED TO TELL YOU HOW I FEEL TOWARDS HIM NOW!
PLEASE DON'T UPSET YOURSELF.
EEP?
10

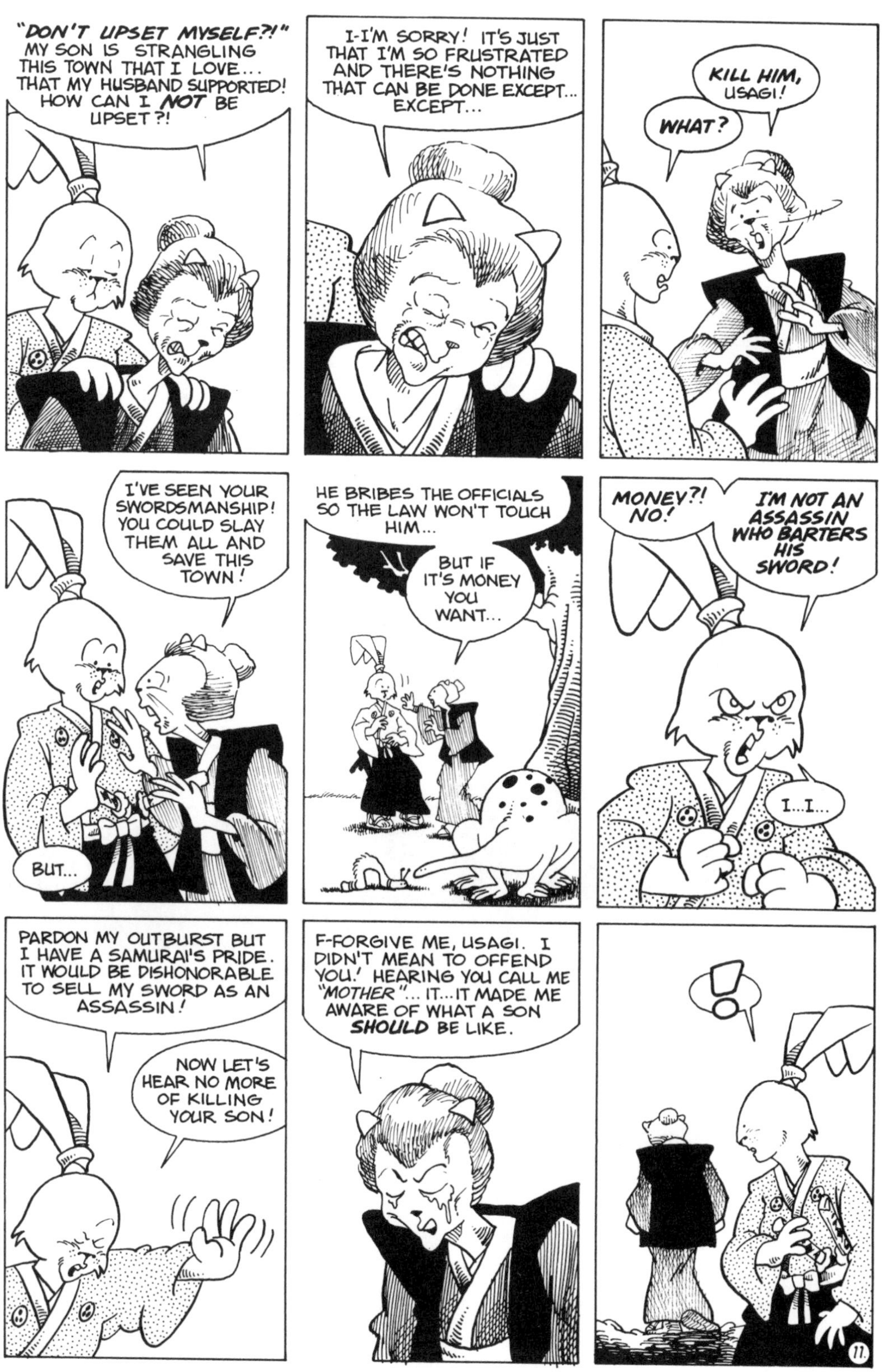
"DON'T UPSET MYSELF?!" MY SON IS STRANGLING THIS TOWN THAT I LOVE... THAT MY HUSBAND SUPPORTED! HOW CAN I NOT BE UPSET?!
I-I'M SORRY! IT'S JUST THAT I'M SO FRUSTRATED AND THERE'S NOTHING THAT CAN BE DONE EXCEPT... EXCEPT...
KILL HIM, USAGI!
WHAT?
I'VE SEEN YOUR SWORDSMANSHIP! YOU COULD SLAY THEM ALL AND SAVE THIS TOWN!
BUT...
HE BRIBES THE OFFICIALS SO THE LAW WON'T TOUCH HIM...
BUT IF IT'S MONEY YOU WANT...
MONEY?! NO!
I'M NOT AN ASSASSIN WHO BARTERS HIS SWORD!
I...I...
PARDON MY OUTBURST BUT I HAVE A SAMURAI'S PRIDE. IT WOULD BE DISHONORABLE TO SELL MY SWORD AS AN ASSASSIN!
NOW LET'S HEAR NO MORE OF KILLING YOUR SON!
F-FORGIVE ME, USAGI. I DIDN'T MEAN TO OFFEND YOU! HEARING YOU CALL ME "MOTHER"... IT...IT MADE ME AWARE OF WHAT A SON SHOULD BE LIKE.
11.

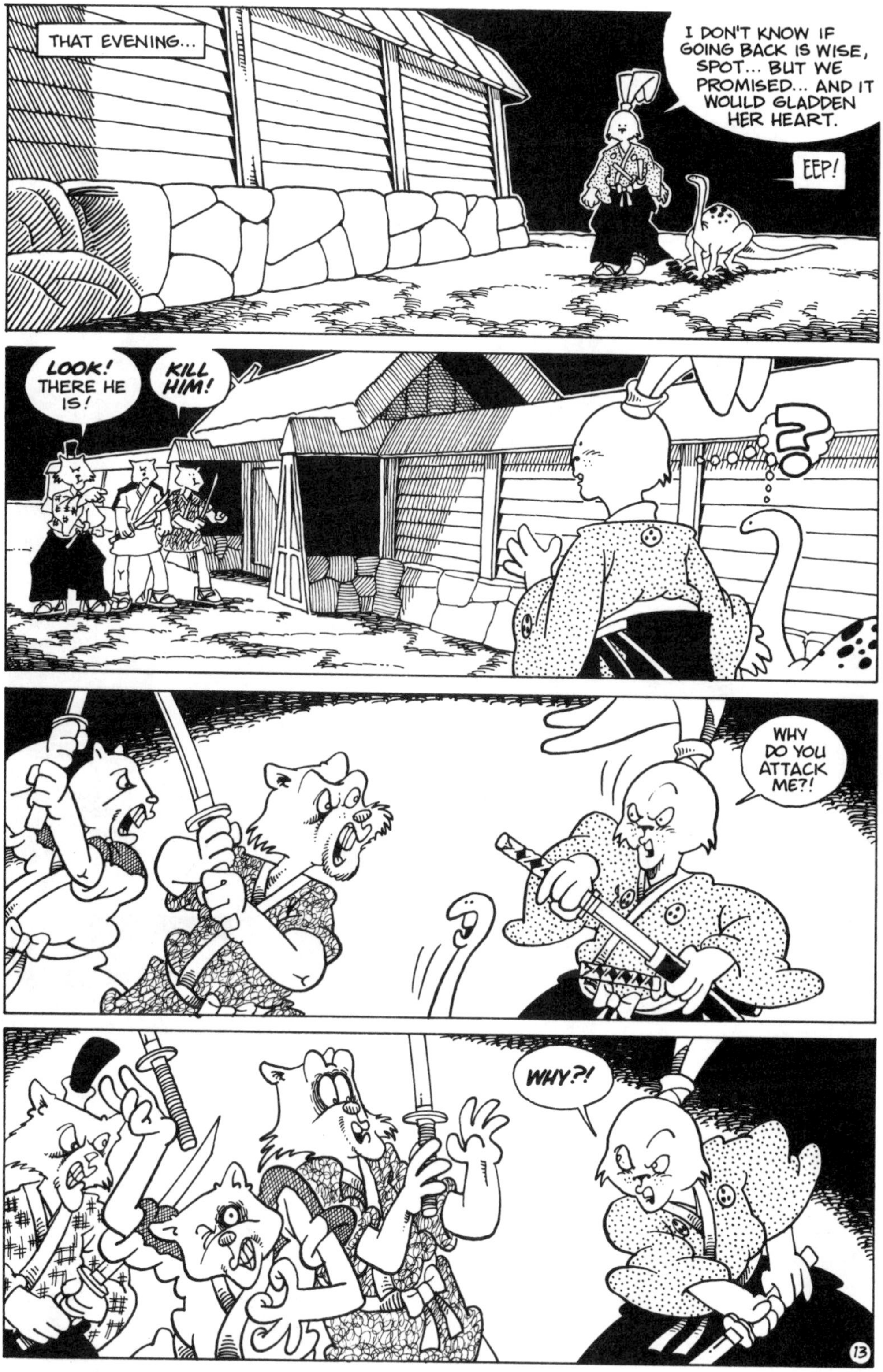
THAT EVENING...
I DON'T KNOW IF GOING BACK IS WISE, SPOT... BUT WE PROMISED... AND IT WOULD GLADDEN HER HEART.
EEP!
LOOK! THERE HE IS!
KILL HIM!
?
WHY DO YOU ATTACK ME?!
WHY?!
13

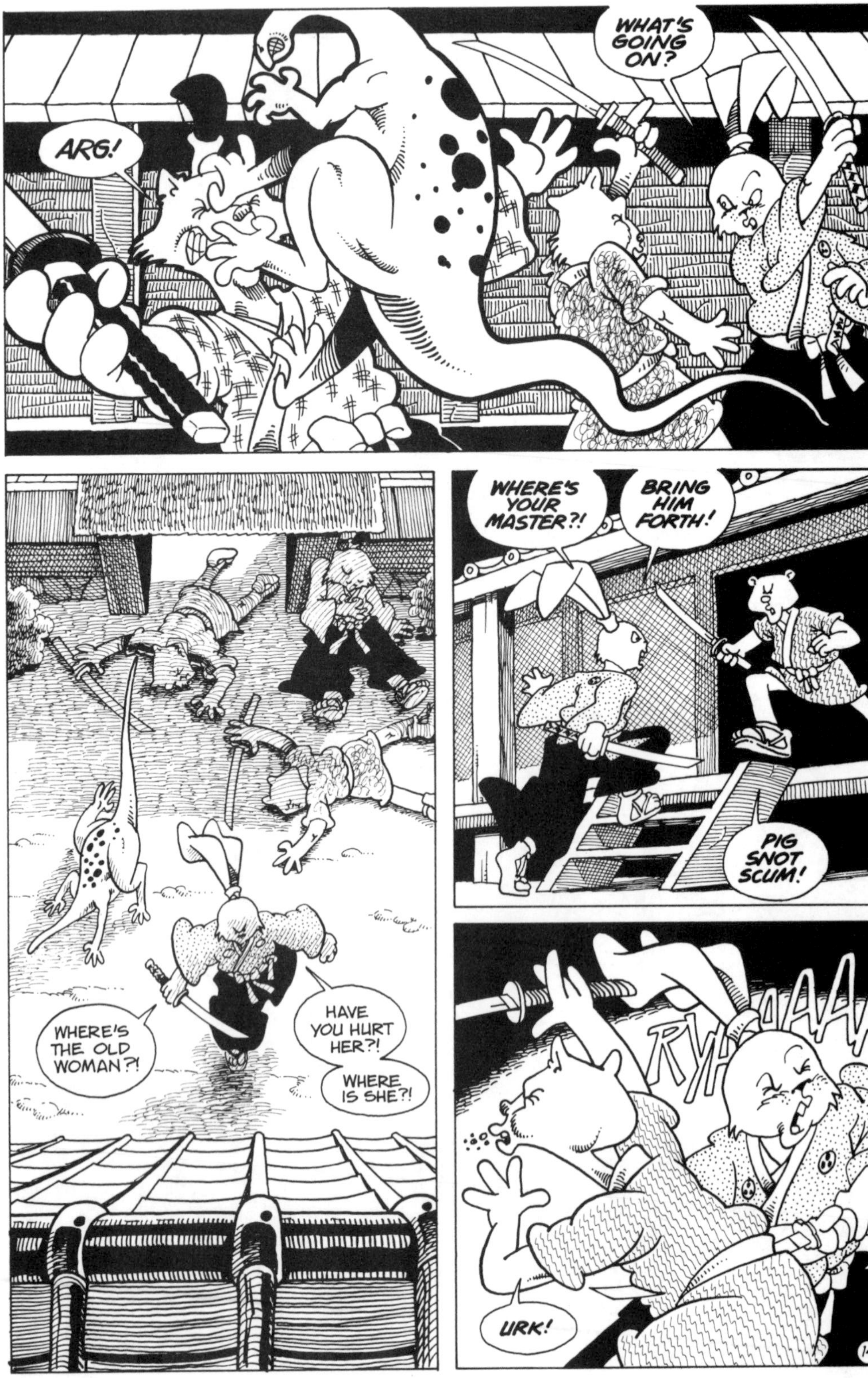

ARG!
WHAT'S GOING ON?
WHERE'S YOUR MASTER?!
BRING HIM FORTH!
PIG SNOT SCUM!
WHERE'S THE OLD WOMAN?!
HAVE YOU HURT HER?!
WHERE IS SHE?!
RYAAAAA
URK!
14

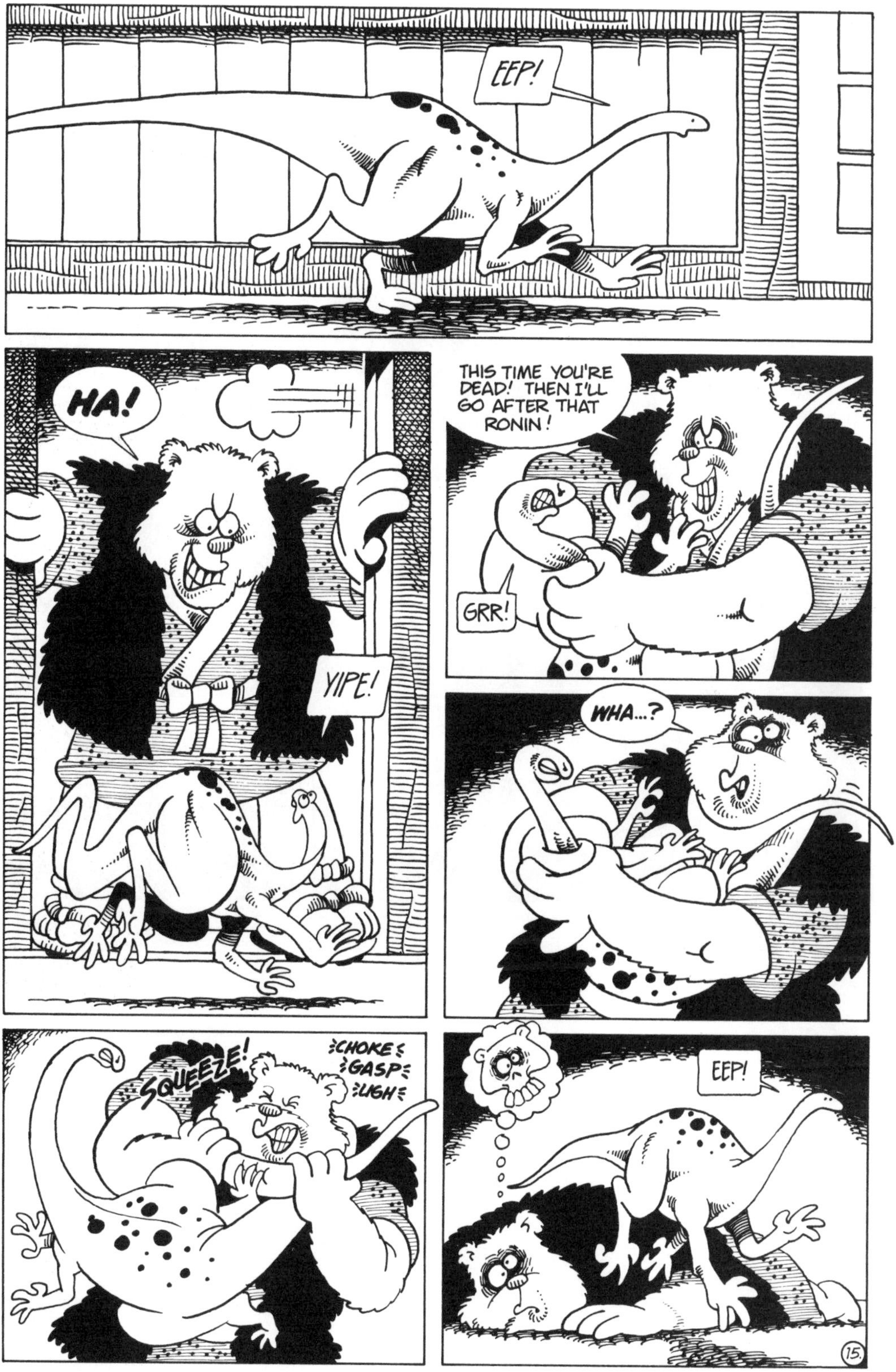
EEP!
HA!
YIPE!
THIS TIME YOU'RE DEAD! THEN I'LL GO AFTER THAT RONIN!
GRR!
WHA...?
SQUEEZE!
CHOKE
GASP
UGH
EEP!
15.

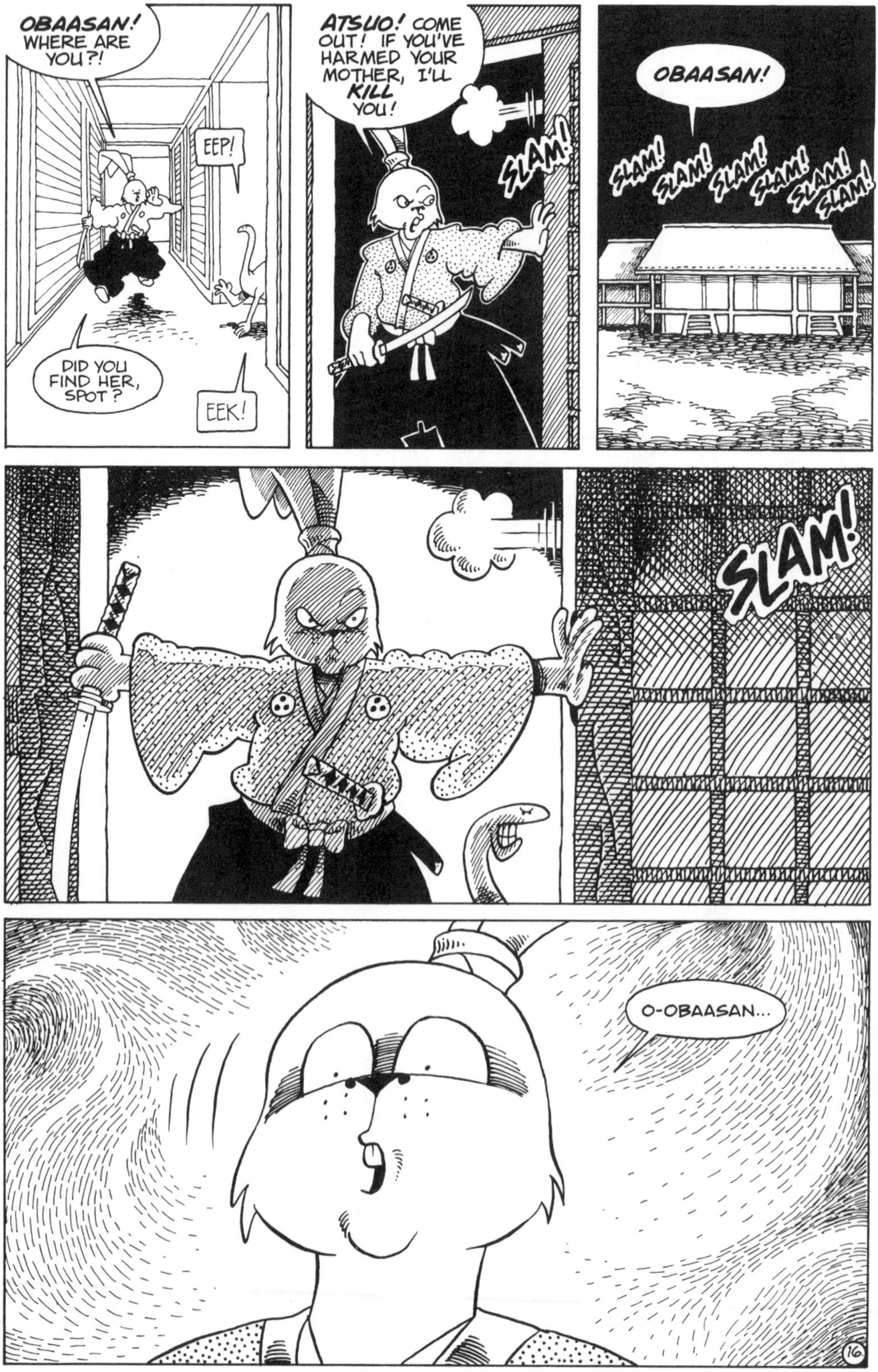
OBAASAN! WHERE ARE YOU?!
EEP!
DID YOU FIND HER, SPOT?
EEK!
ATSUO! COME OUT! IF YOU'VE HARMED YOUR MOTHER, I'LL KILL YOU!
SLAM!
OBAASAN!
SLAM! SLAM! SLAM! SLAM! SLAM! SLAM!
SLAM!
O-OBAASAN...
16

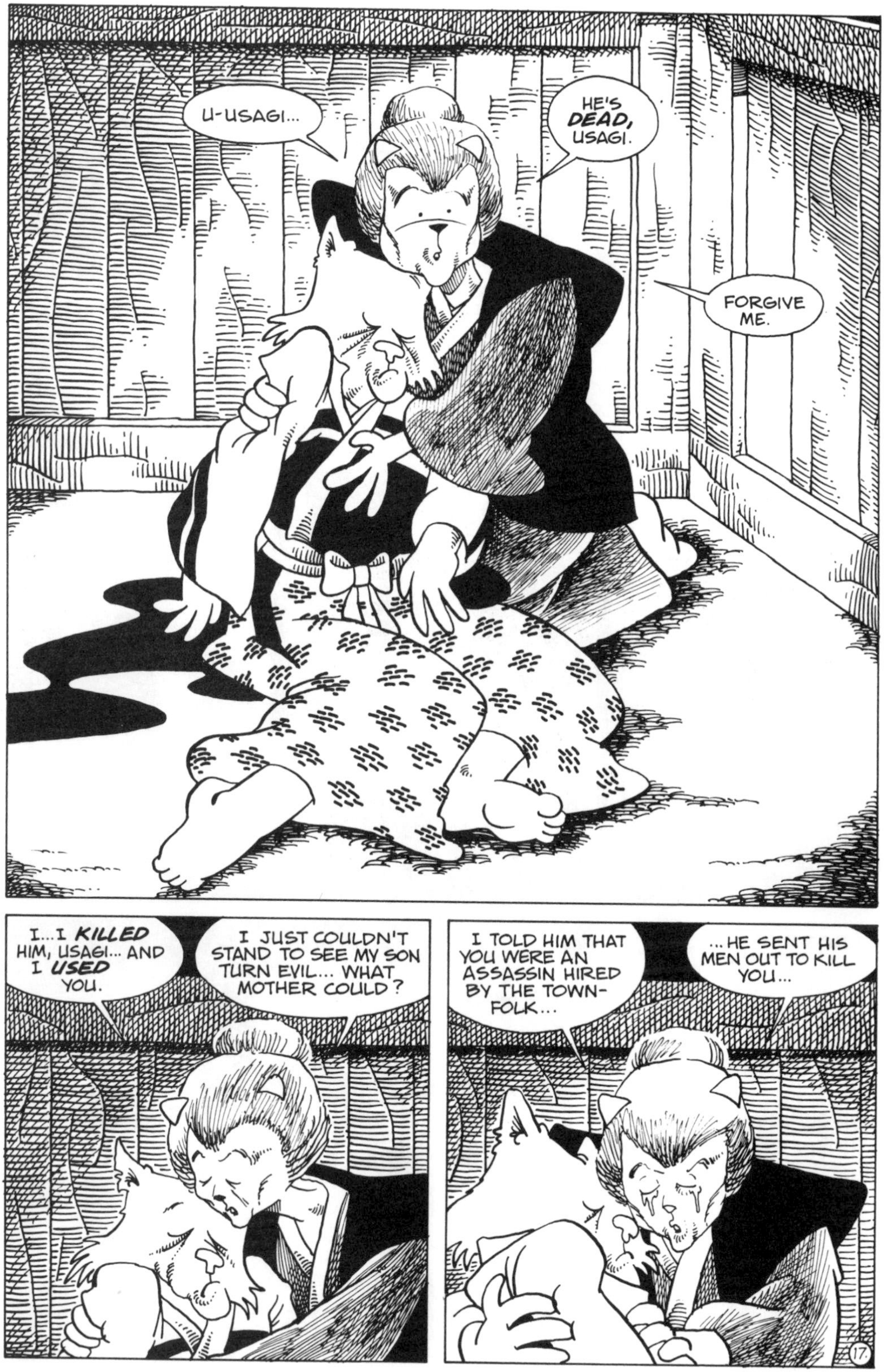
U-USAGI...
HE'S **DEAD,** USAGI.
FORGIVE ME.
I...I ***KILLED*** HIM, USAGI... AND I ***USED*** YOU.
I JUST COULDN'T STAND TO SEE MY SON TURN EVIL... WHAT MOTHER COULD?
I TOLD HIM THAT YOU WERE AN ASSASSIN HIRED BY THE TOWN-FOLK...
...HE SENT HIS MEN OUT TO KILL YOU...
17.

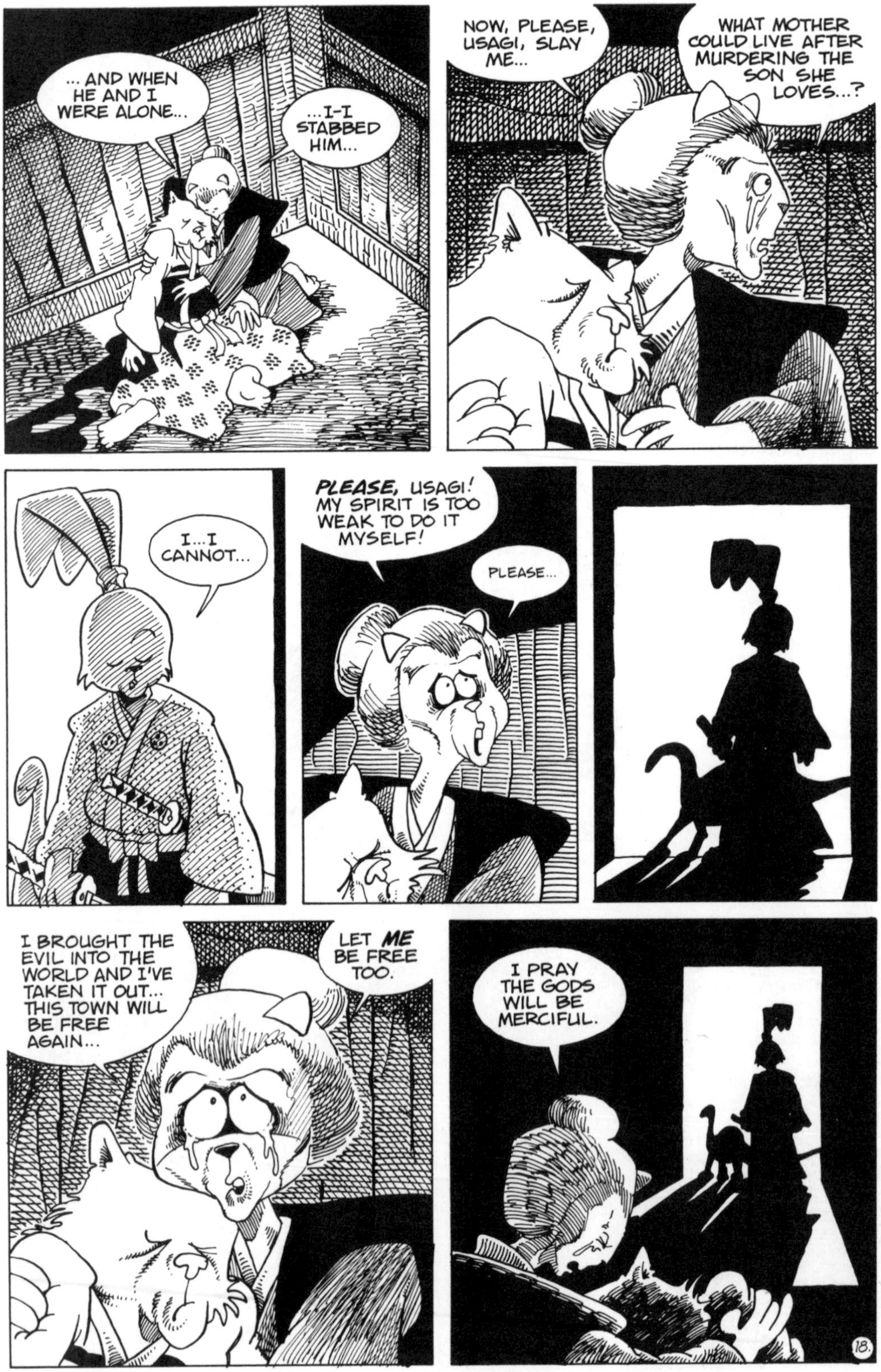
... AND WHEN HE AND I WERE ALONE...
...I-I STABBED HIM...
NOW, PLEASE, USAGI, SLAY ME...
WHAT MOTHER COULD LIVE AFTER MURDERING THE SON SHE LOVES...?
I...I CANNOT...
PLEASE, USAGI! MY SPIRIT IS TOO WEAK TO DO IT MYSELF!
PLEASE...
I BROUGHT THE EVIL INTO THE WORLD AND I'VE TAKEN IT OUT... THIS TOWN WILL BE FREE AGAIN...
LET *ME* BE FREE TOO.
I PRAY THE GODS WILL BE MERCIFUL.
18.

I'LL HOLD YOU TIGHT, MY SON... AND SING TO YOU-- JUST LIKE I USED TO...

The grass of summertime Grows long and green...

But it withers Before autumn's cold, harsh wind...

Winter covers all With a blanket of snow...

But lo how they reappear With the spring thaw...

All has its seasons Life is a cycle. It goes round and round Round and round Round and rou--※

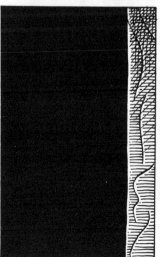

19.

43

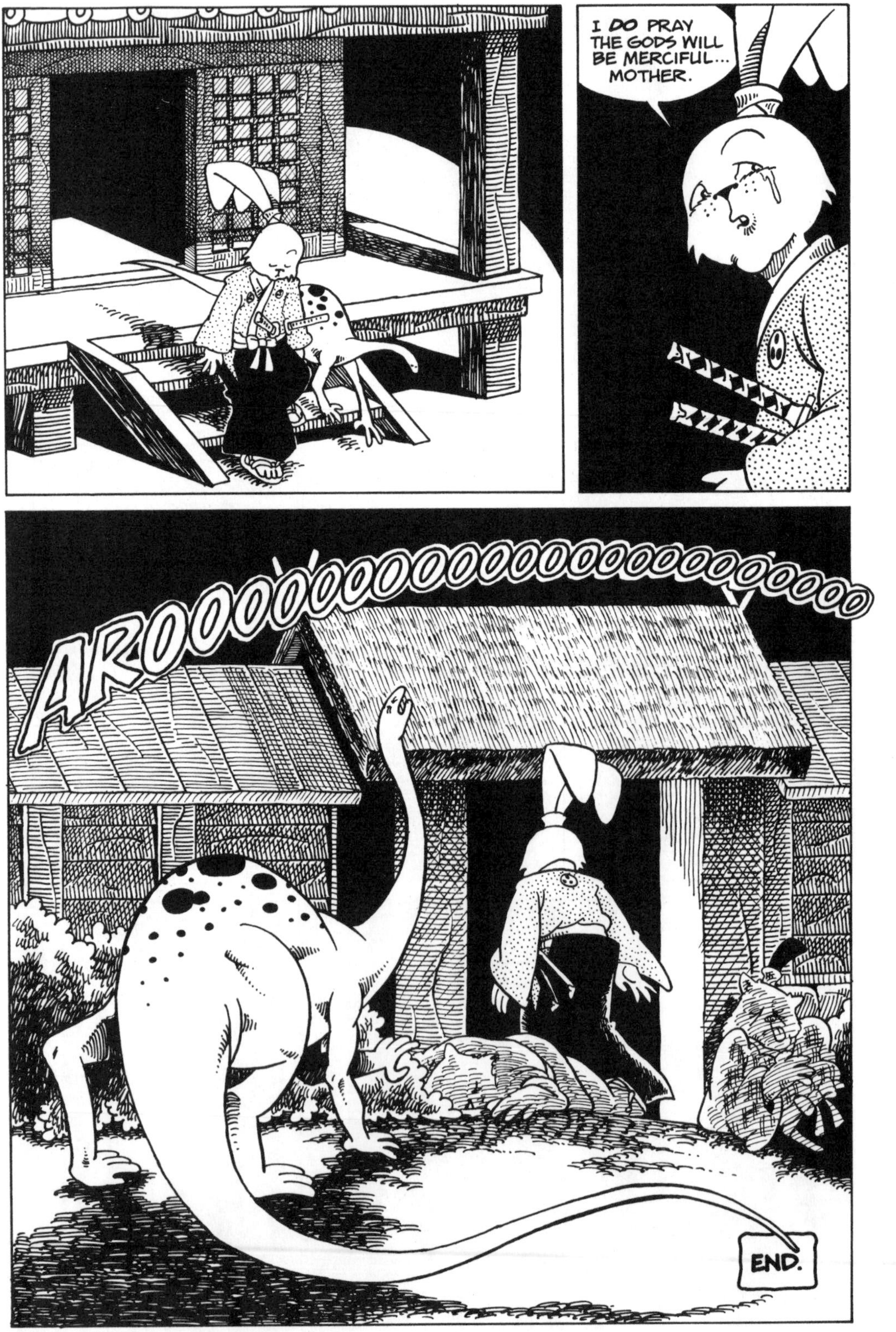
I DO PRAY THE GODS WILL BE MERCIFUL... MOTHER.
AROOOOOOOOOOOOOOOOOOOOOOOOOOOOO
END.

CHAPTER THREE

"Return of the Blind Swordspig"

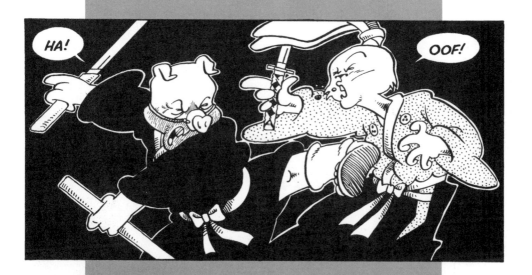

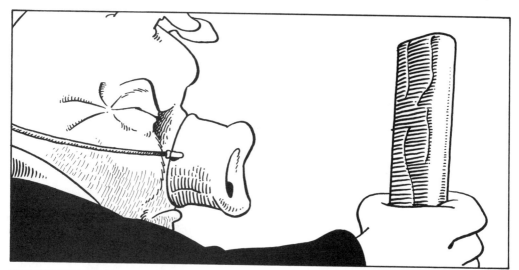

A LIFE OF SOLITUDE IS WHAT I LEAD... COMPANIONSHIP LEADS TO BETRAYAL AND DESPAIR...

OTHERS ARE CONTENT TO COMPLICATE THEIR LIVES... BUT FOR ME, THE SWORD IS MY ONLY FRIEND...

CHIRP!

≶SNIFF SNIFF≶ *PHAW!* PEASANTS FERTILIZING THE FIELDS! I HATE THIS TIME OF YEAR! IT RUINS MY DELICATE SENSE OF SMELL...

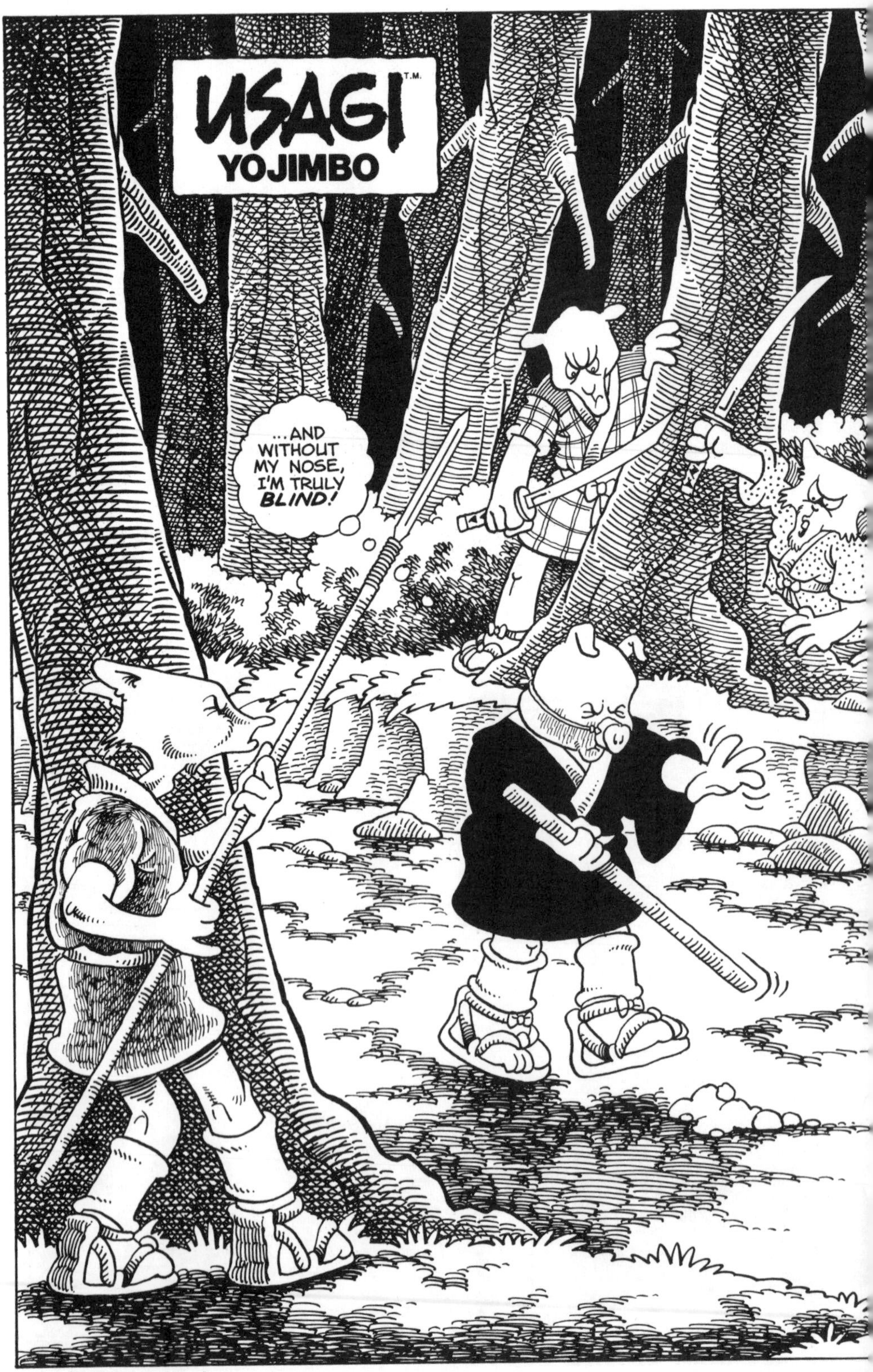
USAGI™
YOJIMBO
...AND WITHOUT MY NOSE, I'M TRULY BLIND!

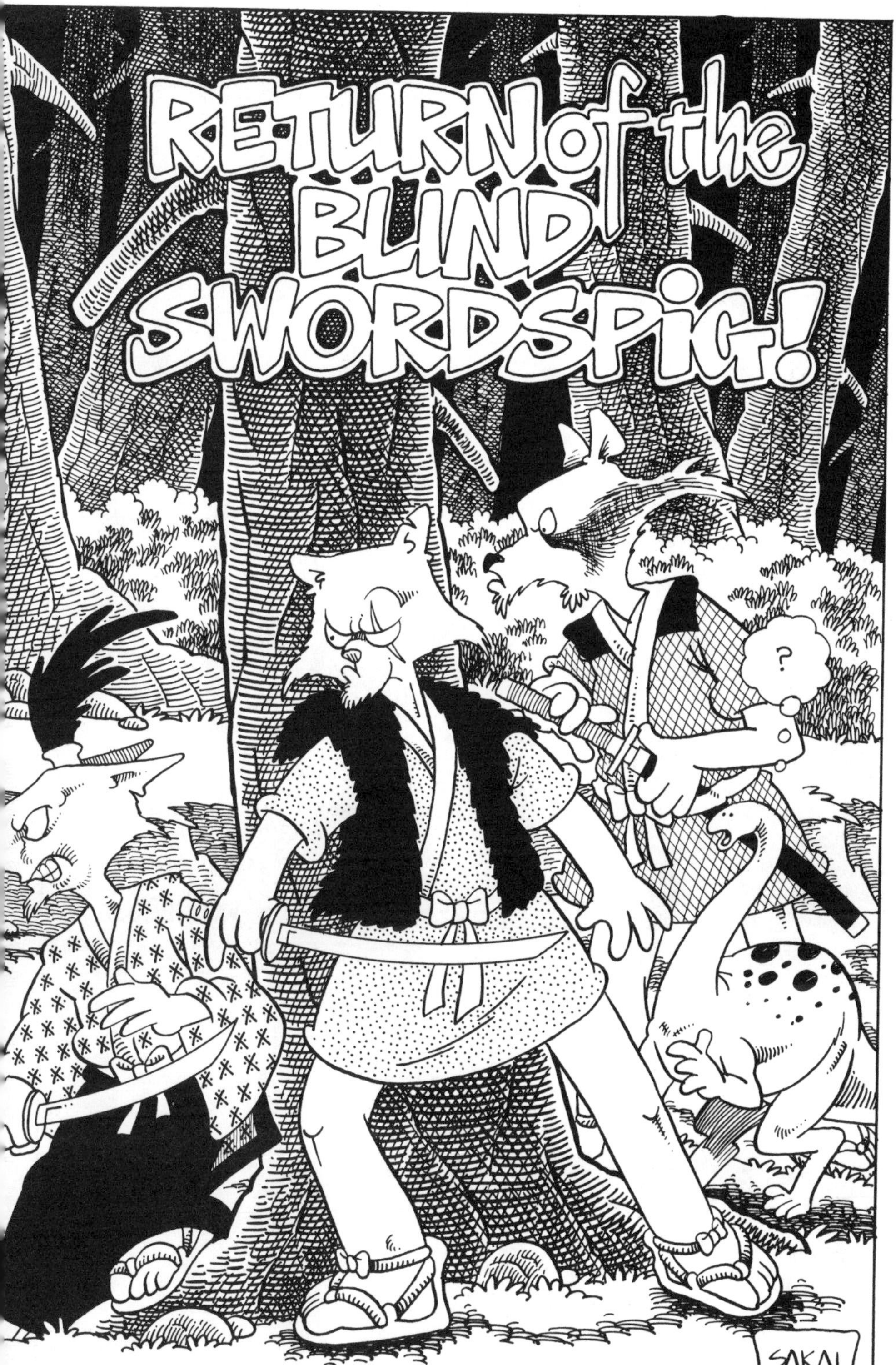
RETURN of the BLIND SWORDSPIG!
?
SAKAI

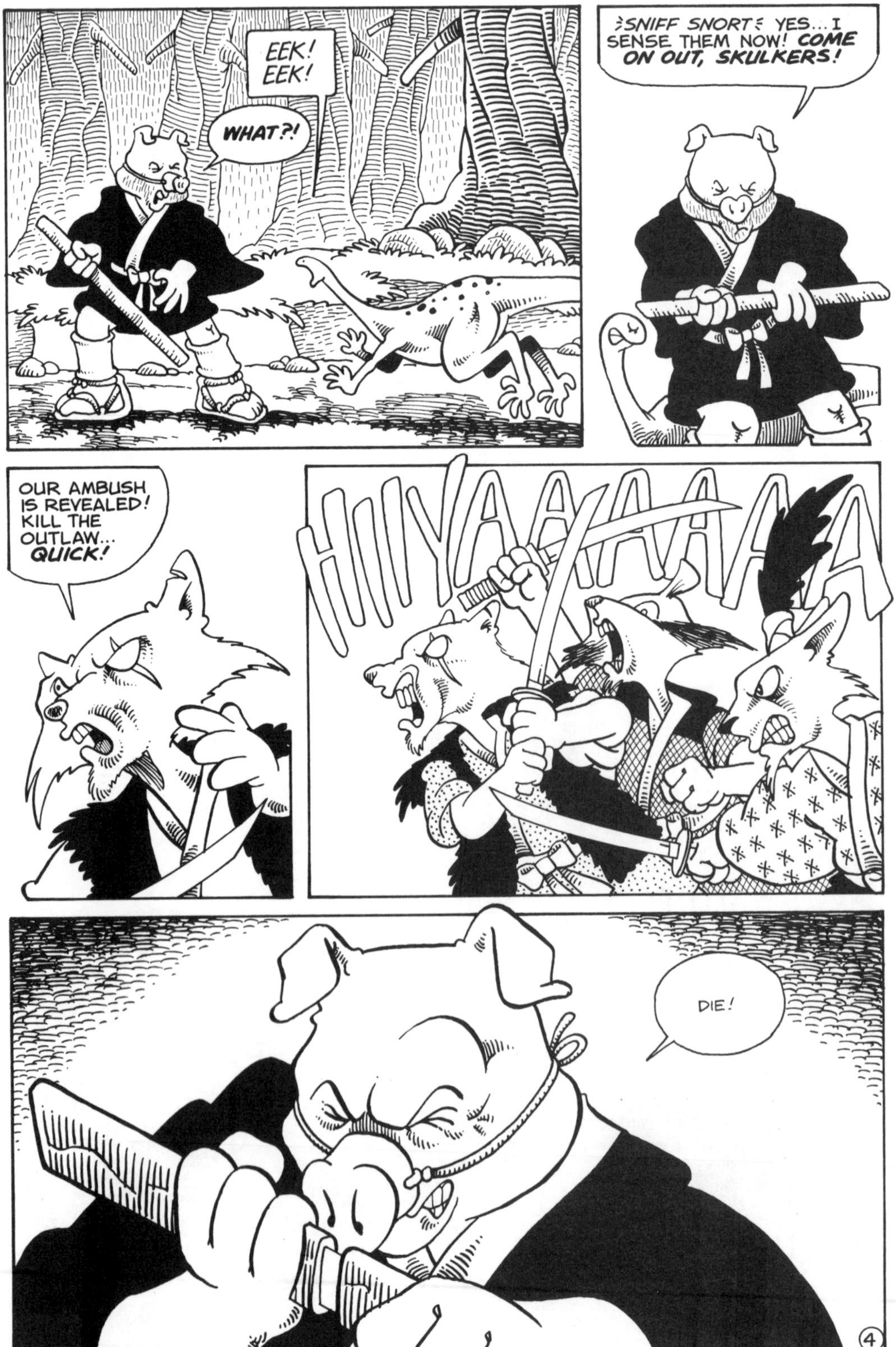
EEK! EEK!
WHAT?!
≥SNIFF SNORT≤ YES... I SENSE THEM NOW! COME ON OUT, SKULKERS!
OUR AMBUSH IS REVEALED! KILL THE OUTLAW... QUICK!
HIIYAAAAAAA
DIE!
4

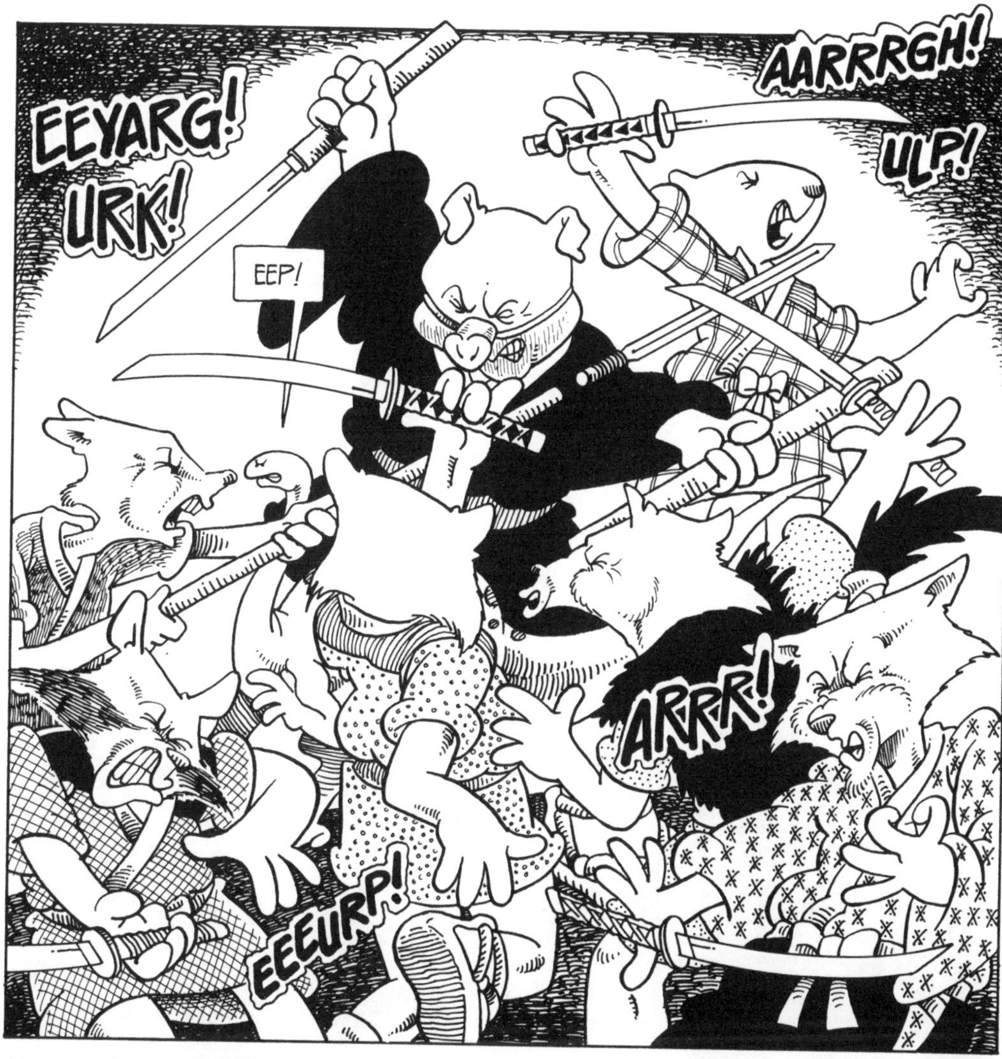
EEYARG!
URK!
AARRRGH!
ULP!
EEP!
ARRR!
EEEURP!

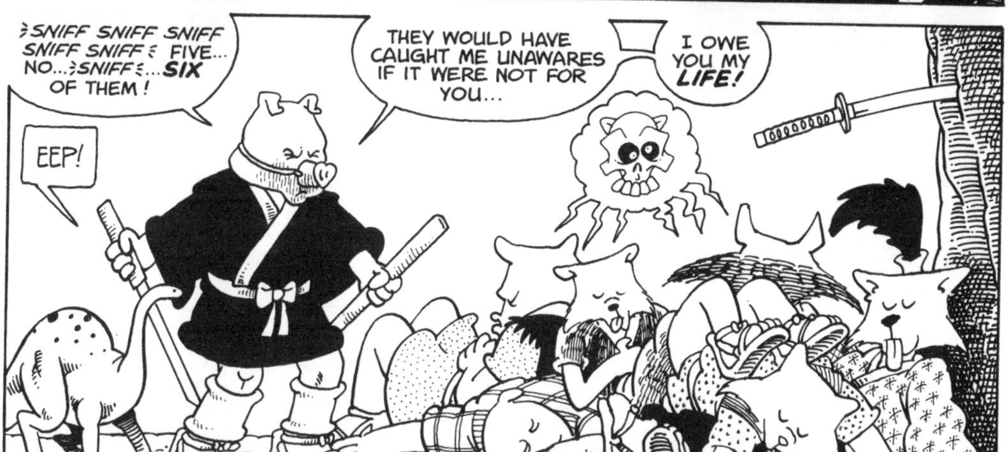
SNIFF SNIFF SNIFF SNIFF SNIFF FIVE... NO... *SNIFF* ...SIX OF THEM!
THEY WOULD HAVE CAUGHT ME UNAWARES IF IT WERE NOT FOR YOU...
I OWE YOU MY LIFE!
EEP!
5

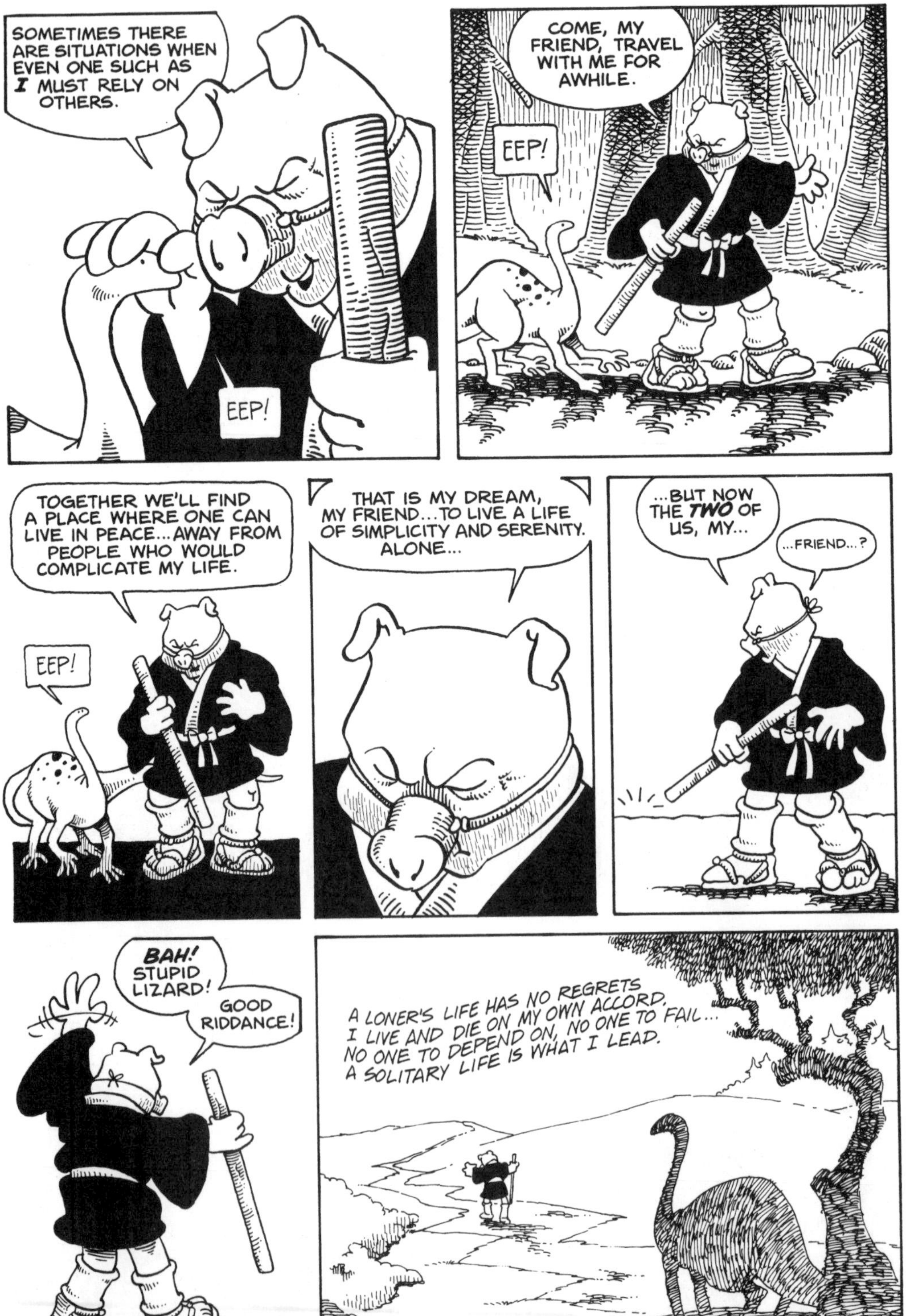
SOMETIMES THERE ARE SITUATIONS WHEN EVEN ONE SUCH AS *I* MUST RELY ON OTHERS.
EEP!
COME, MY FRIEND, TRAVEL WITH ME FOR AWHILE.
EEP!
TOGETHER WE'LL FIND A PLACE WHERE ONE CAN LIVE IN PEACE... AWAY FROM PEOPLE WHO WOULD COMPLICATE MY LIFE.
EEP!
THAT IS MY DREAM, MY FRIEND... TO LIVE A LIFE OF SIMPLICITY AND SERENITY. ALONE...
...BUT NOW THE *TWO* OF US, MY...
...FRIEND...?
BAH! STUPID LIZARD!
GOOD RIDDANCE!
A LONER'S LIFE HAS NO REGRETS
I LIVE AND DIE ON MY OWN ACCORD,
NO ONE TO DEPEND ON, NO ONE TO FAIL...
A SOLITARY LIFE IS WHAT I LEAD.
6

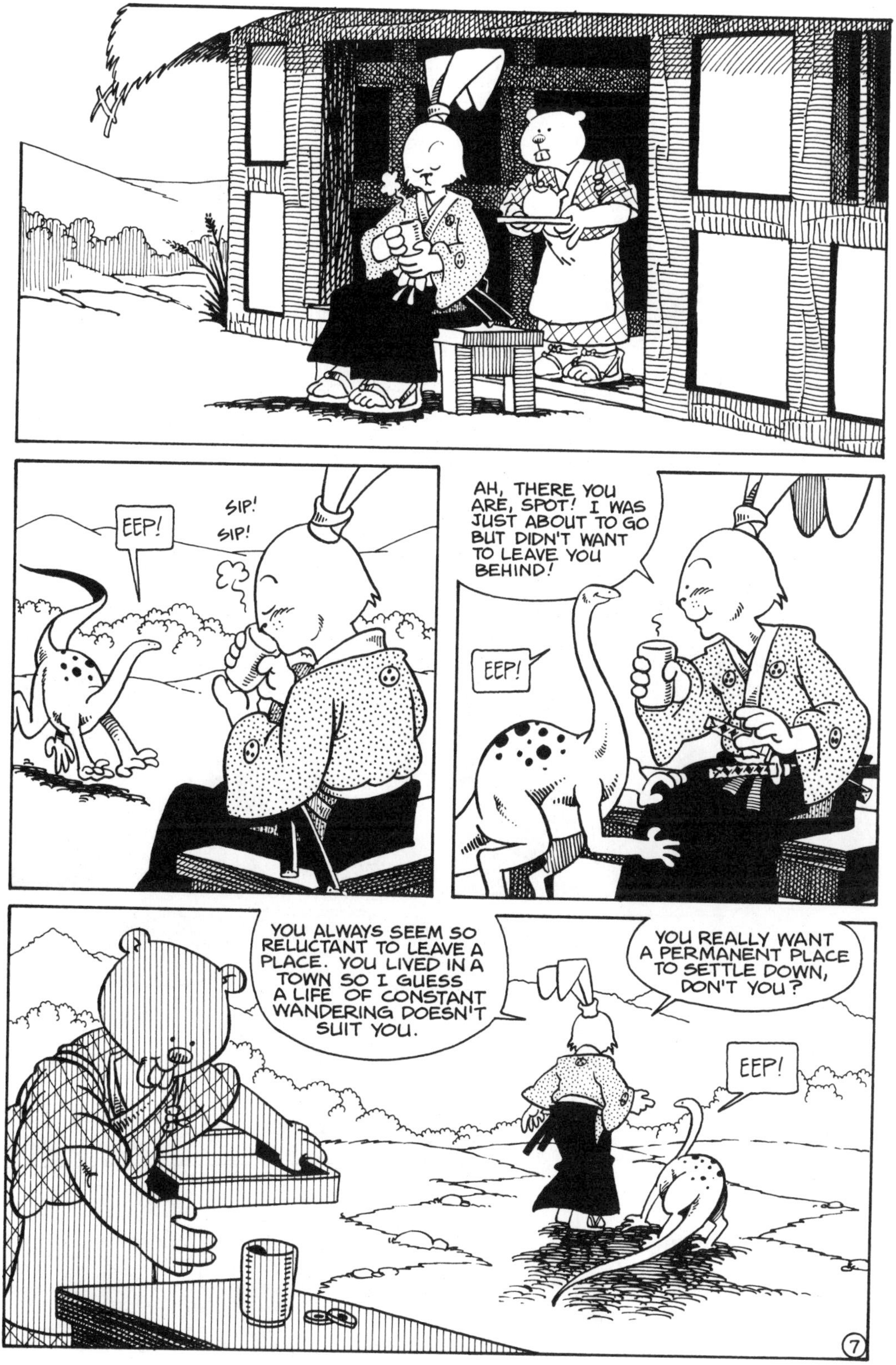
EEP!
SIP!
SIP!
AH, THERE YOU ARE, SPOT! I WAS JUST ABOUT TO GO BUT DIDN'T WANT TO LEAVE YOU BEHIND!
EEP!
YOU ALWAYS SEEM SO RELUCTANT TO LEAVE A PLACE. YOU LIVED IN A TOWN SO I GUESS A LIFE OF CONSTANT WANDERING DOESN'T SUIT YOU.
YOU REALLY WANT A PERMANENT PLACE TO SETTLE DOWN, DON'T YOU?
EEP!
7

54

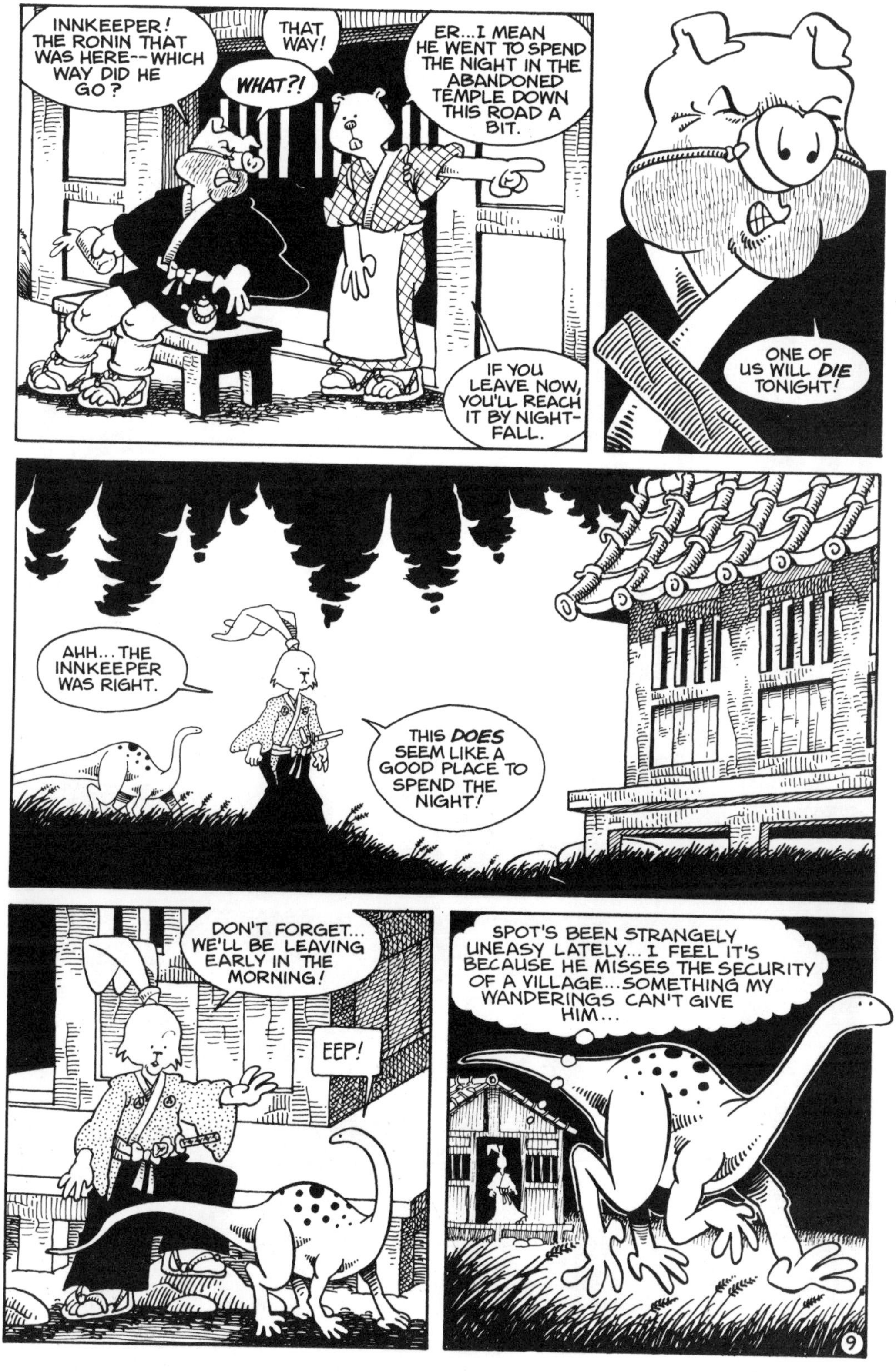

INNKEEPER! THE RONIN THAT WAS HERE-- WHICH WAY DID HE GO?
WHAT?!
THAT WAY!
ER...I MEAN HE WENT TO SPEND THE NIGHT IN THE ABANDONED TEMPLE DOWN THIS ROAD A BIT.
IF YOU LEAVE NOW, YOU'LL REACH IT BY NIGHT-FALL.
ONE OF US WILL DIE TONIGHT!
AHH... THE INNKEEPER WAS RIGHT.
THIS DOES SEEM LIKE A GOOD PLACE TO SPEND THE NIGHT!
DON'T FORGET... WE'LL BE LEAVING EARLY IN THE MORNING!
EEP!
SPOT'S BEEN STRANGELY UNEASY LATELY... I FEEL IT'S BECAUSE HE MISSES THE SECURITY OF A VILLAGE... SOMETHING MY WANDERINGS CAN'T GIVE HIM...
9

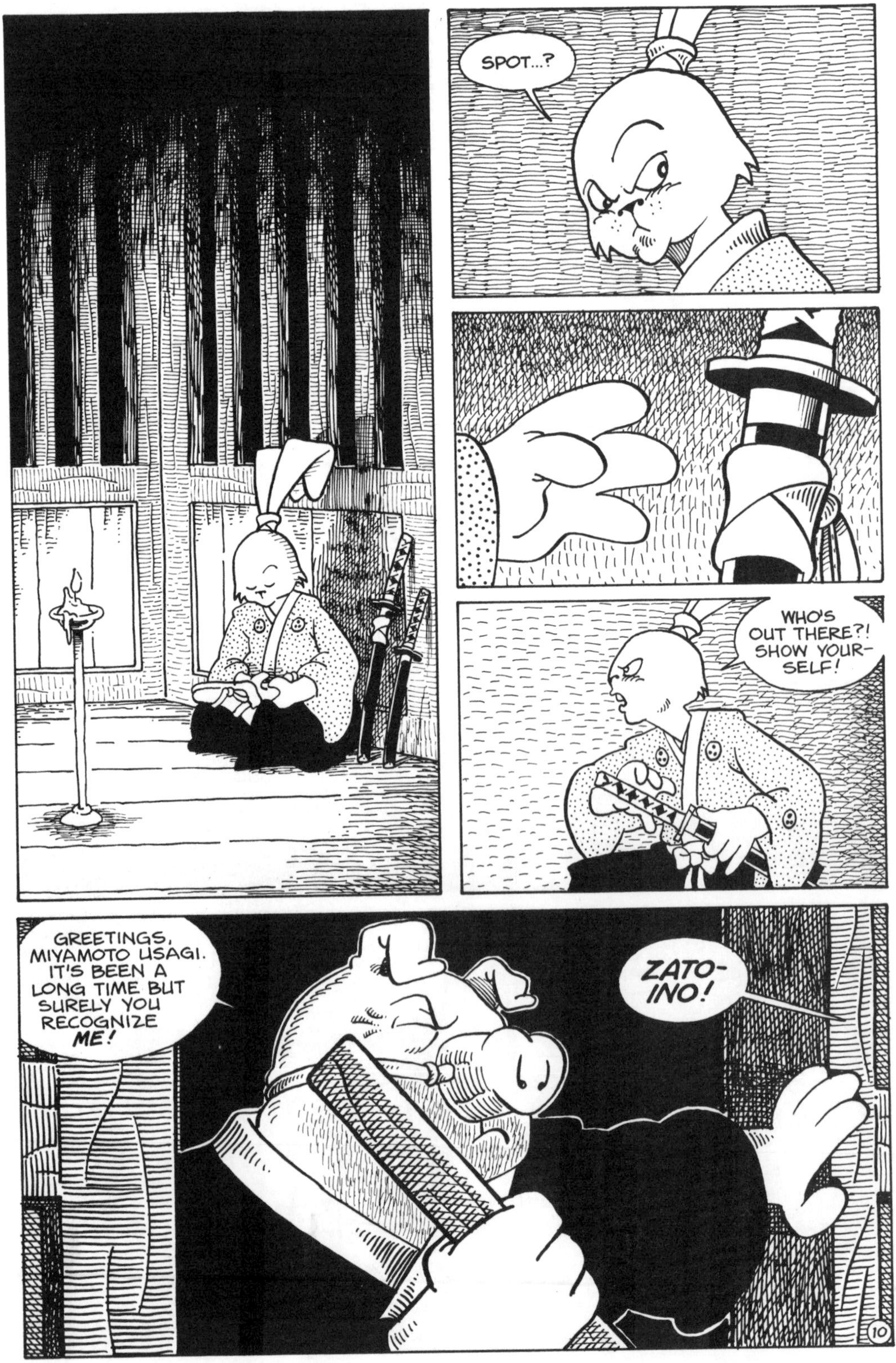
SPOT...?
WHO'S OUT THERE?! SHOW YOUR-SELF!
GREETINGS, MIYAMOTO USAGI. IT'S BEEN A LONG TIME BUT SURELY YOU RECOGNIZE ME!
ZATO-INO!
10

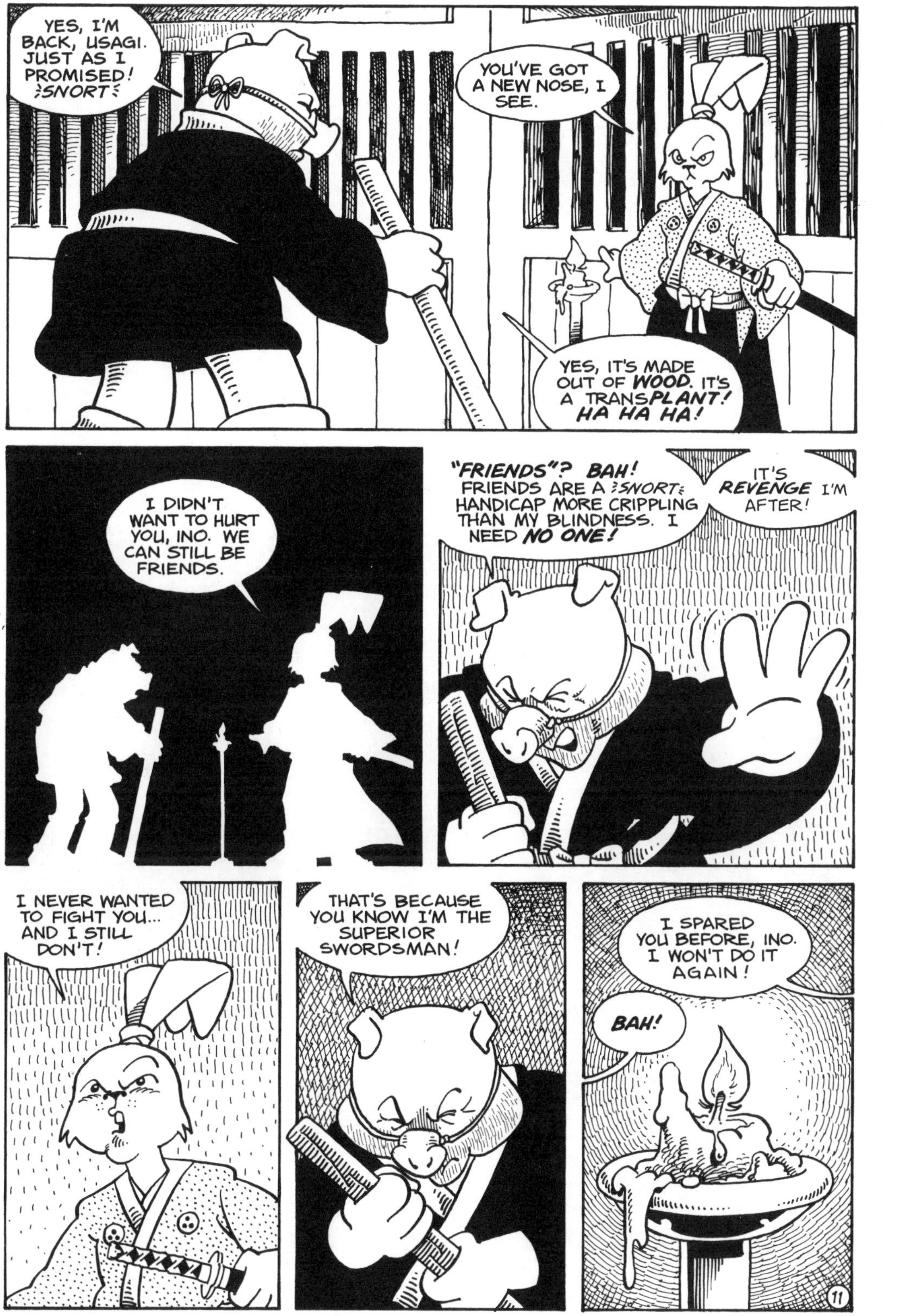
YES, I'M BACK, USAGI. JUST AS I PROMISED! SNORT
YOU'VE GOT A NEW NOSE, I SEE.
YES, IT'S MADE OUT OF WOOD. IT'S A TRANSPLANT! HA HA HA!
I DIDN'T WANT TO HURT YOU, INO. WE CAN STILL BE FRIENDS.
"FRIENDS"? BAH! FRIENDS ARE A SNORT HANDICAP MORE CRIPPLING THAN MY BLINDNESS. I NEED NO ONE!
IT'S REVENGE I'M AFTER!
I NEVER WANTED TO FIGHT YOU... AND I STILL DON'T!
THAT'S BECAUSE YOU KNOW I'M THE SUPERIOR SWORDSMAN!
I SPARED YOU BEFORE, INO. I WON'T DO IT AGAIN!
BAH!
11

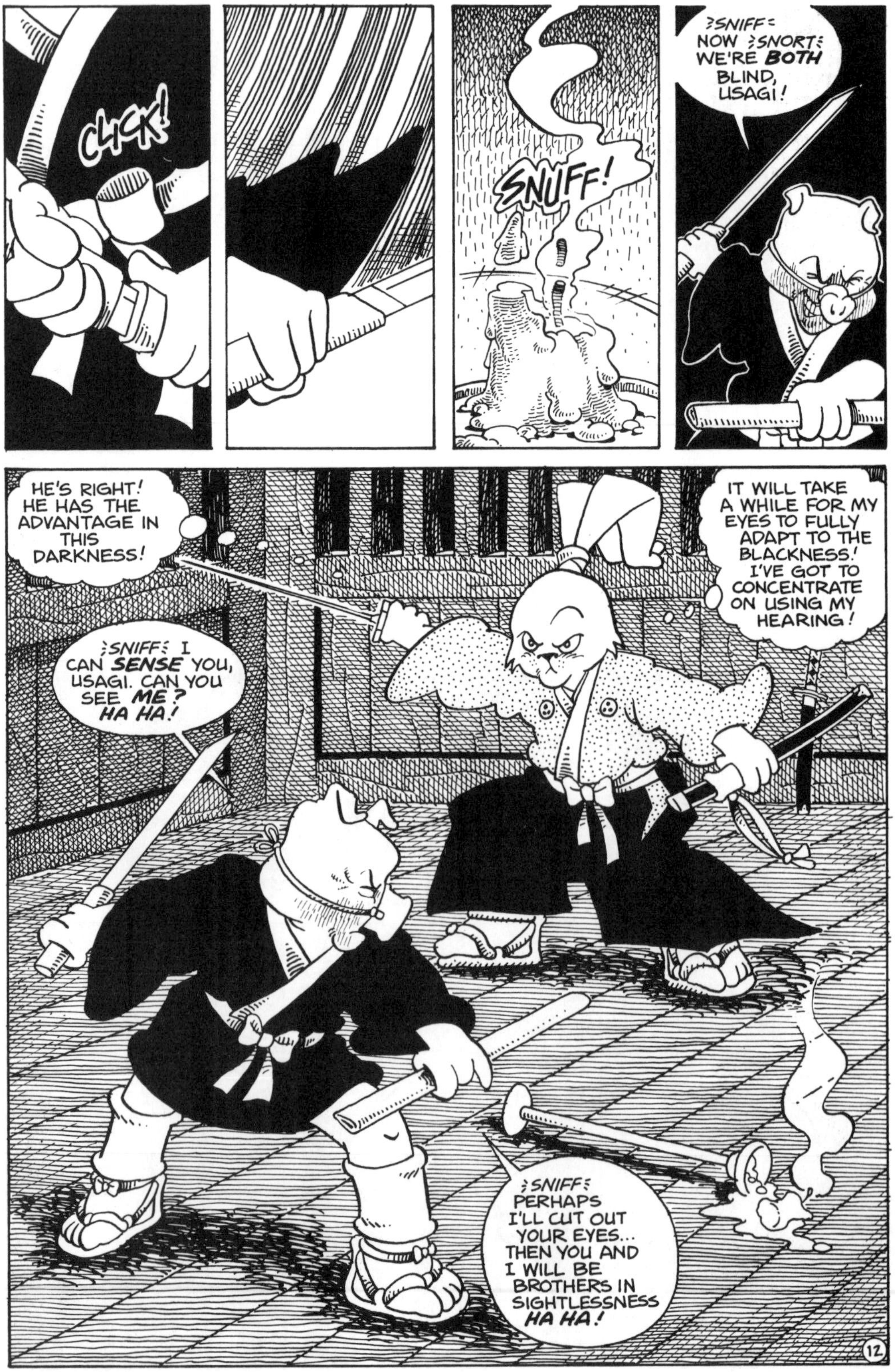
CLICK!
SNUFF!
≋SNIFF≋ NOW ≋SNORT≋ WE'RE BOTH BLIND, USAGI!
HE'S RIGHT! HE HAS THE ADVANTAGE IN THIS DARKNESS!
IT WILL TAKE A WHILE FOR MY EYES TO FULLY ADAPT TO THE BLACKNESS! I'VE GOT TO CONCENTRATE ON USING MY HEARING!
≋SNIFF≋ I CAN SENSE YOU, USAGI. CAN YOU SEE ME? HA HA!
≋SNIFF≋ PERHAPS I'LL CUT OUT YOUR EYES... THEN YOU AND I WILL BE BROTHERS IN SIGHTLESSNESS HA HA!
12

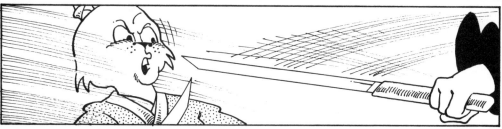

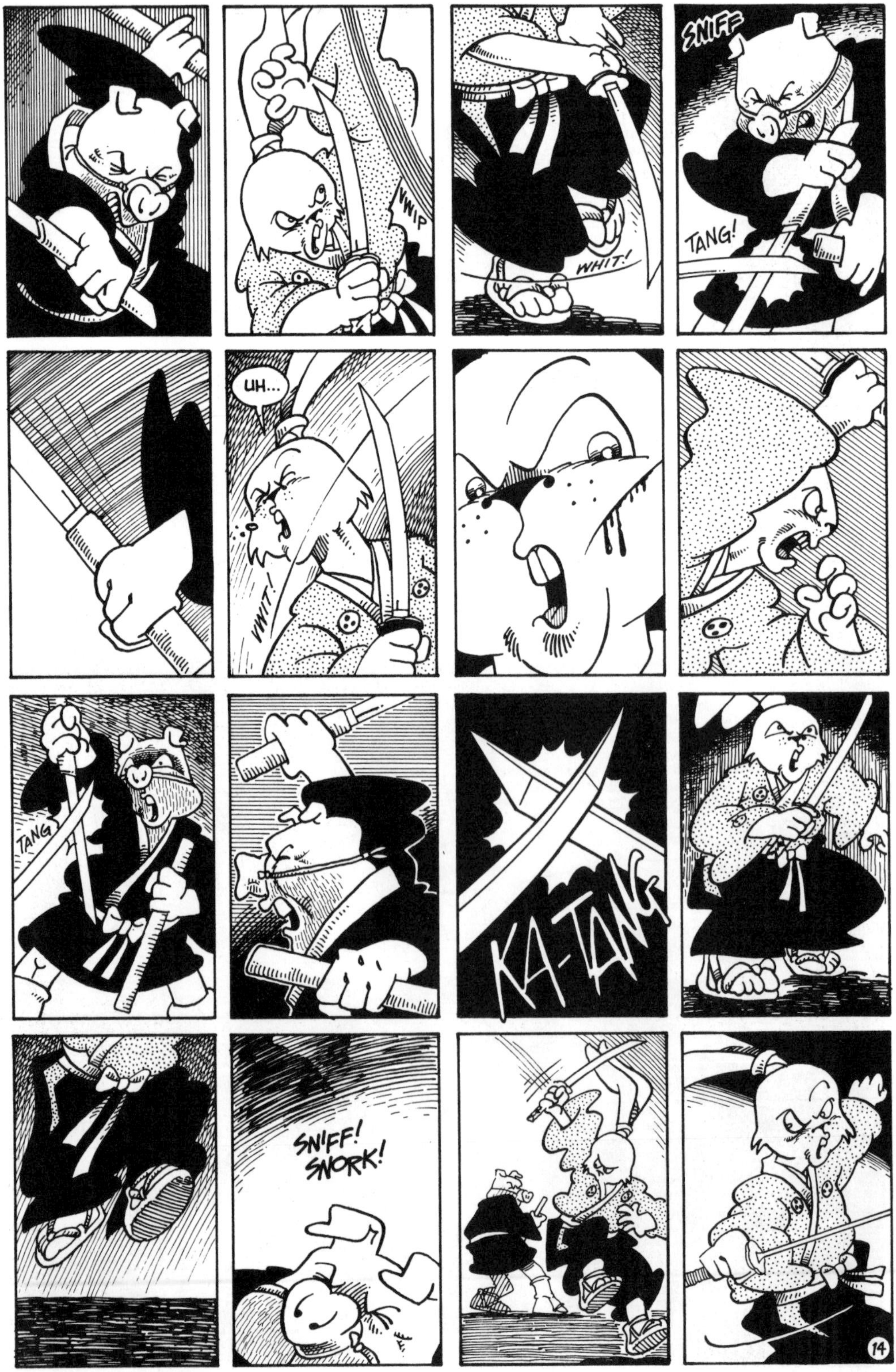
VWIP
WHIT!
SNIFF
TANG!
UH...
VWIT!
TANG
KA-TANG
SNIFF!
SNORK!
14

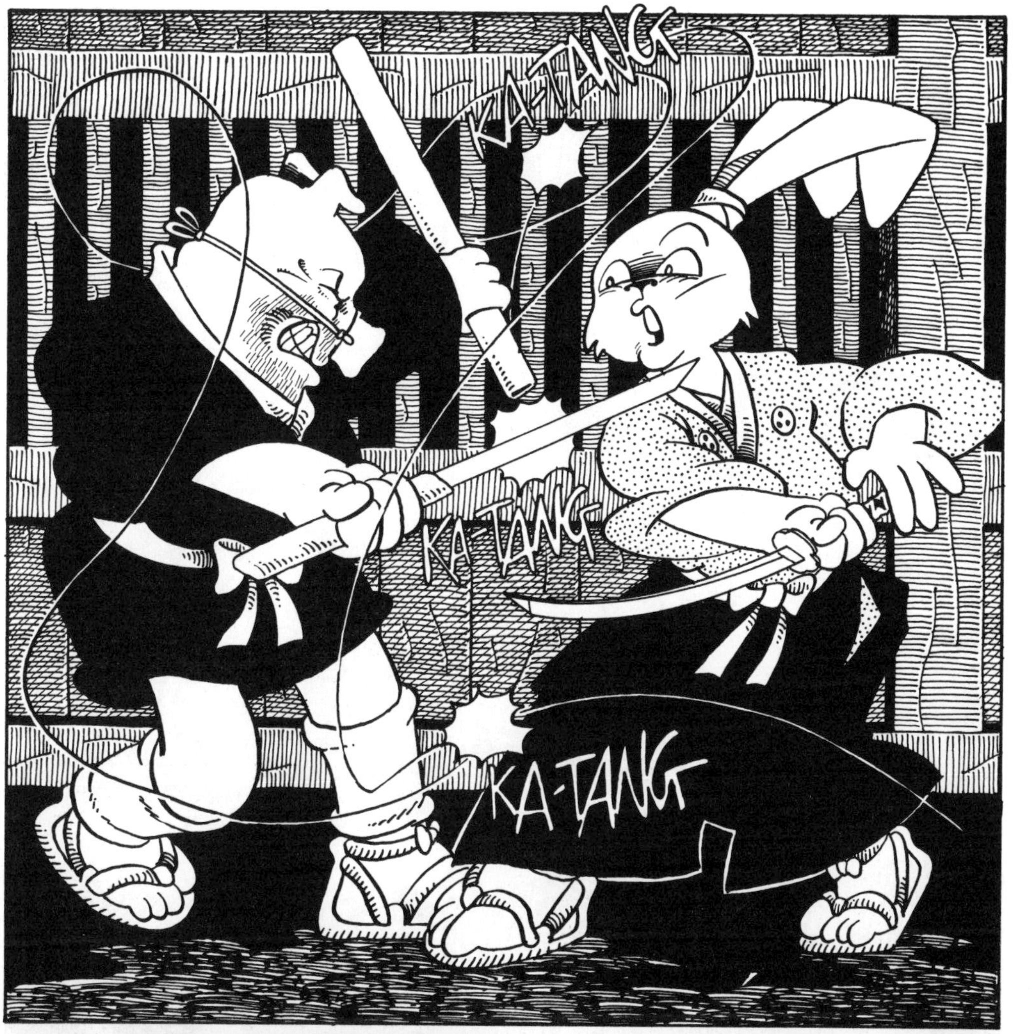
KA-TANG
KA-TANG
KA-TANG

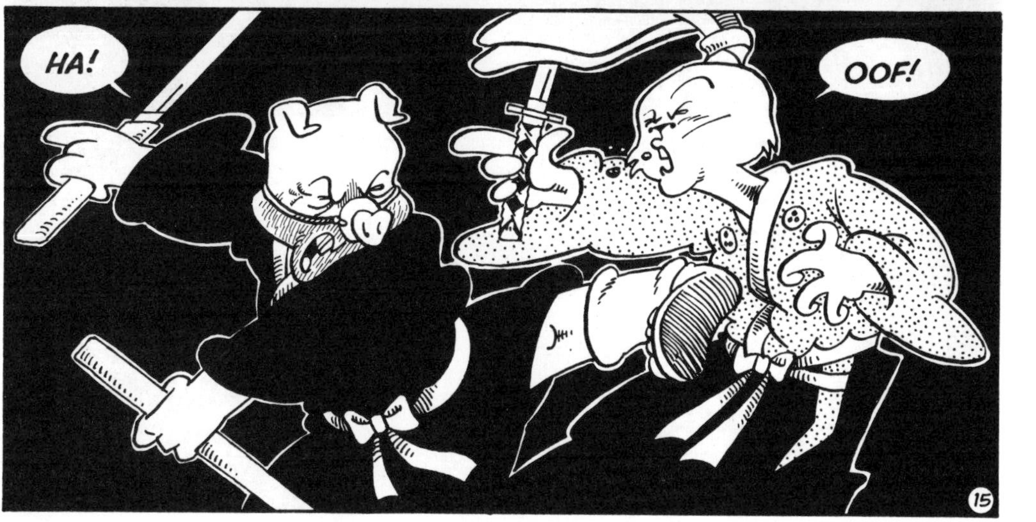
HA!
OOF!
15

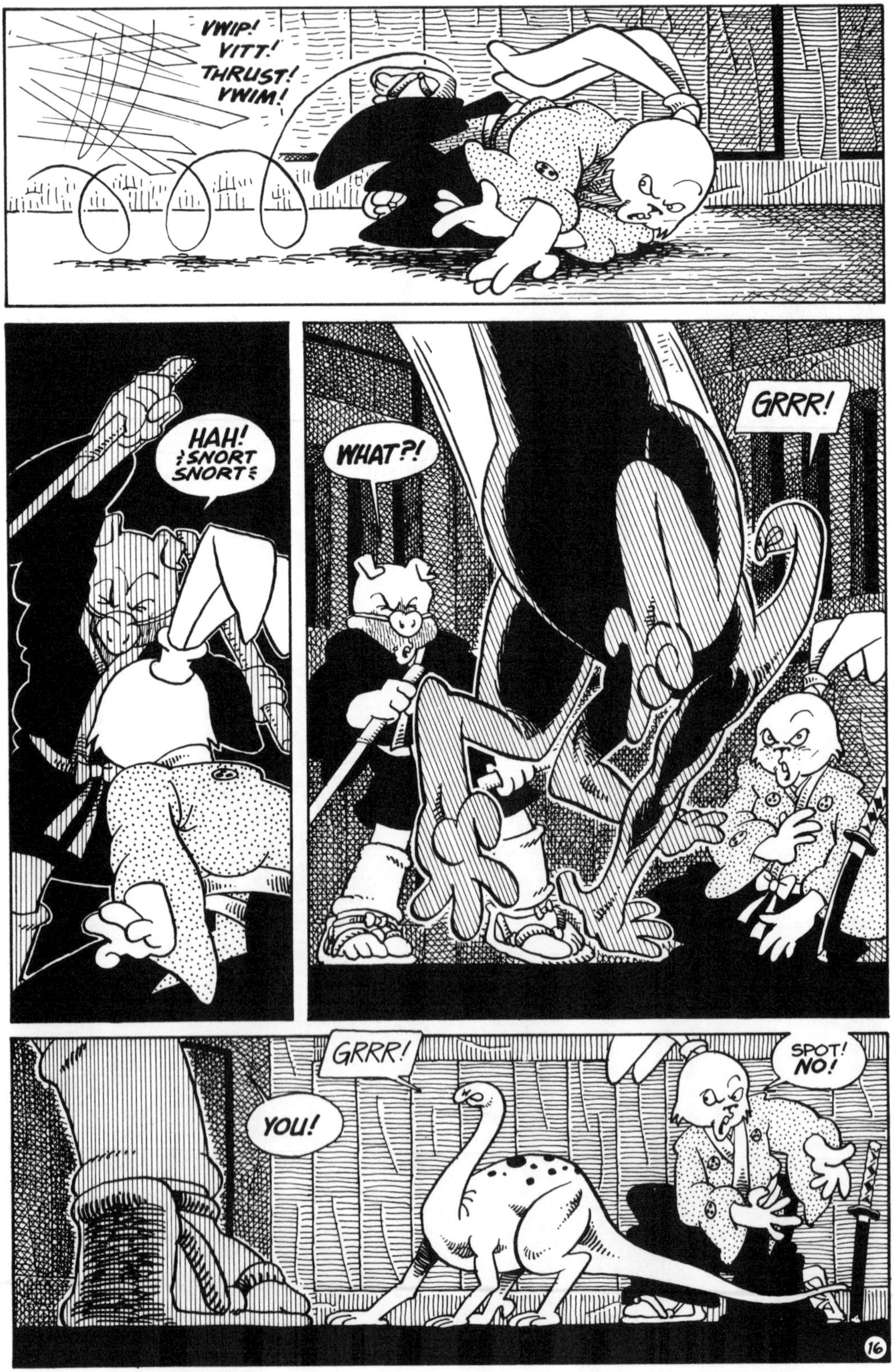
VWIP! VITT! THRUST! VWIM!
HAH! SNORT SNORT
WHAT?!
GRRR!
GRRR!
YOU!
SPOT! NO!
16

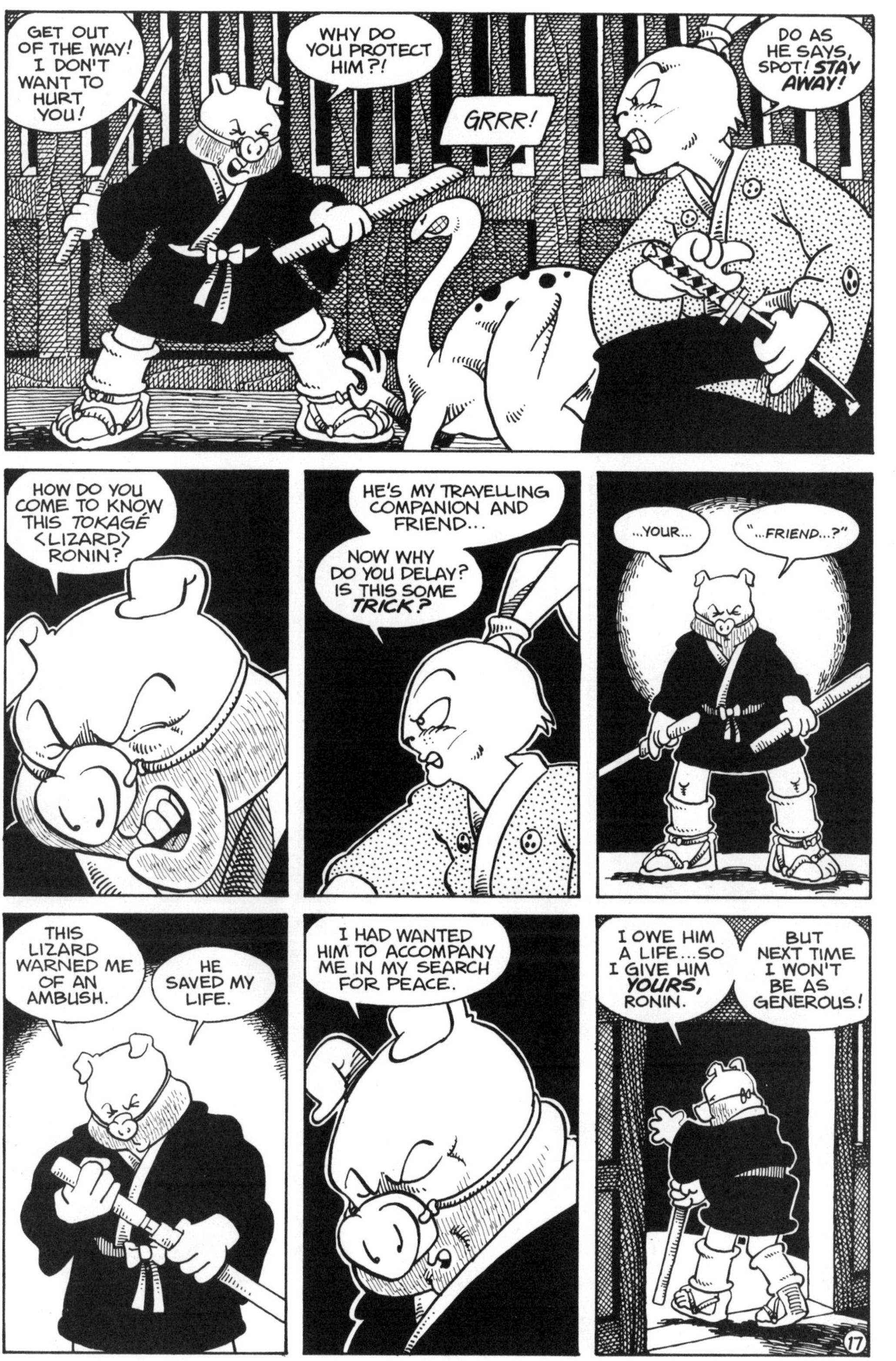
GET OUT OF THE WAY! I DON'T WANT TO HURT YOU!
WHY DO YOU PROTECT HIM?!
GRRR!
DO AS HE SAYS, SPOT! **STAY AWAY!**
HOW DO YOU COME TO KNOW THIS *TOKAGÉ* <LIZARD> RONIN?
HE'S MY TRAVELLING COMPANION AND FRIEND...
NOW WHY DO YOU DELAY? IS THIS SOME **TRICK?**
...YOUR...
"...FRIEND...?"
THIS LIZARD WARNED ME OF AN AMBUSH.
HE SAVED MY LIFE.
I HAD WANTED HIM TO ACCOMPANY ME IN MY SEARCH FOR PEACE.
I OWE HIM A LIFE...SO I GIVE HIM **YOURS,** RONIN.
BUT NEXT TIME I WON'T BE AS GENEROUS!
17

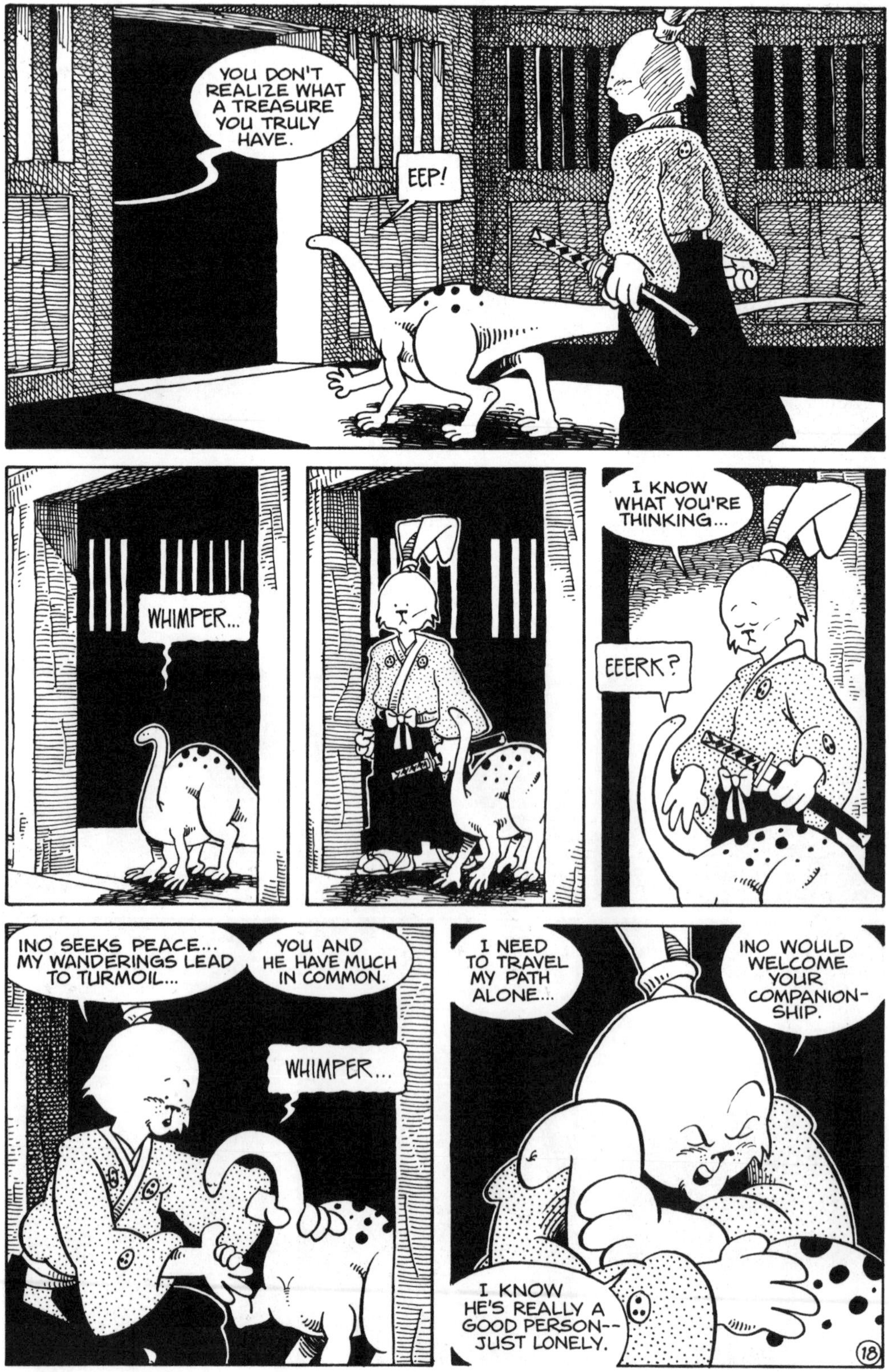
YOU DON'T REALIZE WHAT A TREASURE YOU TRULY HAVE.
EEP!
WHIMPER...
I KNOW WHAT YOU'RE THINKING...
EEERK?
INO SEEKS PEACE... MY WANDERINGS LEAD TO TURMOIL...
YOU AND HE HAVE MUCH IN COMMON.
WHIMPER...
I NEED TO TRAVEL MY PATH ALONE...
INO WOULD WELCOME YOUR COMPANIONSHIP.
I KNOW HE'S REALLY A GOOD PERSON-- JUST LONELY.
18

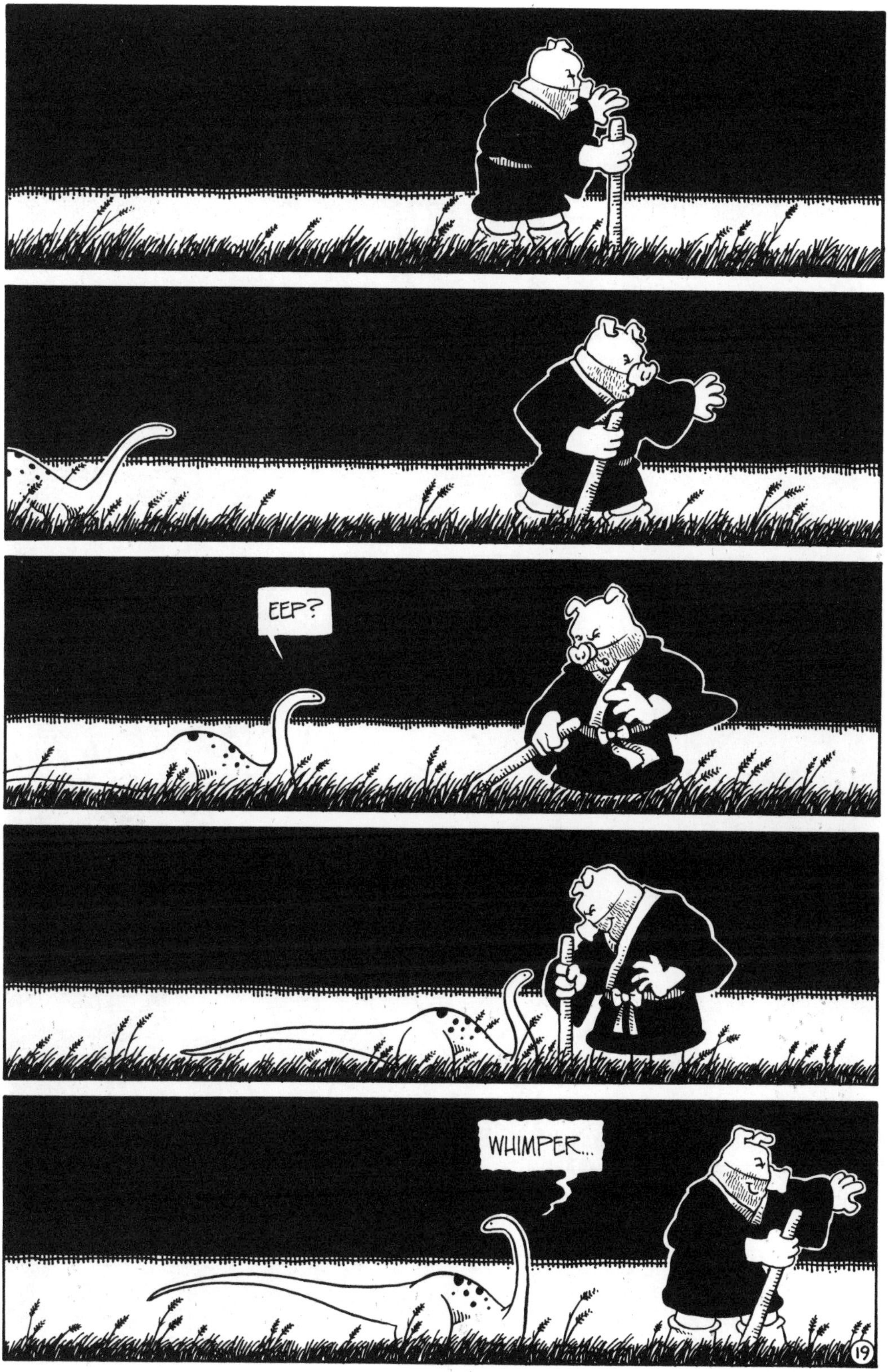
EEP?
WHIMPER...
19

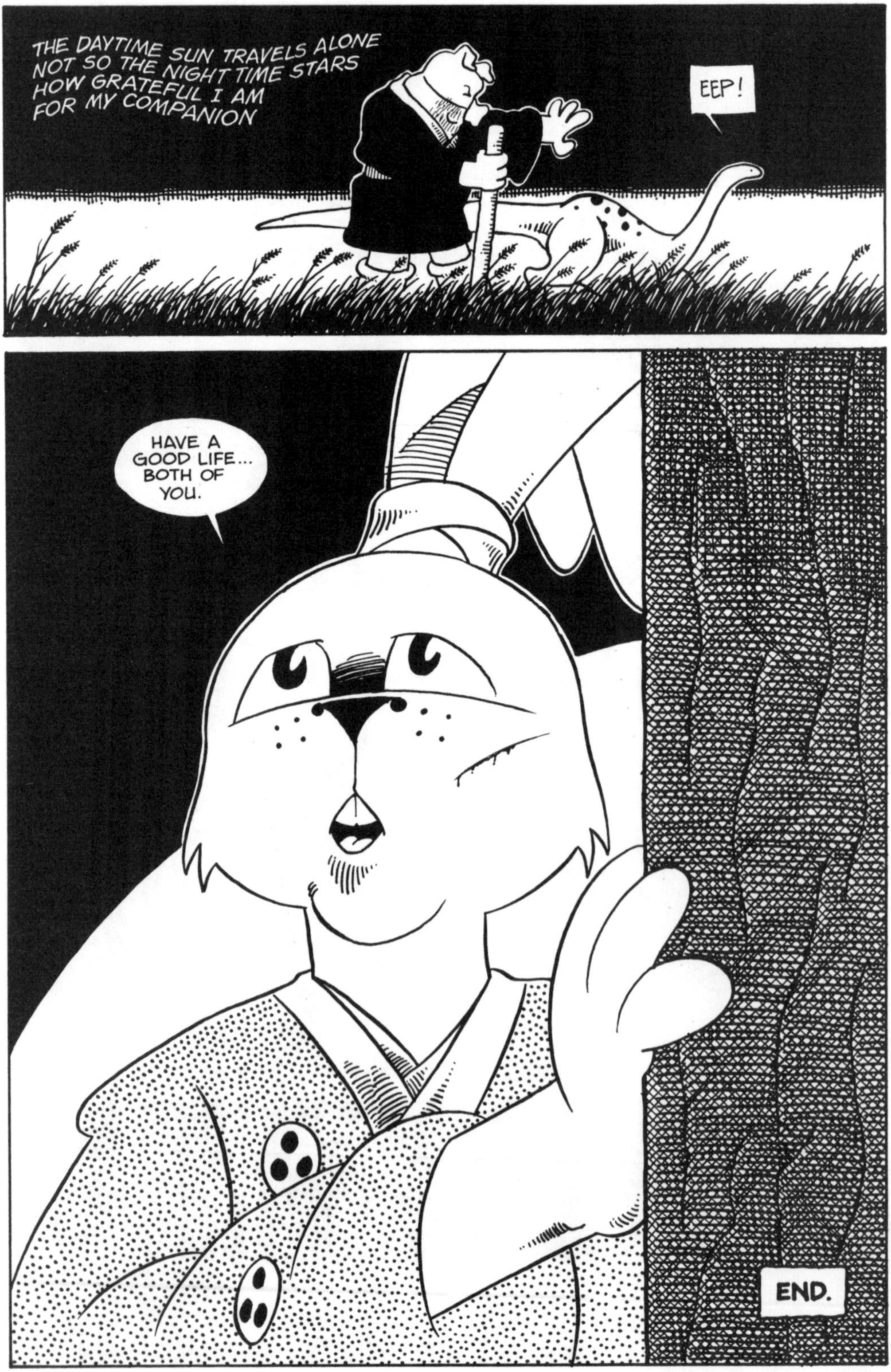
THE DAYTIME SUN TRAVELS ALONE
NOT SO THE NIGHT TIME STARS
HOW GRATEFUL I AM
FOR MY COMPANION
EEP!
HAVE A GOOD LIFE... BOTH OF YOU.
END.

CHAPTER FOUR

"Blade of the Gods"

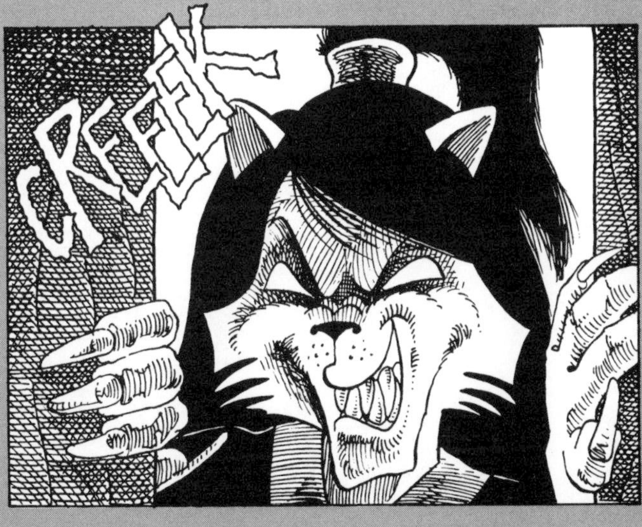
CREEEK

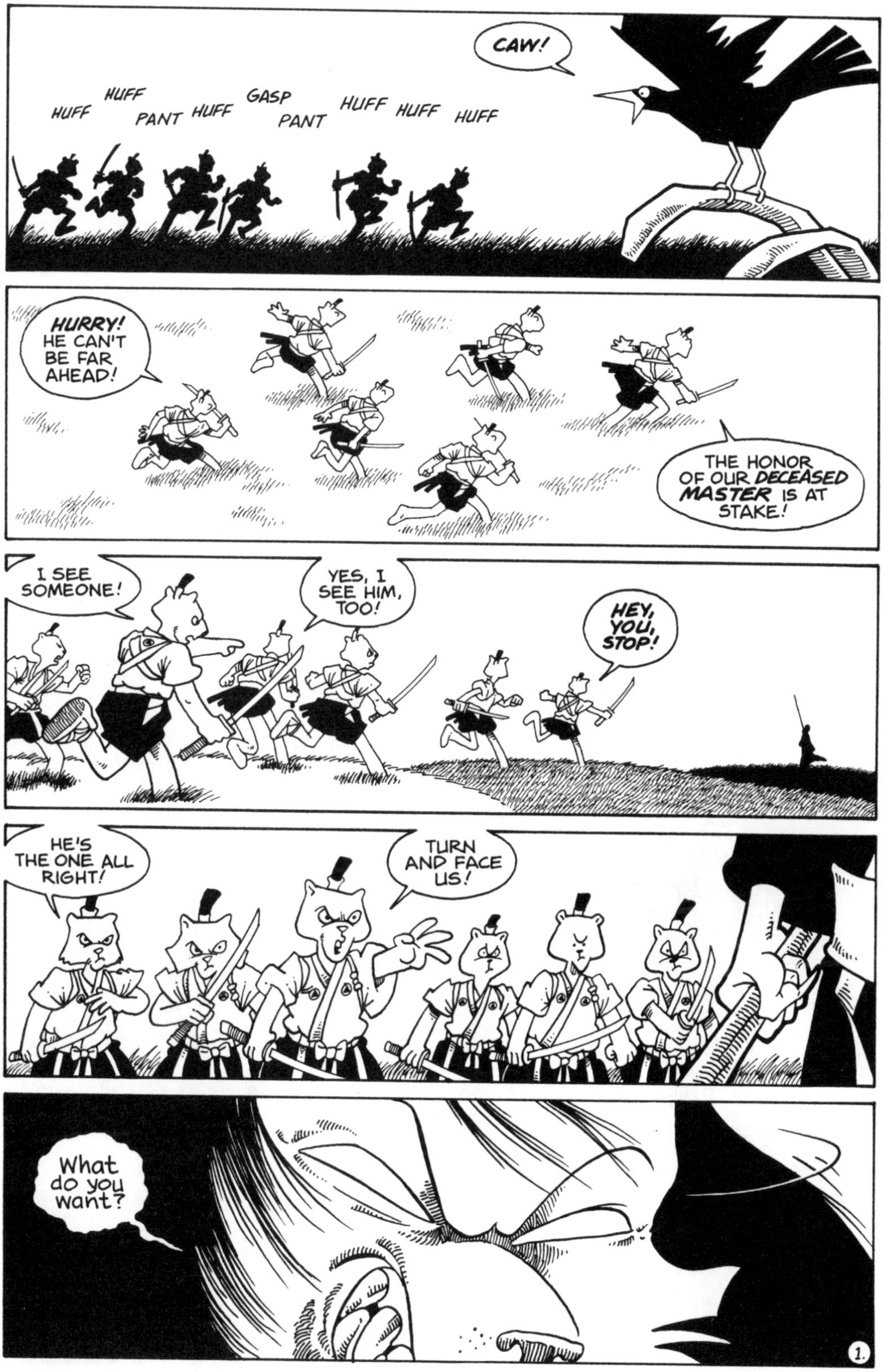
CAW!
HUFF HUFF PANT HUFF GASP PANT HUFF HUFF HUFF
HURRY! HE CAN'T BE FAR AHEAD!
THE HONOR OF OUR DECEASED MASTER IS AT STAKE!
I SEE SOMEONE!
YES, I SEE HIM, TOO!
HEY, YOU, STOP!
HE'S THE ONE ALL RIGHT!
TURN AND FACE US!
What do you want?
1.

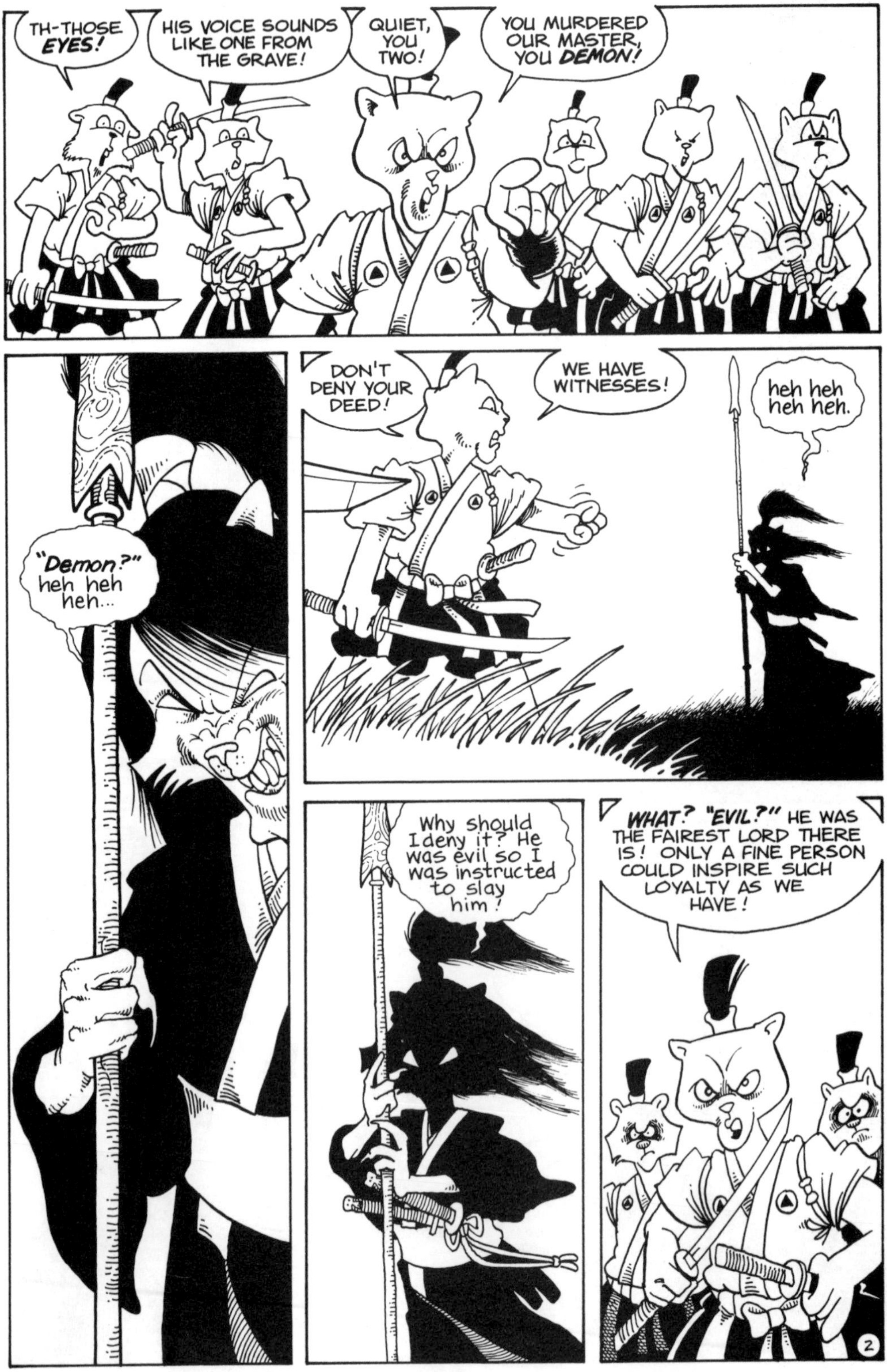
TH-THOSE EYES!
HIS VOICE SOUNDS LIKE ONE FROM THE GRAVE!
QUIET, YOU TWO!
YOU MURDERED OUR MASTER, YOU DEMON!
"Demon?" heh heh heh...
DON'T DENY YOUR DEED!
WE HAVE WITNESSES!
heh heh heh heh.
Why should I deny it? He was evil so I was instructed to slay him!
WHAT? "EVIL?" HE WAS THE FAIREST LORD THERE IS! ONLY A FINE PERSON COULD INSPIRE SUCH LOYALTY AS WE HAVE!
2

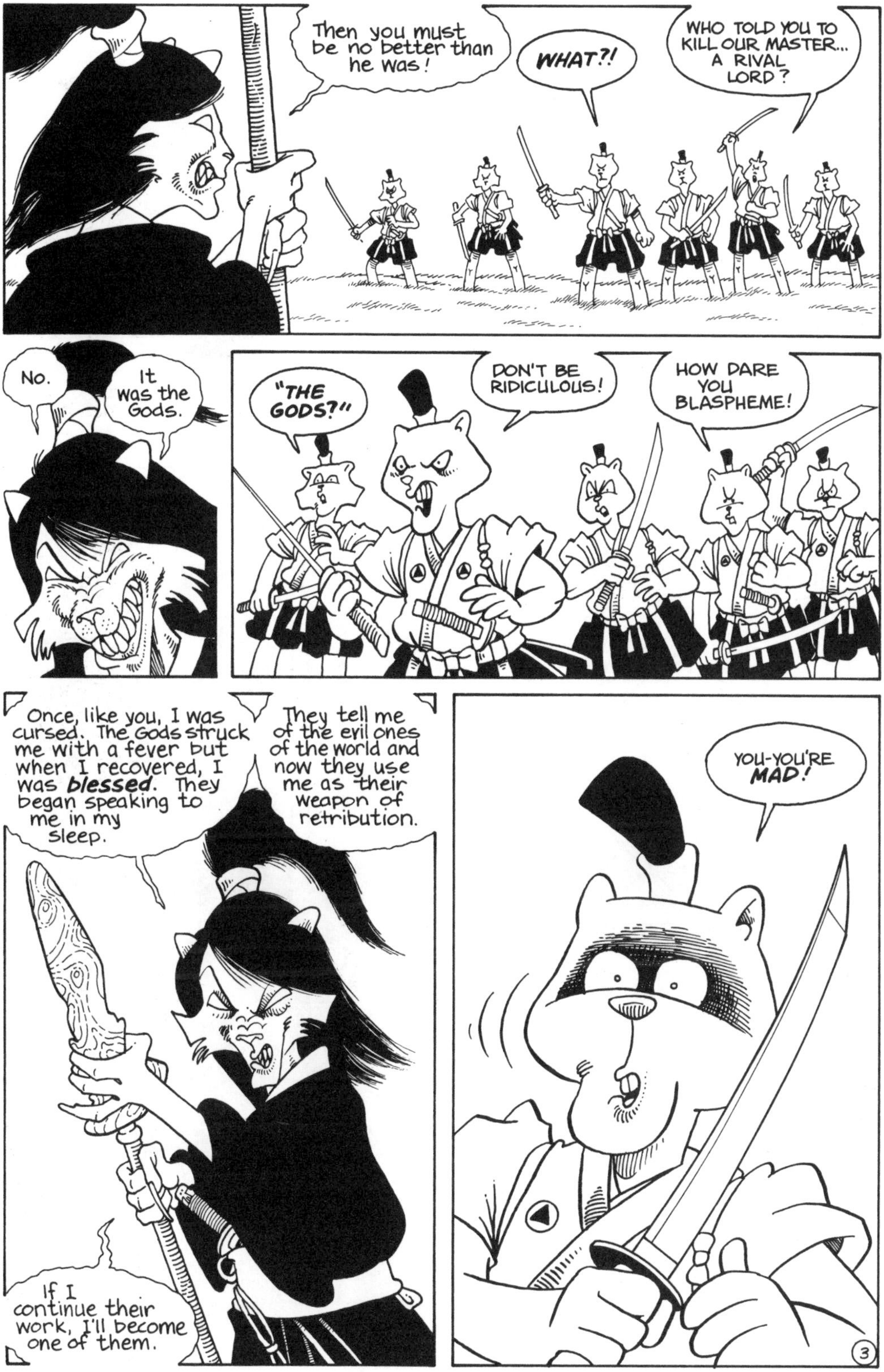

Then you must be no better than he was!
WHAT?!
WHO TOLD YOU TO KILL OUR MASTER... A RIVAL LORD?
No.
It was the Gods.
"THE GODS?"
DON'T BE RIDICULOUS!
HOW DARE YOU BLASPHEME!
Once, like you, I was cursed. The Gods struck me with a fever but when I recovered, I was blessed. They began speaking to me in my sleep.
They tell me of the evil ones of the world and now they use me as their weapon of retribution.
If I continue their work, I'll become one of them.
YOU-YOU'RE MAD!
3

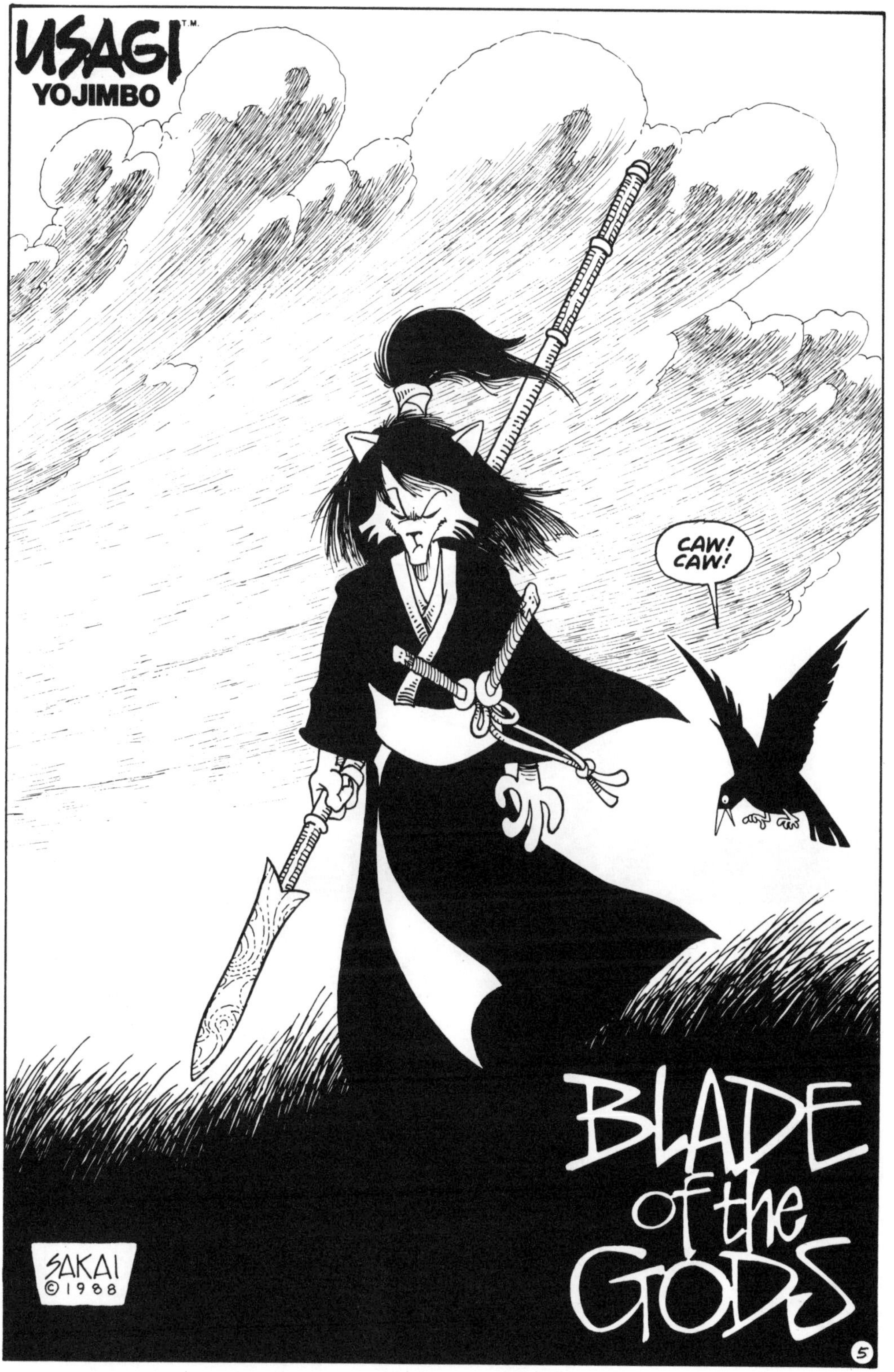
USAGI YOJIMBO
CAW! CAW!
BLADE of the GODS
SAKAI ©1988
5

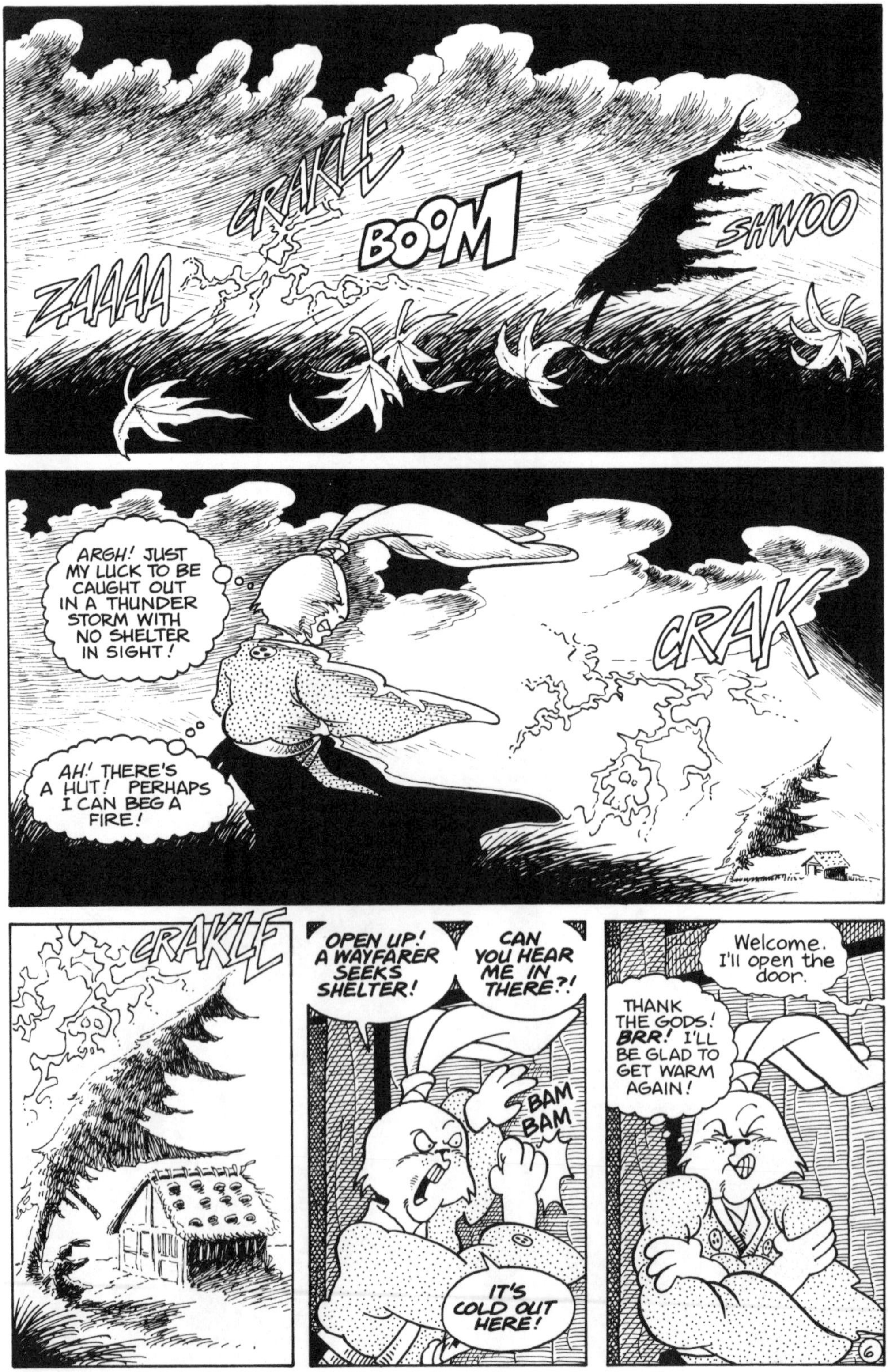
ZAAAA
CRAKLE
BOOM
SHWOO
ARGH! JUST MY LUCK TO BE CAUGHT OUT IN A THUNDER STORM WITH NO SHELTER IN SIGHT!
AH! THERE'S A HUT! PERHAPS I CAN BEG A FIRE!
CRAK
CRAKLE
OPEN UP! A WAYFARER SEEKS SHELTER!
CAN YOU HEAR ME IN THERE?!
BAM BAM
IT'S COLD OUT HERE!
Welcome. I'll open the door.
THANK THE GODS! BRR! I'LL BE GLAD TO GET WARM AGAIN!
6

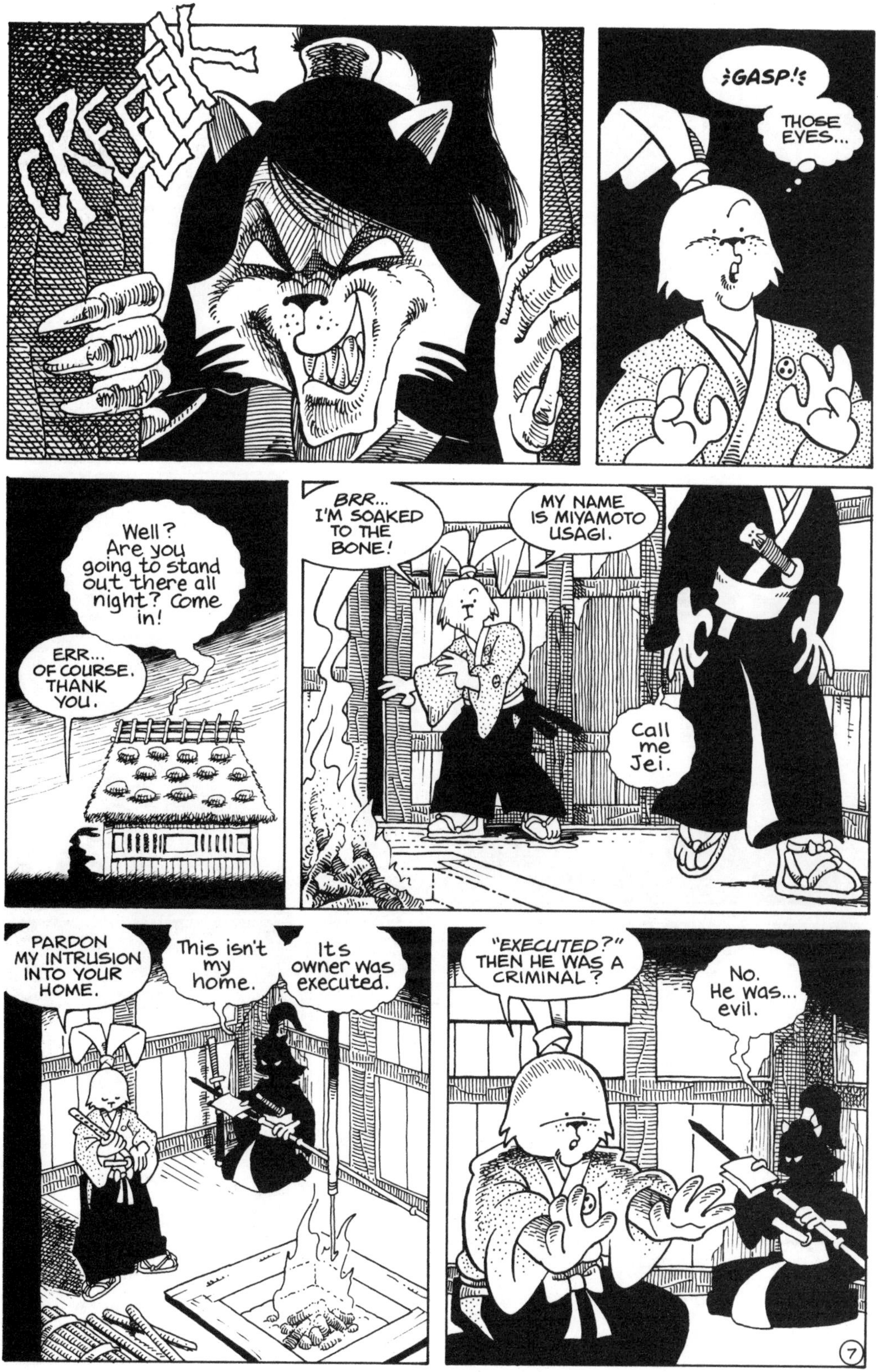
CREEEK
GASP!
THOSE EYES...
Well? Are you going to stand out there all night? Come in!
ERR... OF COURSE. THANK YOU.
BRR... I'M SOAKED TO THE BONE!
MY NAME IS MIYAMOTO USAGI.
Call me Jei.
PARDON MY INTRUSION INTO YOUR HOME.
This isn't my home.
It's owner was executed.
"EXECUTED?" THEN HE WAS A CRIMINAL?
No. He was... evil.
7

"EVIL?" I DON'T UNDER-STAND.

Heh, heh. Don't mind me. I was just making conversation.

BLACK! YOUR BLADE IS BLACK!

What?!

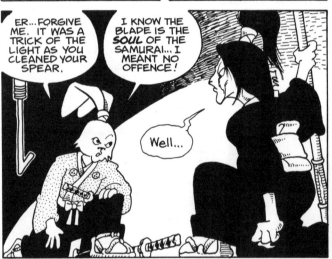

ER...FORGIVE ME. IT WAS A TRICK OF THE LIGHT AS YOU CLEANED YOUR SPEAR.

I KNOW THE BLADE IS THE SOUL OF THE SAMURAI... I MEANT NO OFFENCE!

Well...

Forget it. Let's blame it on the flickering fire.

THANK YOU.

RUB RUB RUB

BRR...THE FIRE IS RAGING BUT IT STILL FEELS LIKE IT'S FREEZING IN HERE!

Oh really? I haven't noticed.

≷Yawn≷ My inner fires are enough to warm me...but you can add more wood if you wish.

8

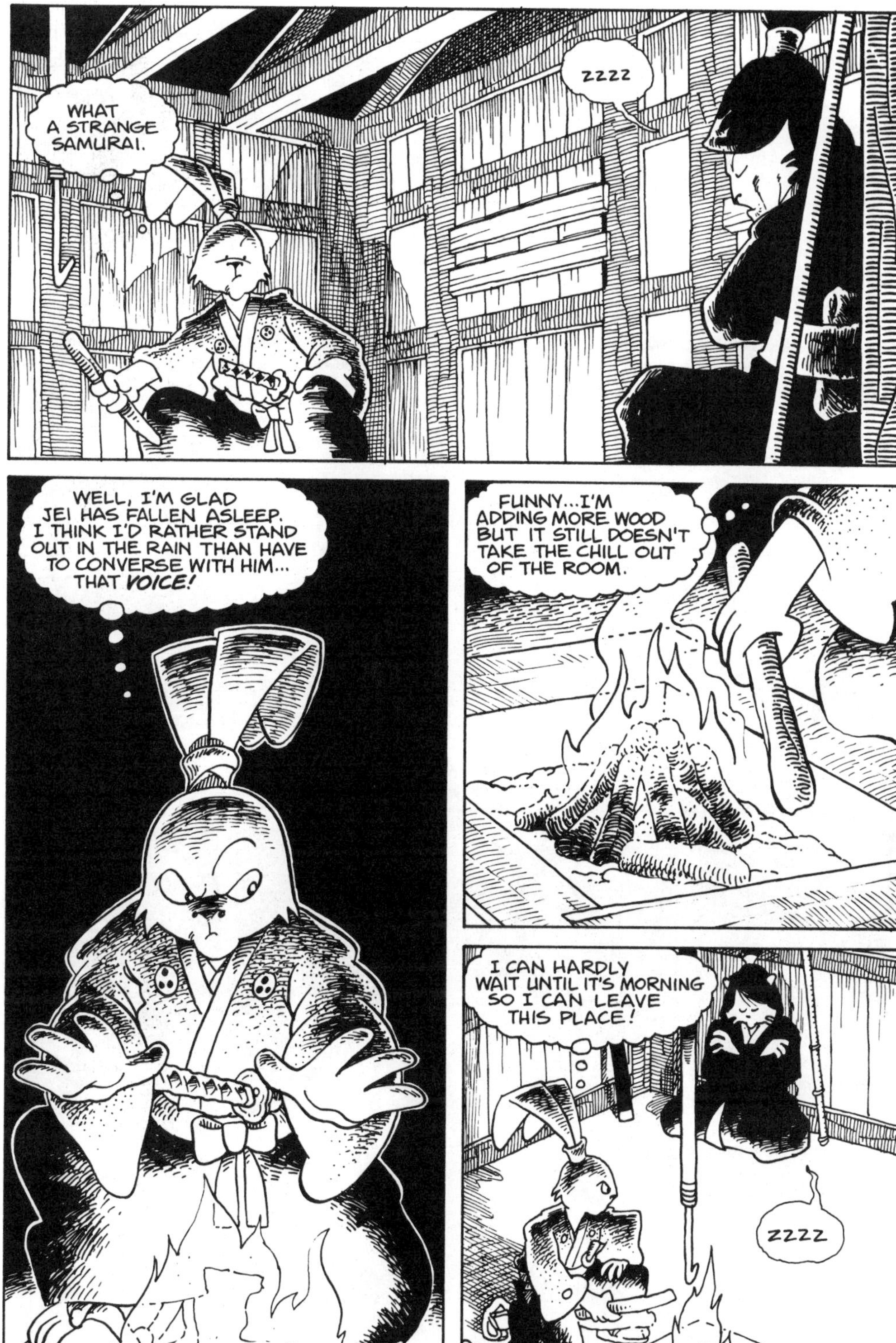
WHAT A STRANGE SAMURAI.
ZZZZ
WELL, I'M GLAD JEI HAS FALLEN ASLEEP. I THINK I'D RATHER STAND OUT IN THE RAIN THAN HAVE TO CONVERSE WITH HIM... THAT *VOICE!*
FUNNY...I'M ADDING MORE WOOD BUT IT STILL DOESN'T TAKE THE CHILL OUT OF THE ROOM.
I CAN HARDLY WAIT UNTIL IT'S MORNING SO I CAN LEAVE THIS PLACE!
ZZZZ
9

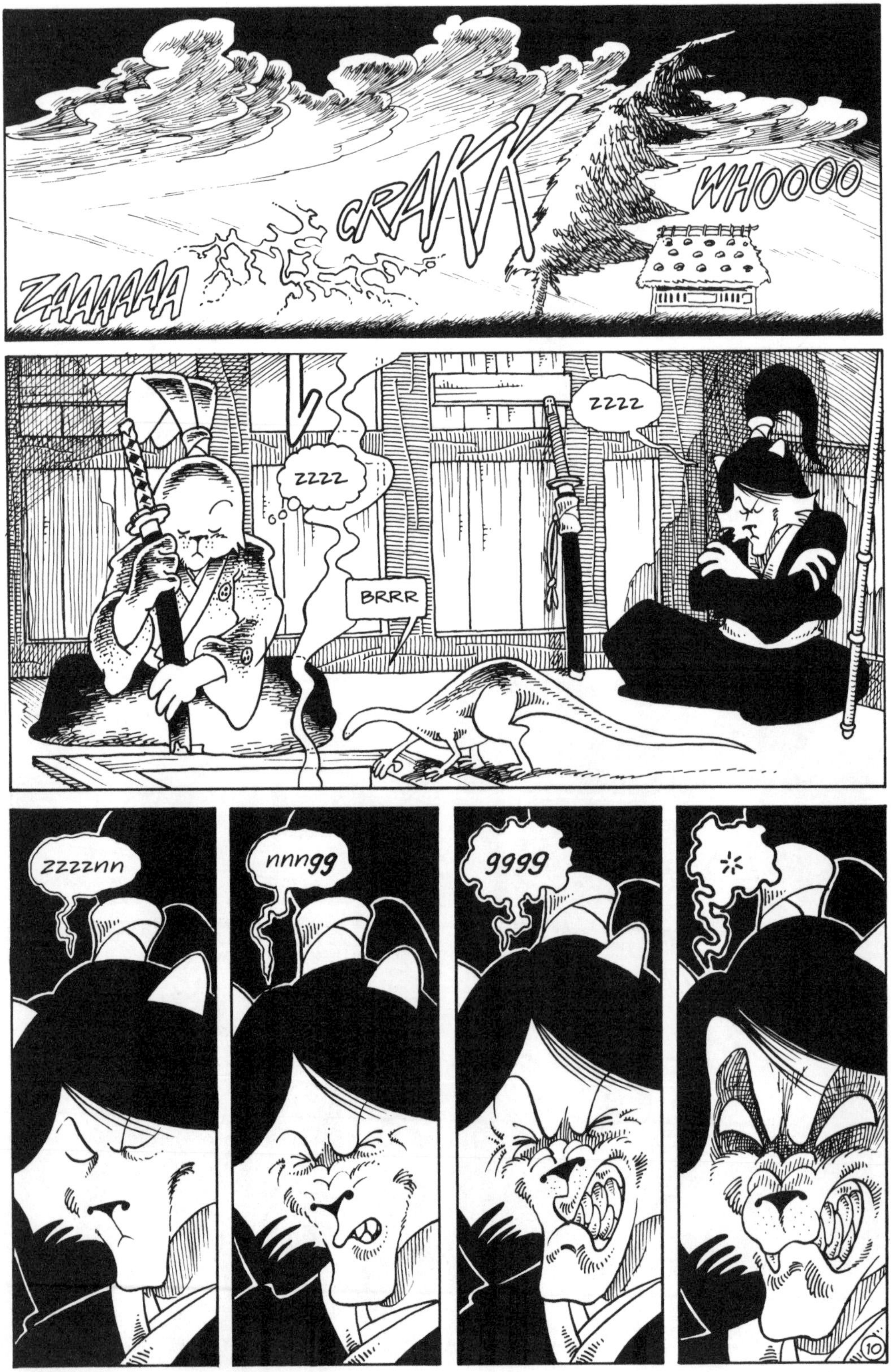
ZAAAAAA
CRAKK
WHOOOOO
zzzz
zzzz
BRRR
zzzznn
nnngg
gggg
10

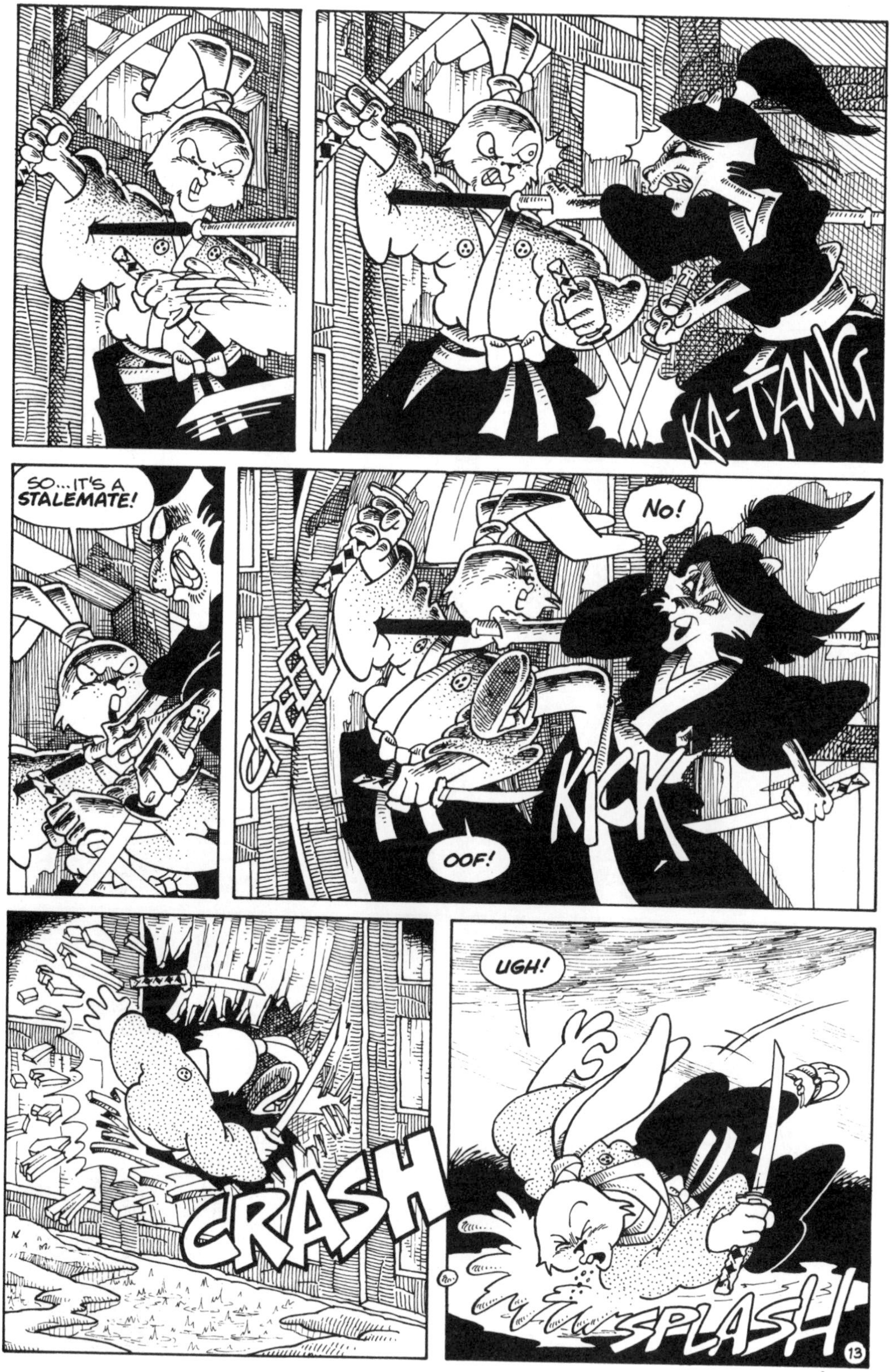
KA-TANG
SO...IT'S A STALEMATE!
No!
CREEEE
KICK
OOF!
CRASH
UGH!
SPLASH
13

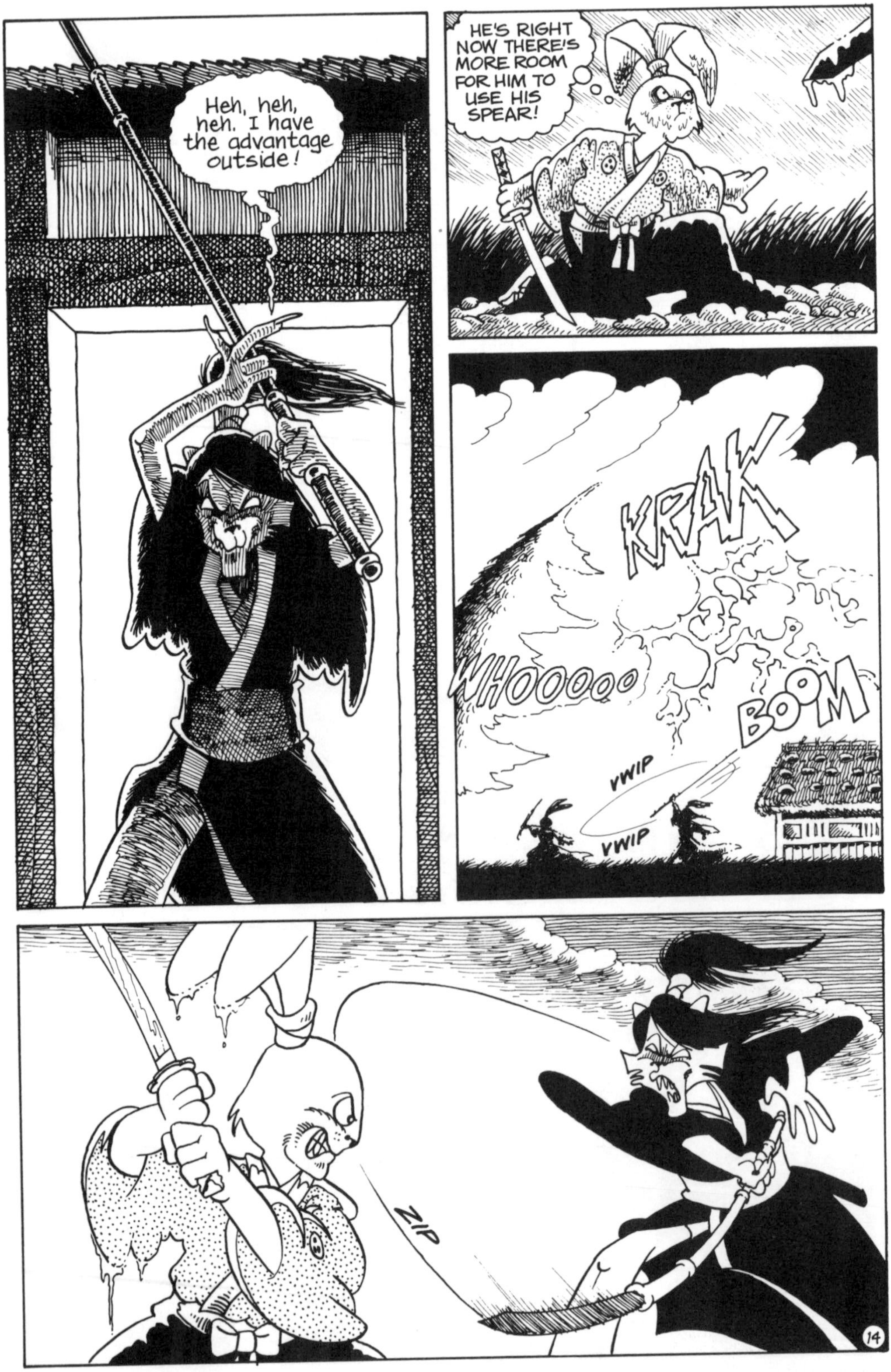
Heh, heh, heh. I have the advantage outside!
HE'S RIGHT NOW THERE'S MORE ROOM FOR HIM TO USE HIS SPEAR!
KRAK
WHOOOOO
BOOM
VWIP
VWIP
ZIP
14

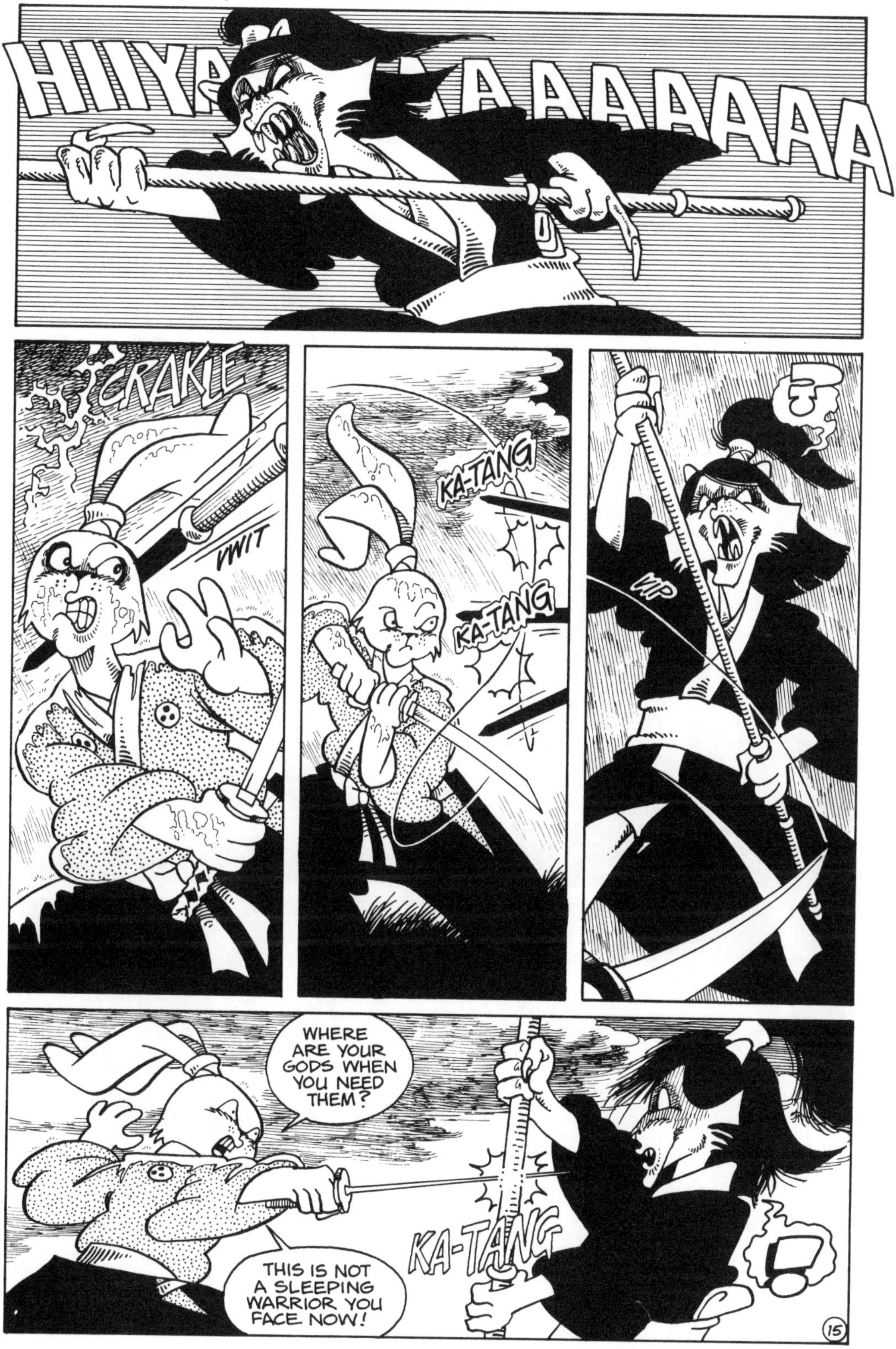
HIIYAAAAAAAAAA
CRAKLE
VWIT
KA-TANG
KA-TANG
VIP
?
WHERE ARE YOUR GODS WHEN YOU NEED THEM?
THIS IS NOT A SLEEPING WARRIOR YOU FACE NOW!
KA-TANG
!
15

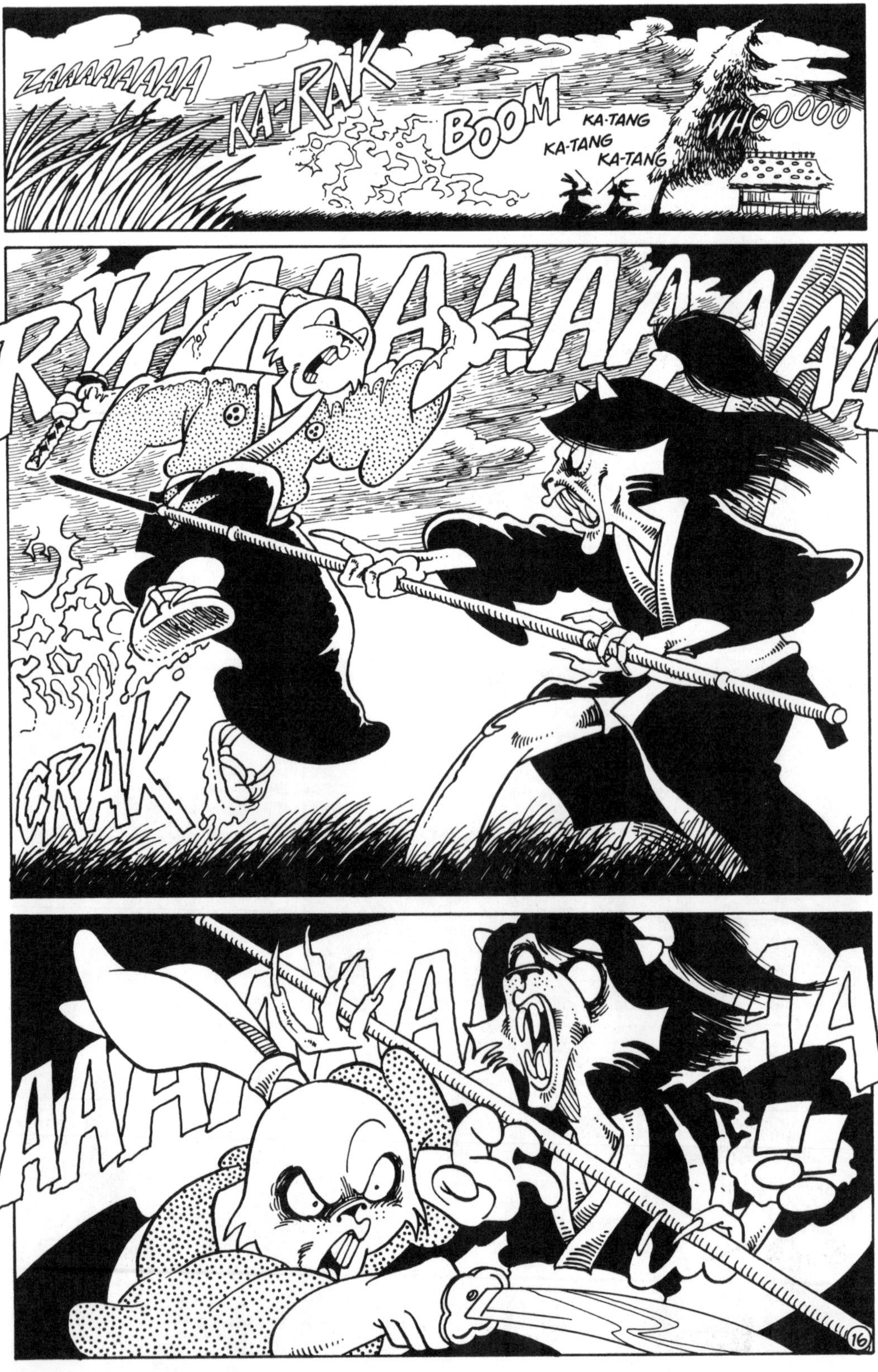
ZAAAAAAAAA
KA-RAK
BOOM
KA-TANG
KA-TANG
KA-TANG
WHOOOOOO
RYAAAAAAAAAAAA
CRAK
AAAAAAAAAAAA
16

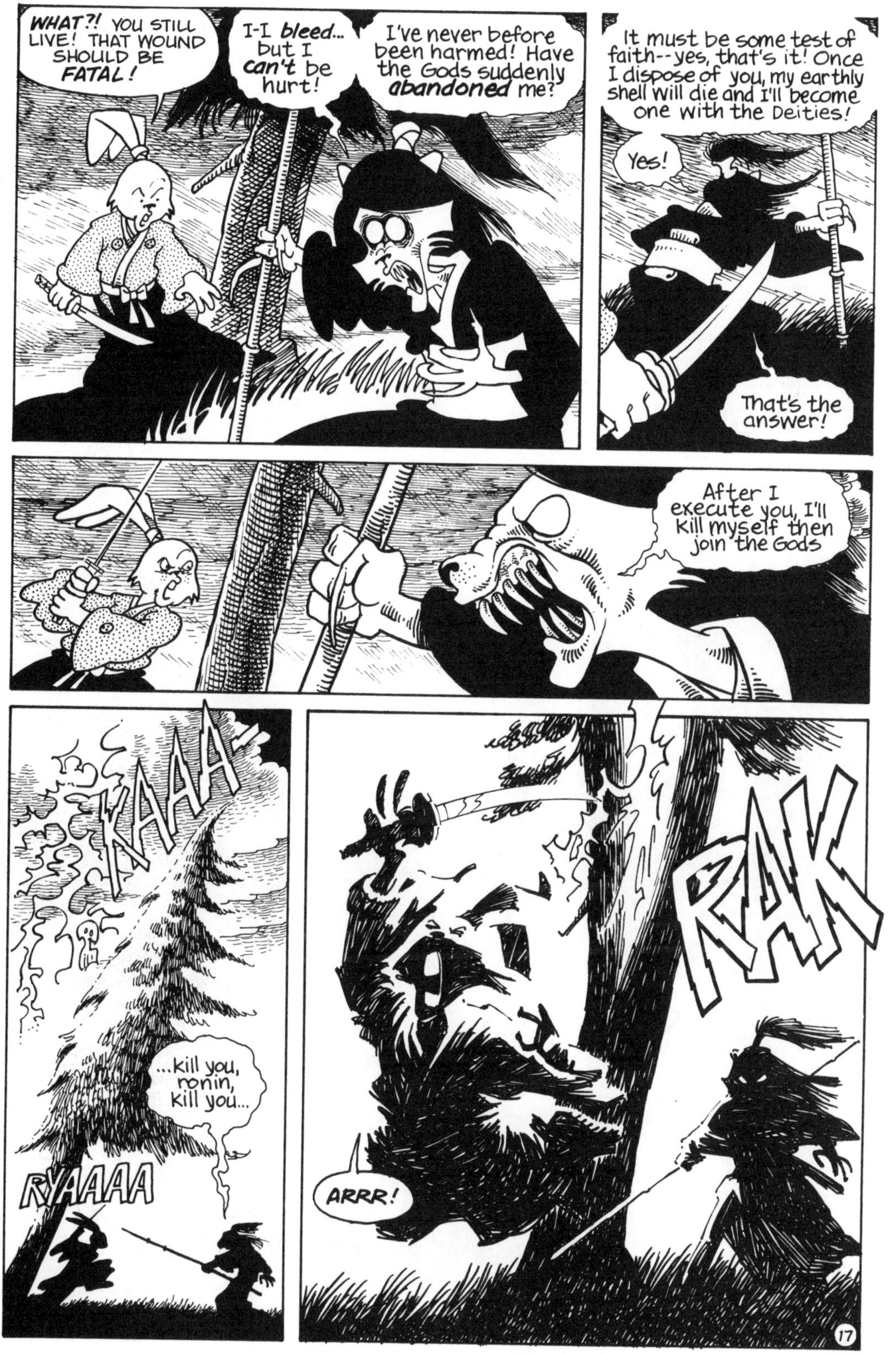
WHAT?! YOU STILL LIVE! THAT WOUND SHOULD BE FATAL!
I-I bleed... but I can't be hurt!
I've never before been harmed! Have the Gods suddenly abandoned me?
It must be some test of faith--yes, that's it! Once I dispose of you, my earthly shell will die and I'll become one with the Deities!
Yes!
That's the answer!
After I execute you, I'll kill myself then join the Gods
KAAAA
...kill you, ronin, kill you...
RYAAAA
RAK
ARRR!
17

SIZZLE

CRAKLE

CRACKLE POP

Usagi!

Heh, heh, heh! See?! That lightning was a sign from above! The Heavens protect me! I am their chosen one... their instrument against evil!

You have only moments to live!

IF IT IS MY KARMA TO DIE NOW, SO BE IT! BUT I'LL FIGHT YOU TO MY LAST BREATH!

Admit the futility of your struggle, ronin!

18

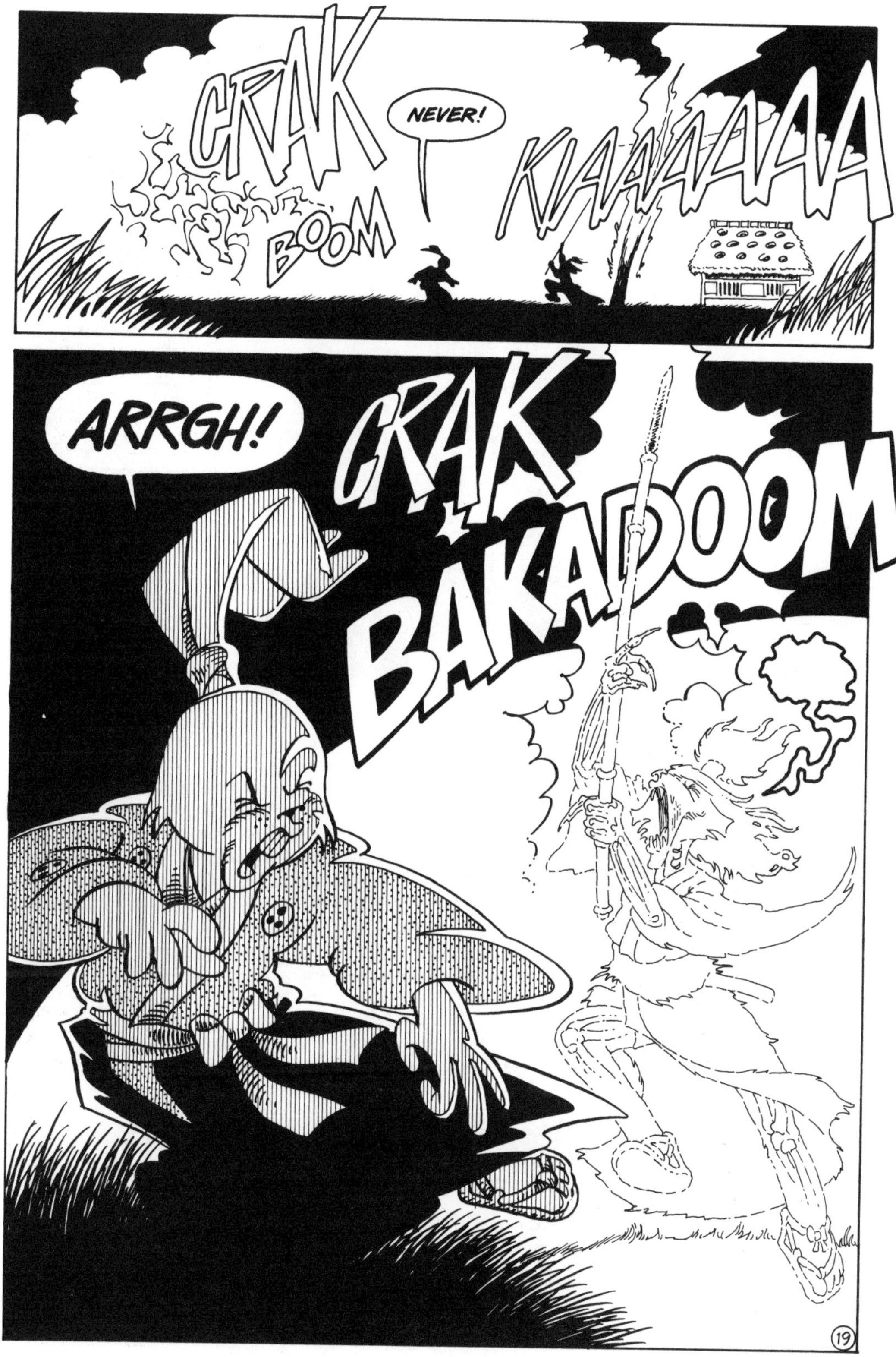
CRAK
BOOM
NEVER!
KIAAAAAAA
ARRGH!
CRAK
BAKADOOM
19

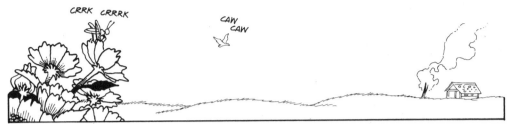

CRRK CRRRK

CAW CAW

CAW CAW

OOH... I'M ALIVE...

...SORT OF...

OWW... MY HEAD.

I CAN'T BELIEVE IT...

...ALMOST STRUCK BY LIGHTNING **TWICE** IN ONE NIGHT!

WHAT ABOUT JEI?

HE-HE'S **GONE**... THE LIGHTNING COMPLETELY **DESTROYED** HIM...

...OR WAS HE **REALLY** AN EMISSARY OF THE GODS NOW GONE TO JOIN THEM?

CAW CAW

I GUESS I'LL NEVER KNOW.

end.

CHAPTER FIVE

"The Tea Cup"

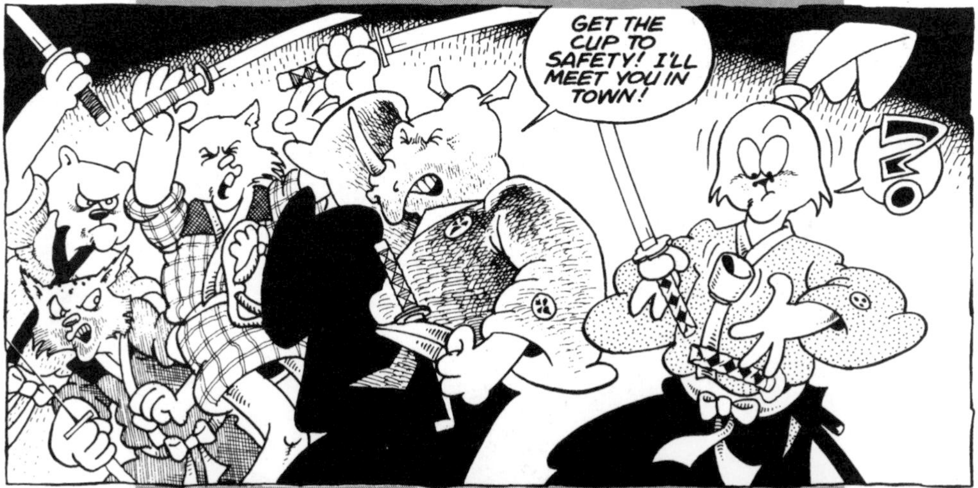
GET THE CUP TO SAFETY! I'LL MEET YOU IN TOWN!

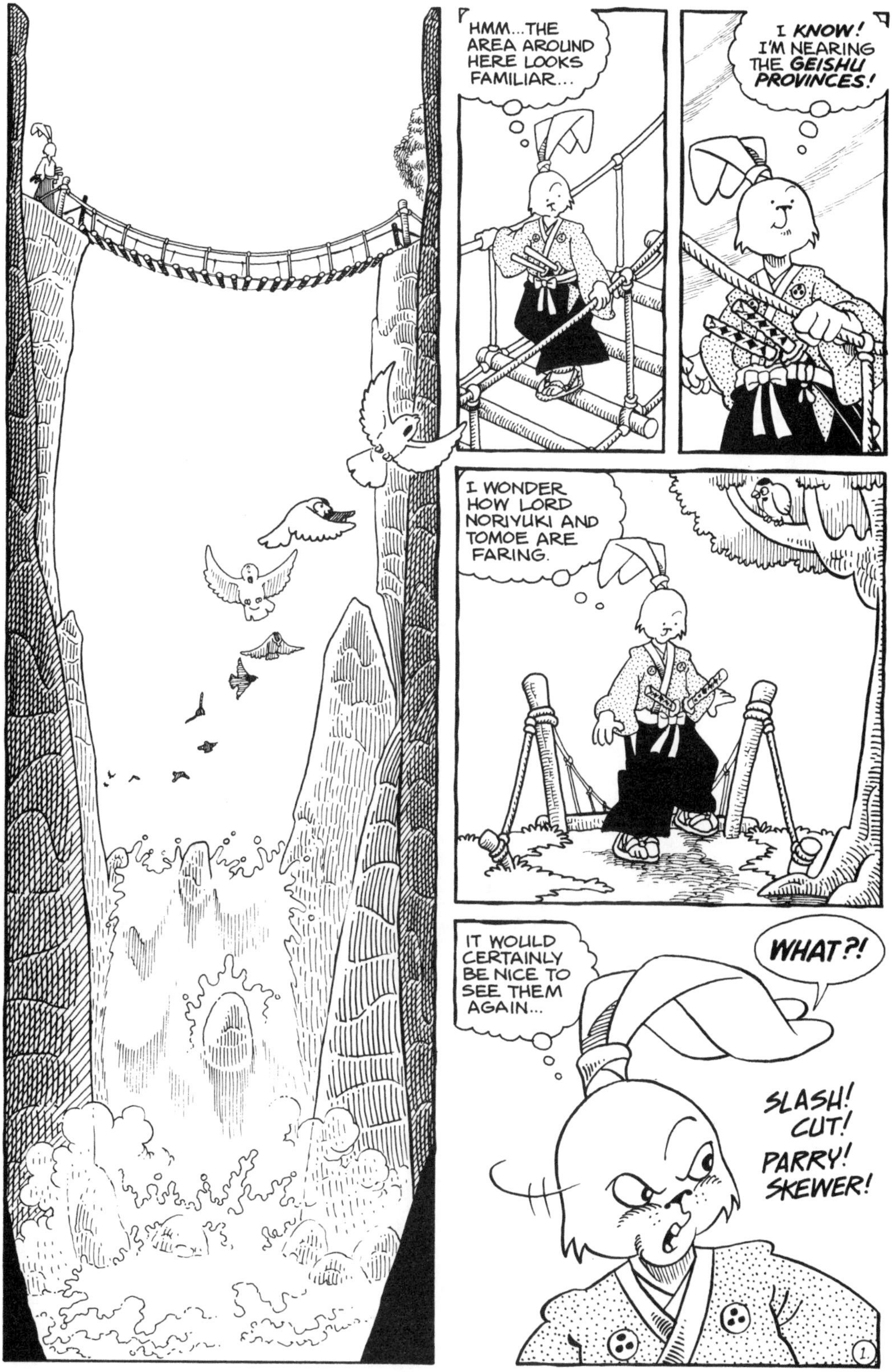
HMM...THE AREA AROUND HERE LOOKS FAMILIAR...
I KNOW! I'M NEARING THE GEISHU PROVINCES!
I WONDER HOW LORD NORIYUKI AND TOMOE ARE FARING.
IT WOULD CERTAINLY BE NICE TO SEE THEM AGAIN...
WHAT?!
SLASH! CUT! PARRY! SKEWER!
1.

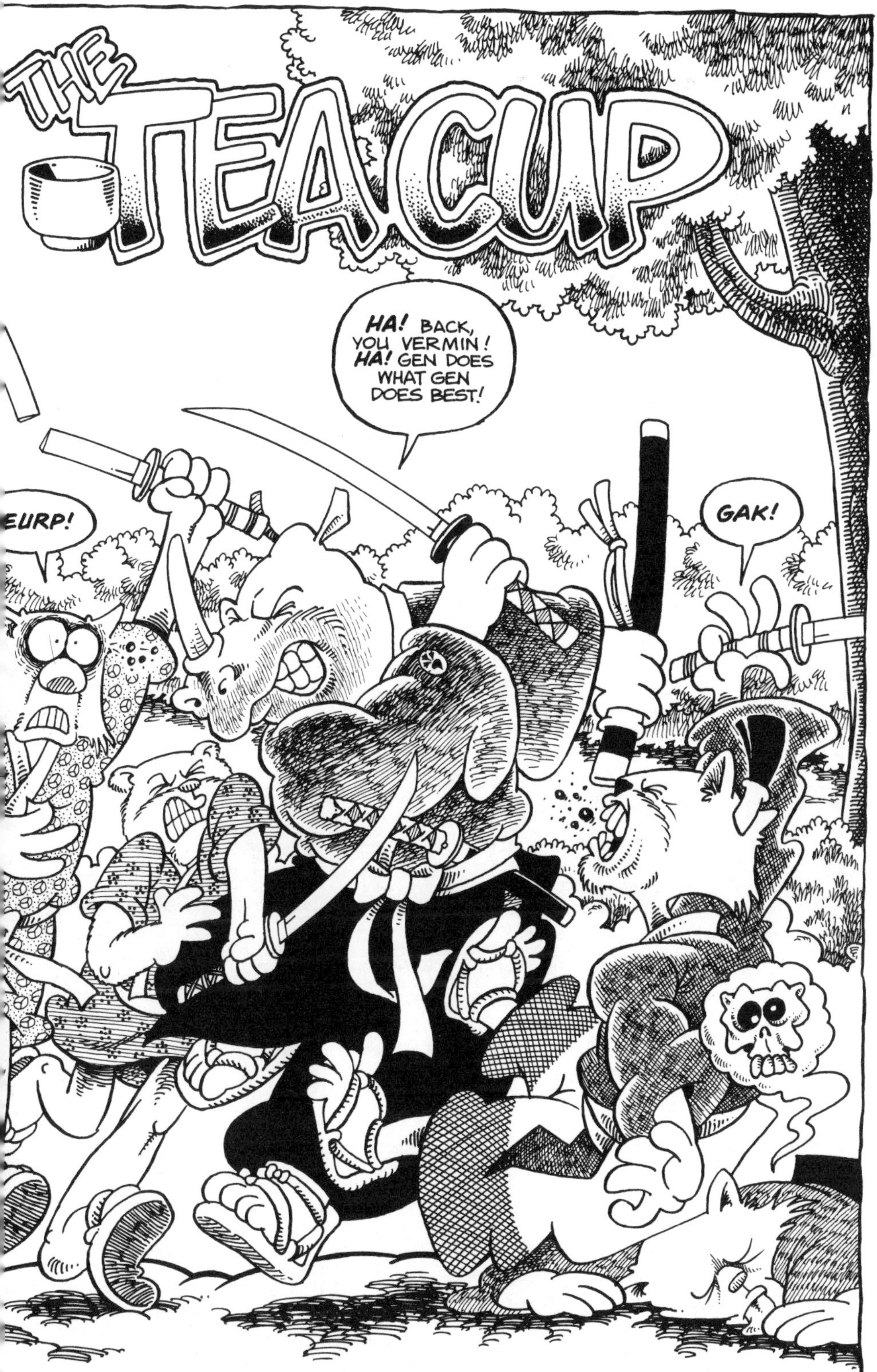
THE TEACUP
EURP!
HA! BACK, YOU VERMIN! HA! GEN DOES WHAT GEN DOES BEST!
GAK!

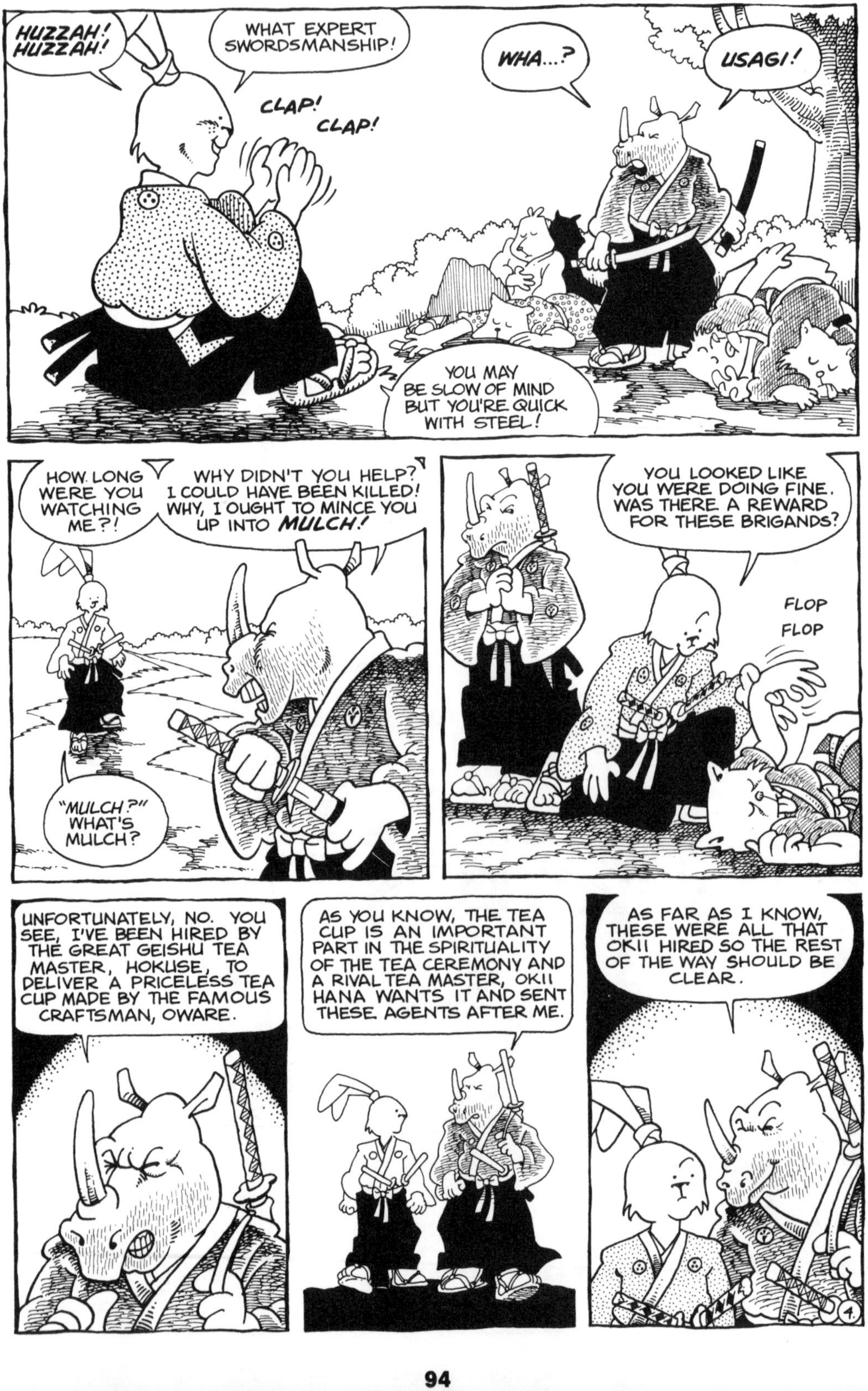
HUZZAH! HUZZAH!
WHAT EXPERT SWORDSMANSHIP!
CLAP! CLAP!
WHA...?
USAGI!
YOU MAY BE SLOW OF MIND BUT YOU'RE QUICK WITH STEEL!
HOW LONG WERE YOU WATCHING ME?!
WHY DIDN'T YOU HELP? I COULD HAVE BEEN KILLED! WHY, I OUGHT TO MINCE YOU UP INTO MULCH!
"MULCH?" WHAT'S MULCH?
YOU LOOKED LIKE YOU WERE DOING FINE. WAS THERE A REWARD FOR THESE BRIGANDS?
FLOP FLOP
UNFORTUNATELY, NO. YOU SEE, I'VE BEEN HIRED BY THE GREAT GEISHU TEA MASTER, HOKUSE, TO DELIVER A PRICELESS TEA CUP MADE BY THE FAMOUS CRAFTSMAN, OWARE.
AS YOU KNOW, THE TEA CUP IS AN IMPORTANT PART IN THE SPIRITUALITY OF THE TEA CEREMONY AND A RIVAL TEA MASTER, OKII HANA WANTS IT AND SENT THESE AGENTS AFTER ME.
AS FAR AS I KNOW, THESE WERE ALL THAT OKII HIRED SO THE REST OF THE WAY SHOULD BE CLEAR.
4.

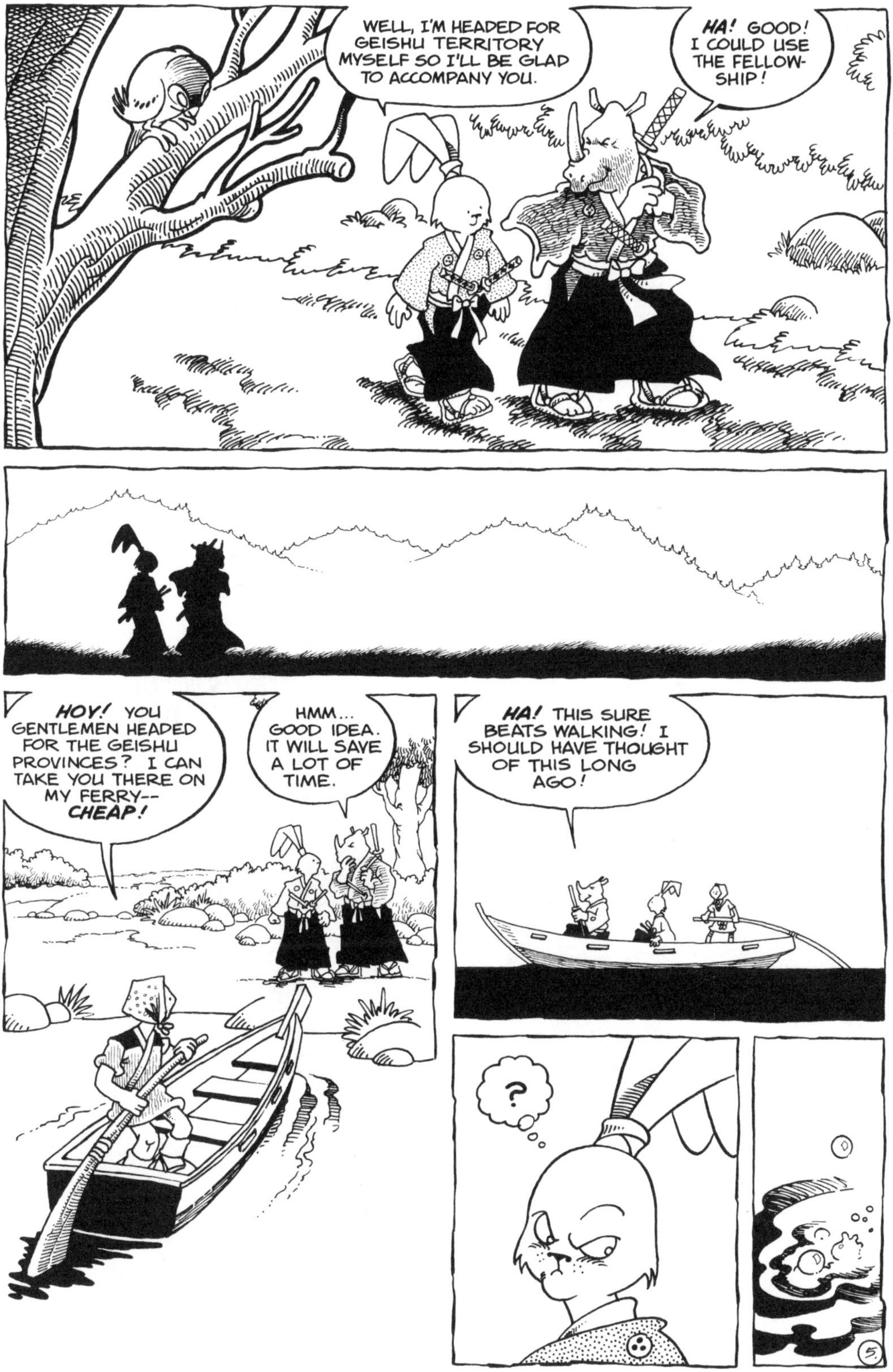
WELL, I'M HEADED FOR GEISHU TERRITORY MYSELF SO I'LL BE GLAD TO ACCOMPANY YOU.
HA! GOOD! I COULD USE THE FELLOW-SHIP!
HOY! YOU GENTLEMEN HEADED FOR THE GEISHU PROVINCES? I CAN TAKE YOU THERE ON MY FERRY-- CHEAP!
HMM... GOOD IDEA. IT WILL SAVE A LOT OF TIME.
HA! THIS SURE BEATS WALKING! I SHOULD HAVE THOUGHT OF THIS LONG AGO!
?
5.

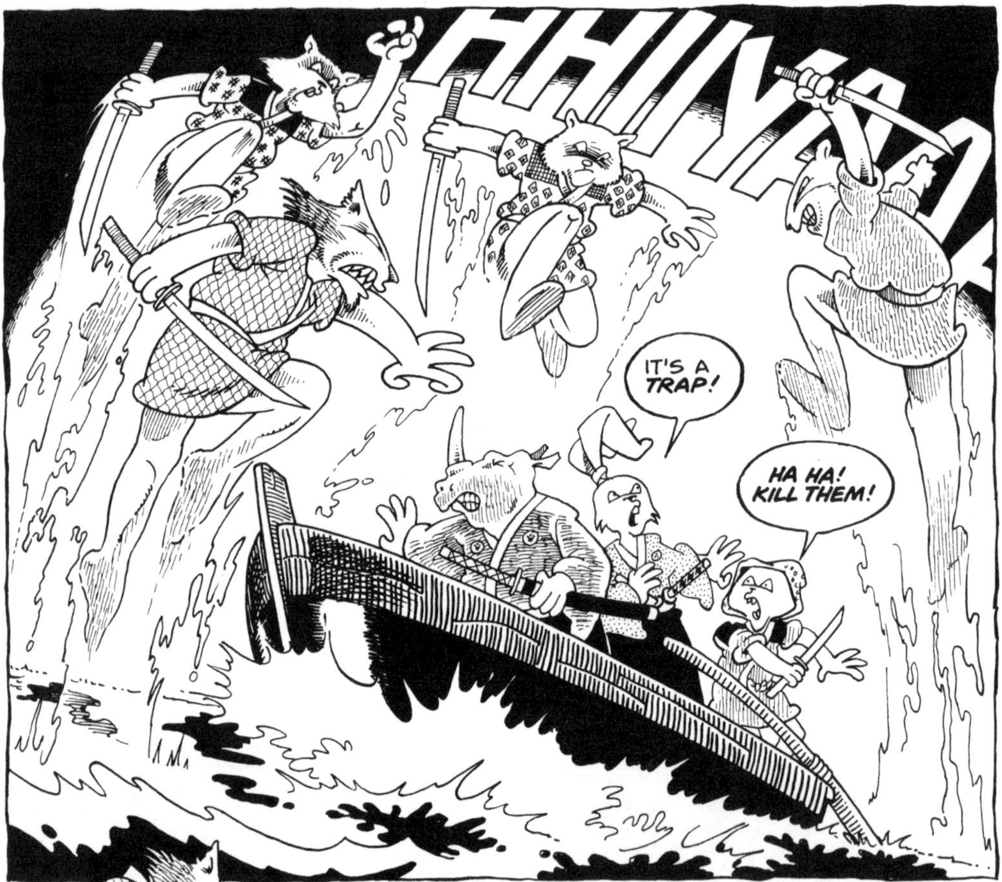
HHIIYAA!
IT'S A TRAP!
HA HA! KILL THEM!

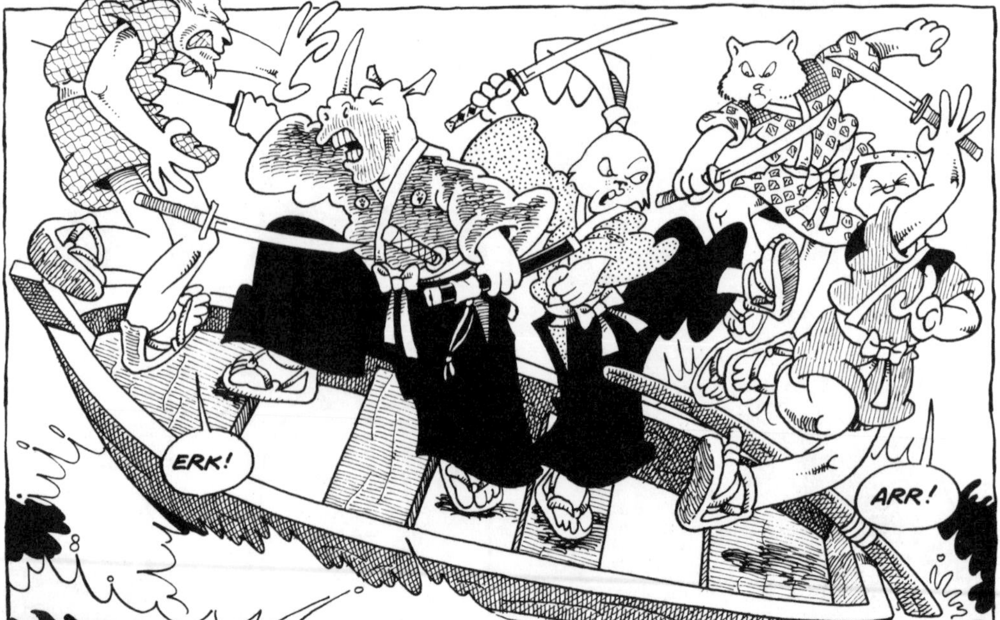
ERK!
ARR!
6

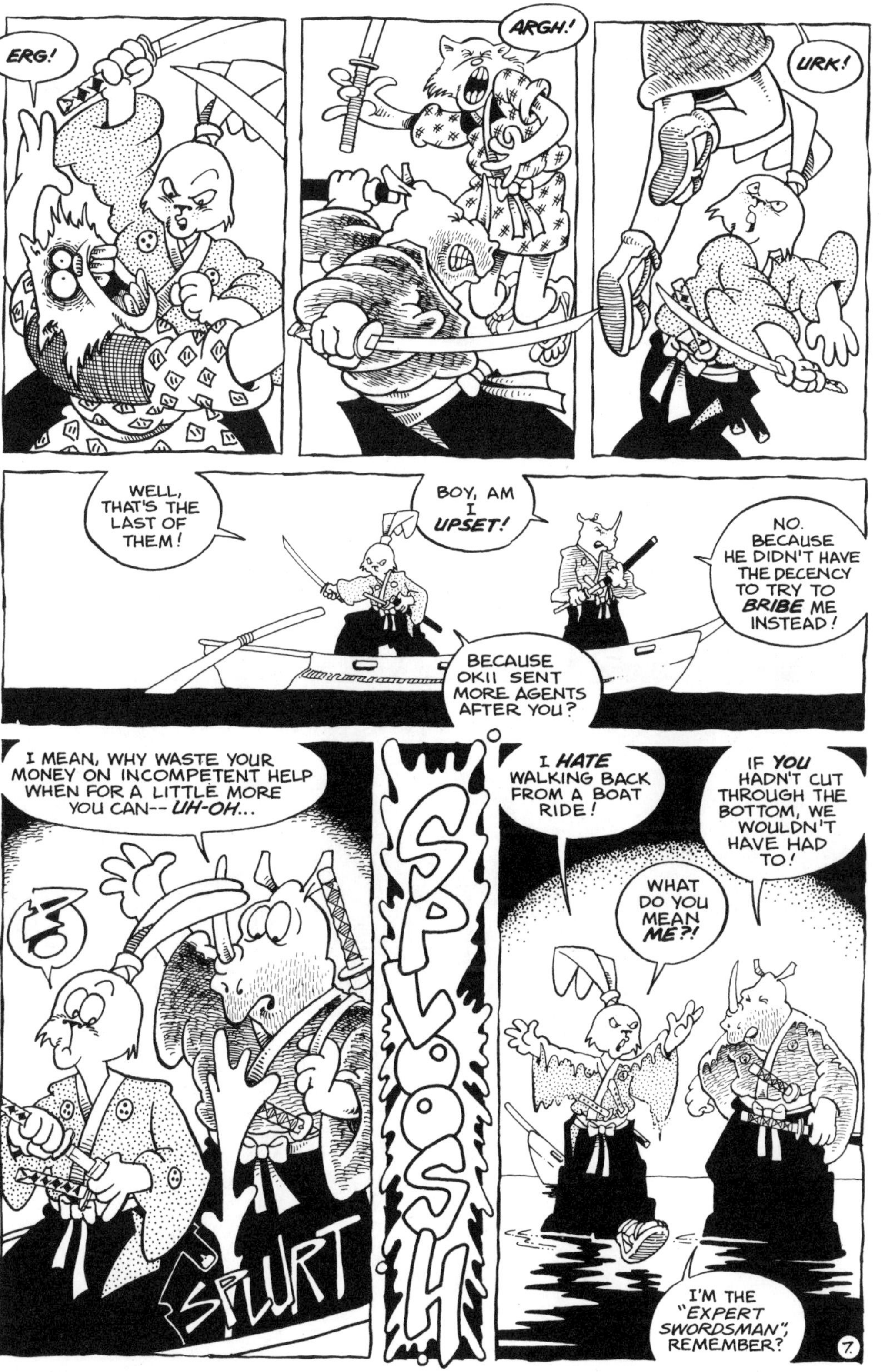
ERG!
ARGH!
URK!
WELL, THAT'S THE LAST OF THEM!
BOY, AM I UPSET!
BECAUSE OKII SENT MORE AGENTS AFTER YOU?
NO. BECAUSE HE DIDN'T HAVE THE DECENCY TO TRY TO BRIBE ME INSTEAD!
I MEAN, WHY WASTE YOUR MONEY ON INCOMPETENT HELP WHEN FOR A LITTLE MORE YOU CAN-- UH-OH...
SPLURT
SPLOOOSH
I HATE WALKING BACK FROM A BOAT RIDE!
IF YOU HADN'T CUT THROUGH THE BOTTOM, WE WOULDN'T HAVE HAD TO!
WHAT DO YOU MEAN ME?!
I'M THE "EXPERT SWORDSMAN", REMEMBER?
7.

THEY'RE OBVIOUSLY FAMISHED! HERE. THIS SHOULD BUY THEM A MEAL.

YES, SIR!

BAH! WHAT A WASTE OF GOOD MONEY!

BAH!

THANK YOU, MR. SAMURAI. IT'S BEEN QUITE A WHILE SINCE WE HAD LAST EATEN!

OH? WHERE ARE YOUR PARENTS?

THEY ARE BOTH DEAD, SIR, AND NOW MY YOUNGER BROTHER AND I ARE TRAVELLING TO THE GEISHU LANDS TO LIVE WITH OUR UNCLE WHO IS A SANDAL REPAIR MAN THERE!

MUNCH! SLURP!

BUT HE MAY NOT ACCEPT US BECAUSE HE IS NOT RICH... AND WITH TWO MORE MOUTHS TO FEED... ≥SIGH≥

SCARF! MUNCH!

BUT OUR MAIN CONCERN IS FIRST GETTING THERE! WE'VE ALREADY TAKEN THE WRONG ROAD-- TWICE!

HIC. HIC. HIC.

WELL, WE'RE GOING TO THE GEISHU PROVINCES OURSELVES. YOU HAD BEST COME WITH US!

HIC. HIC. HIC.

YAY!

WHAT?

WELL, IT'S NOT FAR BUT WE COULDN'T LEAVE THEM TO FEND FOR THEMSELVES, COULD WE?

BAH!

HIC HIC HIC HIC

HIC. HIC. HIC.

BEAT IT, KID! DON'T BOTHER ME!

¡GULP! Y-YES, SIR!

YOU MAY NOT LIKE THE KIDS, GEN, BUT YOU CAN AT LEAST BE CIVIL TO THEM!

IT WAS *YOUR* IDEA TO BRING THEM ALONG. IF YOU WANT TO BABY SIT, THAT'S FINE WITH ME BUT COUNT ME OUT!

BESIDES, I CURED HIS HICCUPS, DIDN'T I?

LATER...

GEN, WHAT HAVE YOU GOT AGAINST THESE KIDS?

THEY'RE POOR, HOMELESS ORPHANS.

WHAT MAKES YOU THINK I'VE GOT ANYTHING AGAINST THEM?

I'M GOING FOR A WALK!

GRUBBY, MENDICANT URCHINS! THERE'S NOTHING WORSE THAN A KID ON HIS OWN...

...I SHOULD KNOW! *I* WAS LIKE THAT! GROWING UP POOR...WITHOUT A HOME OR FAMILY...

I CAN IDENTIFY WITH THEM...*TOO WELL!* MAYBE THAT'S WHY I DISLIKE THEM.

10

USAGI DOESN'T KNOW IT BUT OKII IS STILL AFTER ME AND I NEED HIS HELP TO COMPLETE. MY MISSION.

CHRP CHRP

IF I HAD ANY CON-SCIENCE...IF I WASN'T SO CONNIVING, I'D JUST LEAVE NOW AND LET THEM CONTINUE TO THE GEISHU LANDS IN PEACE.

WHAT KIND OF BEING WOULD I BE IF I KNOWINGLY JEOPARDIZED MY FRIEND'S LIFE FOR THE SAKE OF PROFIT?

CHRP CHRP

I'M THE ONE THAT OKII WANTS. IF I WEREN'T AROUND, THEY'D BE SAFE!

GOOD-BYE, USAGI. I LEAVE YOU NOW BECAUSE OF OUR FRIENDSHIP!

CHRP CHRP

CHRP CHRP

≶SIGH≷ BUT MY LOVE FOR MONEY ALWAYS WINS OUT IN THE END!

CHRP CHRP

≳SNAP!≲

WHAT?! SKULKERS! AN AMBUSH! MAYBE IT'S A GOOD THING I DIDN'T LEAVE AFTER ALL!

USAGI! WE'VE GOT COMPANY!

THANKS FOR THE WARNING, GEN!

URK!

OOF!

THERE'S MORE BEHIND YOU!

11

101

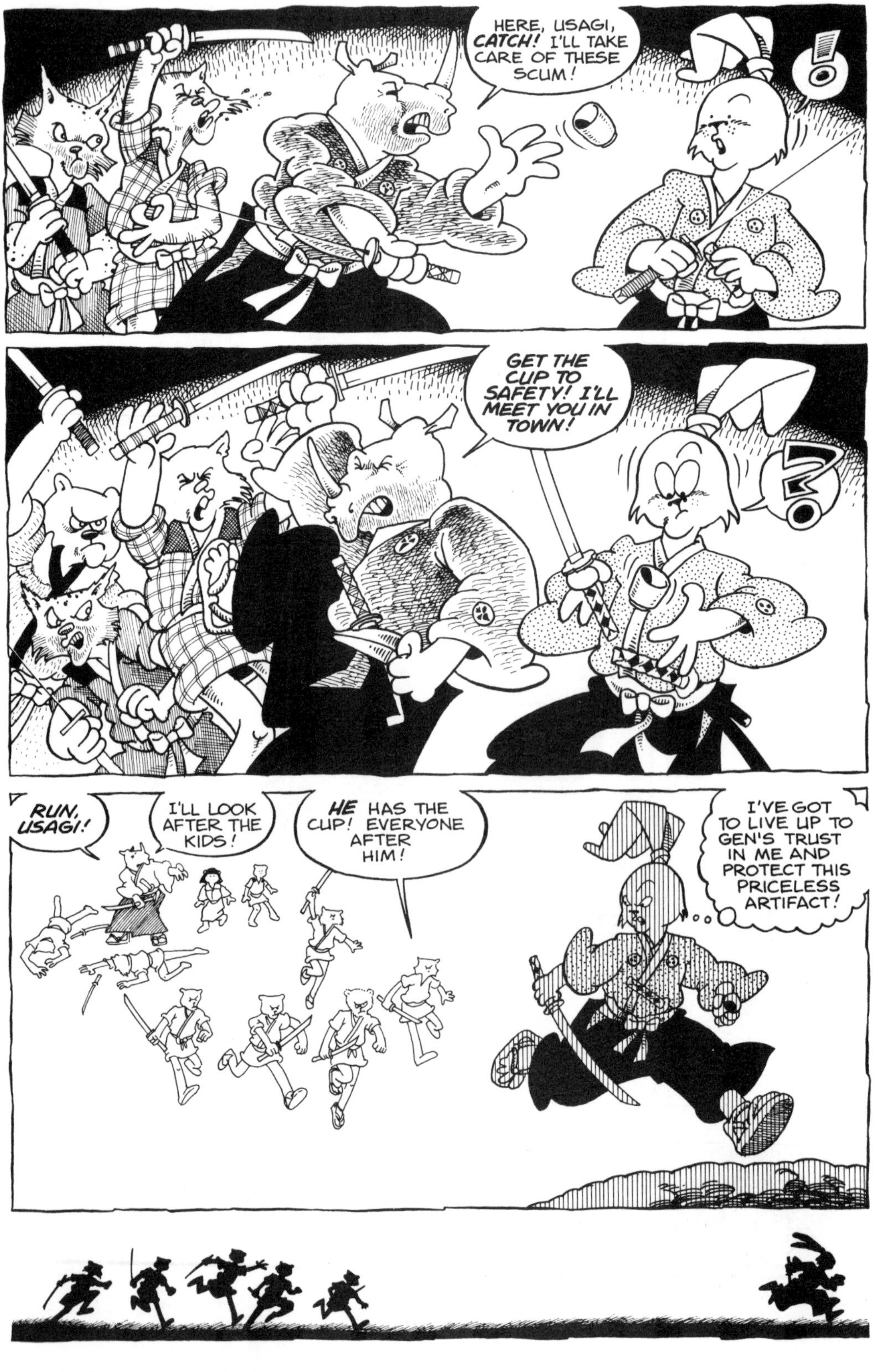
HERE, USAGI, CATCH! I'LL TAKE CARE OF THESE SCUM!
!
GET THE CUP TO SAFETY! I'LL MEET YOU IN TOWN!
?
RUN, USAGI!
I'LL LOOK AFTER THE KIDS!
HE HAS THE CUP! EVERYONE AFTER HIM!
I'VE GOT TO LIVE UP TO GEN'S TRUST IN ME AND PROTECT THIS PRICELESS ARTIFACT!

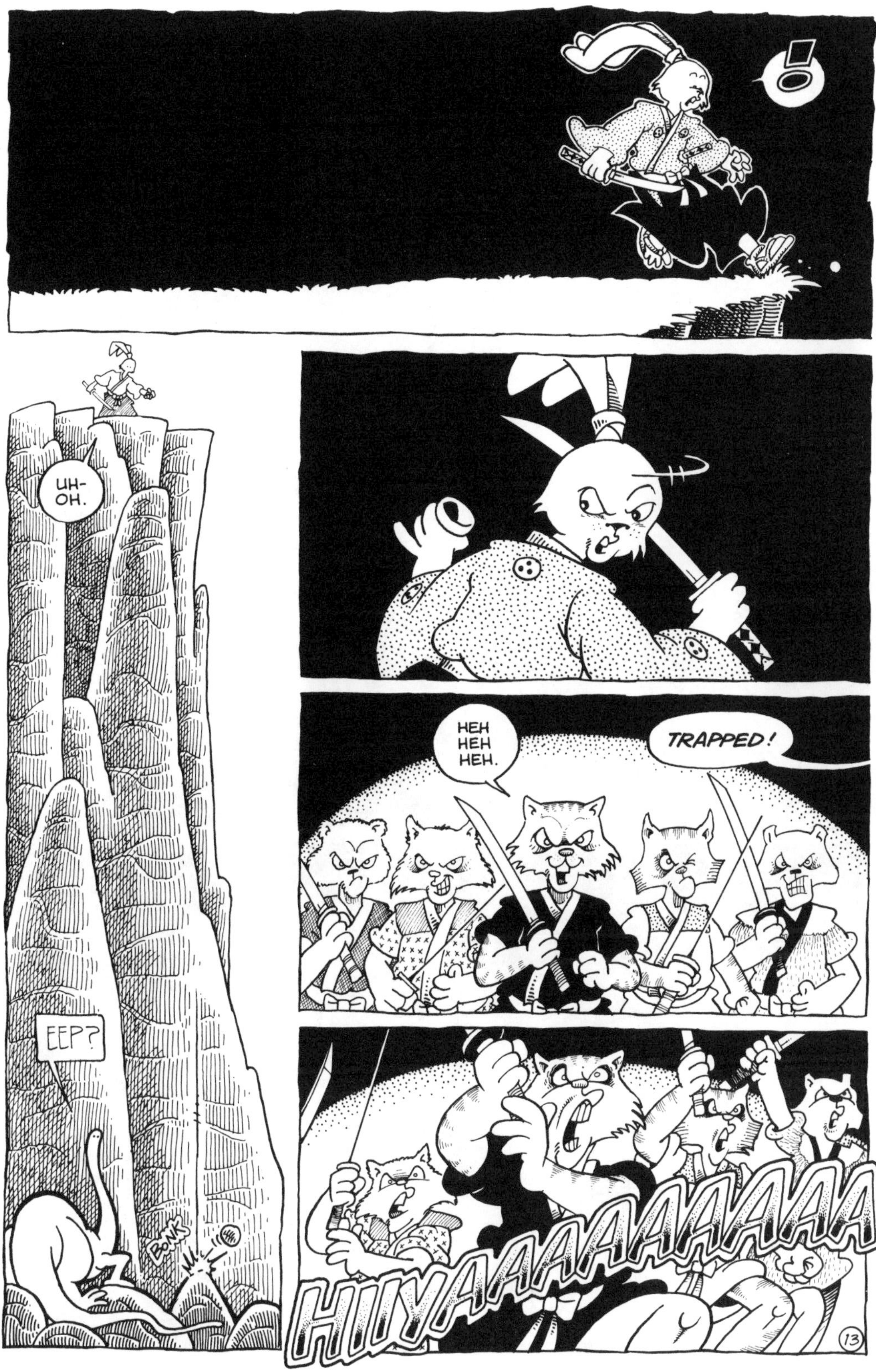
!
UH-OH.
EEP?
BONK
HEH HEH HEH.
TRAPPED!
HIYAAAAAAAAAAAAAA
13

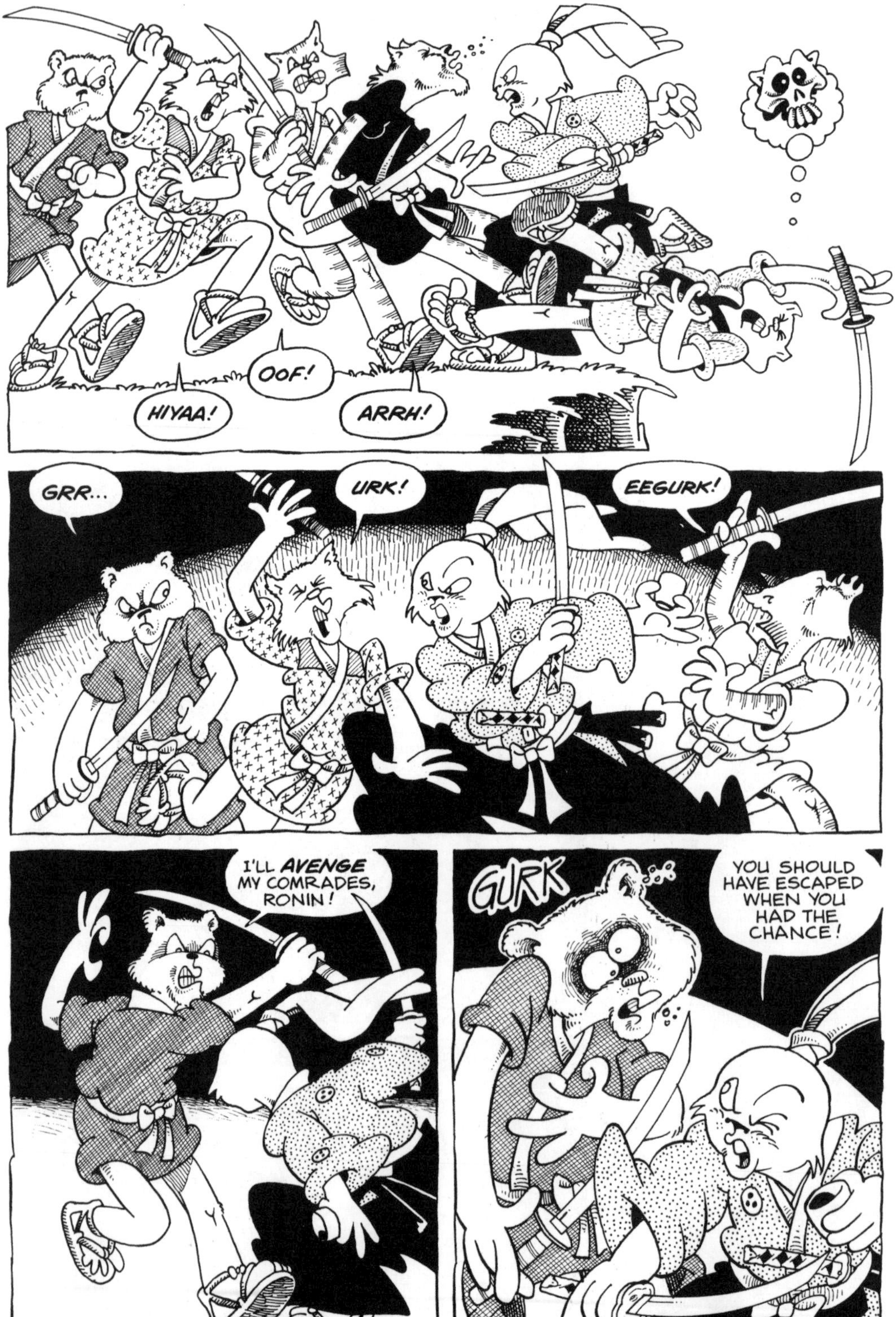
HIYAA!
OOF!
ARRH!
GRR...
URK!
EEGURK!
I'LL AVENGE MY COMRADES, RONIN!
GURK
YOU SHOULD HAVE ESCAPED WHEN YOU HAD THE CHANCE!
14

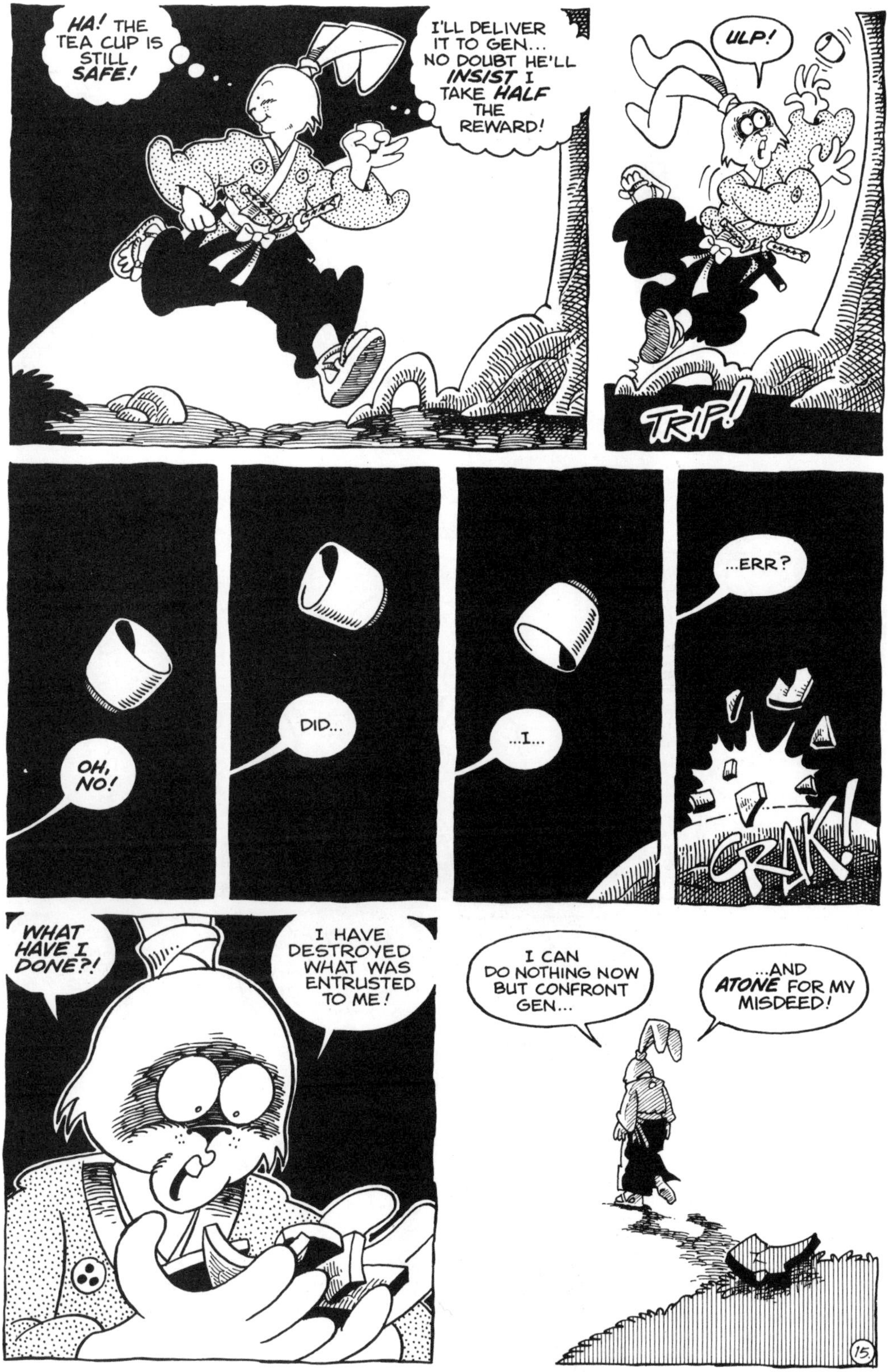
HA! THE TEA CUP IS STILL SAFE!
I'LL DELIVER IT TO GEN... NO DOUBT HE'LL INSIST I TAKE HALF THE REWARD!
ULP!
TRIP!
OH, NO!
DID...
...I...
...ERR?
CRAK!
WHAT HAVE I DONE?!
I HAVE DESTROYED WHAT WAS ENTRUSTED TO ME!
I CAN DO NOTHING NOW BUT CONFRONT GEN...
...AND ATONE FOR MY MISDEED!
15

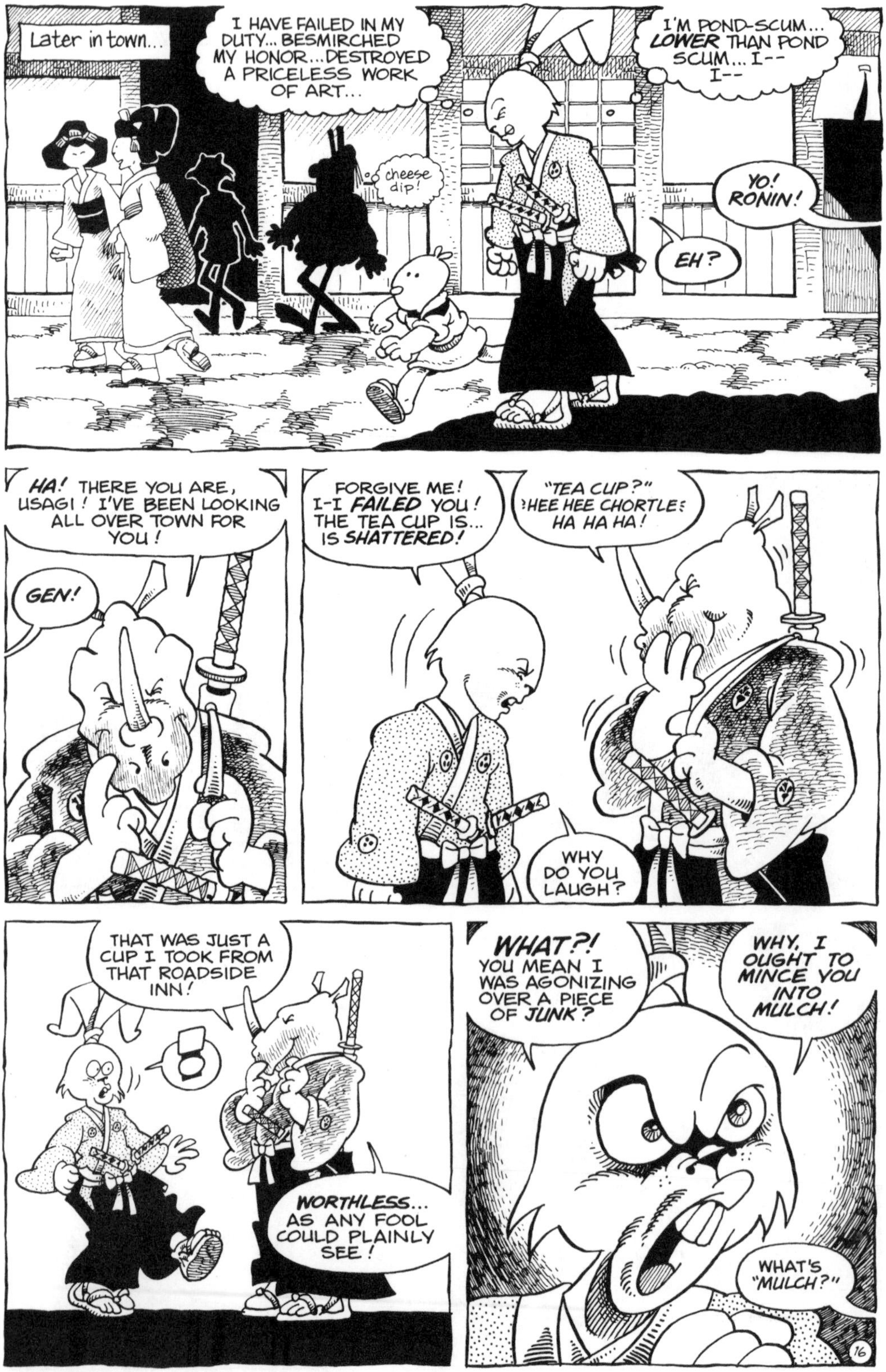
Later in town...
I HAVE FAILED IN MY DUTY... BESMIRCHED MY HONOR... DESTROYED A PRICELESS WORK OF ART...
cheese dip!
I'M POND-SCUM... LOWER THAN POND SCUM... I-- I--
YO! RONIN!
EH?
HA! THERE YOU ARE, USAGI! I'VE BEEN LOOKING ALL OVER TOWN FOR YOU!
GEN!
FORGIVE ME! I-I FAILED YOU! THE TEA CUP IS... IS SHATTERED!
"TEA CUP?" HEE HEE CHORTLE HA HA HA!
WHY DO YOU LAUGH?
THAT WAS JUST A CUP I TOOK FROM THAT ROADSIDE INN!
WORTHLESS... AS ANY FOOL COULD PLAINLY SEE!
WHAT?! YOU MEAN I WAS AGONIZING OVER A PIECE OF JUNK?
WHY, I OUGHT TO MINCE YOU INTO MULCH!
WHAT'S "MULCH?"
16

HA HA HA! COME LET'S HAVE A DRINK TO COOL YOU OFF!

A *DRINK*?! I SHOULD *SLAY* YOU FOR DECEIVING ME!

GRRRR... SO YOU KEEP TELLING ME!

INNKEEPER! FOOD AND DRINK FOR TWO!

YES, SIR!

YOU CAN'T DO THAT! I'M YOUR BEST FRIEND!

FORGIVE ME, USAGI BUT I KNEW THE BRIGANDS WOULD GO AFTER YOU IF THEY THOUGHT YOU HAD THE TEA CUP...

...AND SO I WAS FREE TO COMPLETE MY MISSION AND DELIVER THE *REAL* TEA CUP TO HOKUSE.

INN-KEEPER! MORE SAKE!

HEY, I ALMOST FORGOT...WHAT HAPPENED TO THE KIDS?

OH, *THEM*... WELL... ER...AFTER I DROPPED OFF THE CUP, I...ER... TOOK THEM TO THEIR UNCLE...

ER... WOULD YOU LIKE MORE SAKE?

17.

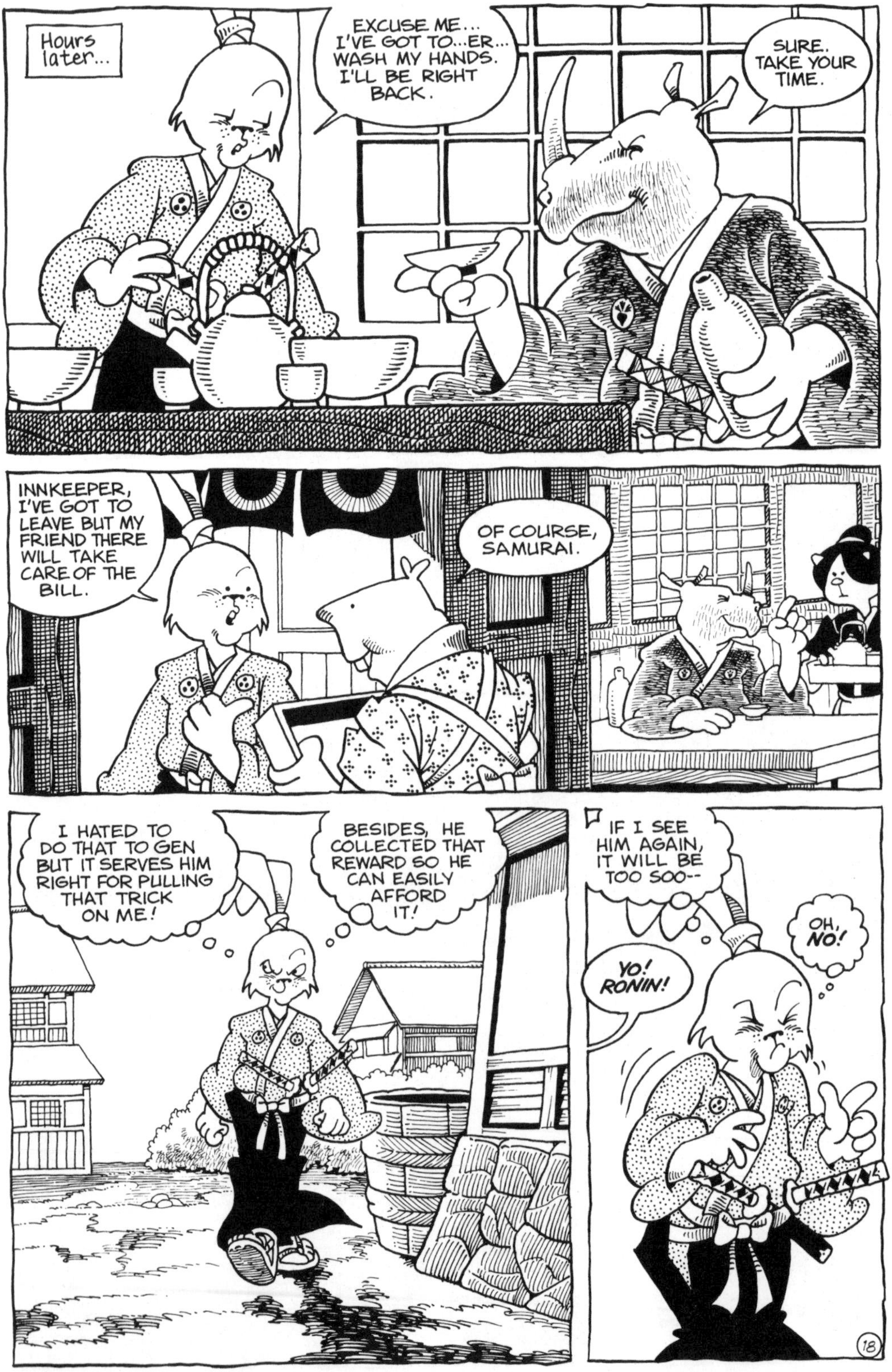
Hours later...
EXCUSE ME... I'VE GOT TO...ER... WASH MY HANDS. I'LL BE RIGHT BACK.
SURE. TAKE YOUR TIME.
INNKEEPER, I'VE GOT TO LEAVE BUT MY FRIEND THERE WILL TAKE CARE OF THE BILL.
OF COURSE, SAMURAI.
I HATED TO DO THAT TO GEN BUT IT SERVES HIM RIGHT FOR PULLING THAT TRICK ON ME!
BESIDES, HE COLLECTED THAT REWARD SO HE CAN EASILY AFFORD IT!
IF I SEE HIM AGAIN, IT WILL BE TOO SOO--
YO! RONIN!
OH, NO!
18

CHAPTER SIX

"The Shogun's Gift"

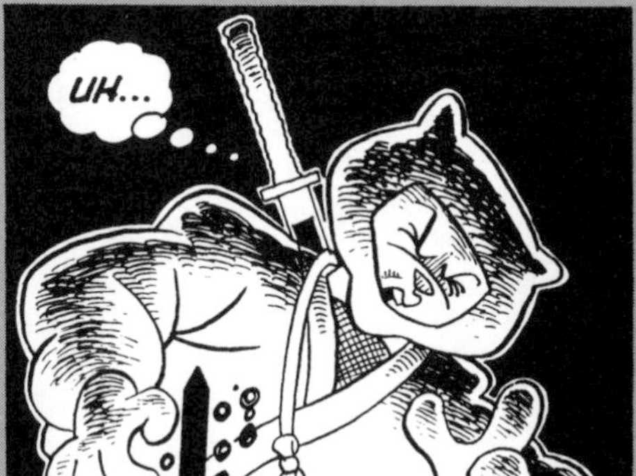
UH...
SHOONK

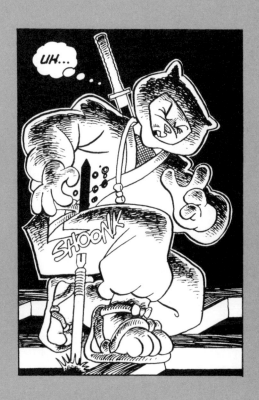

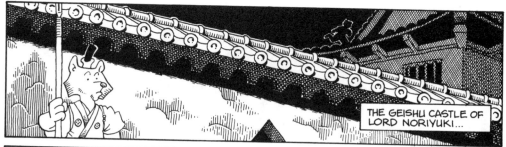

THE GEISHU CASTLE OF LORD NORIYUKI...

THIS, TOMOE, IS THE FAMOUS "MURAMASA BLADE" THAT WILL BE PRESENTED TO THE SHOGUN ON BEHALF OF THE GEISHU CLAN.

IT'S BEAUTIFUL, LORD NORIYUKI. SOME SAY MURAMASA WAS MAD BUT HIS CRAFTSMANSHIP WAS *SUPERB!*

IT IS A *FINE* GIFT!

YES. SUCH A GIFT WILL GIVE OUR CLAN GREAT *PRESTIGE!*

THE SHOGUN WILL BE VERY PLEASED!

HE WOULD ACCEPT NO LESSER SWORD THAN A MURAMASA.

?

1.

113

THE BLADE IS **CLEAN**.

TOMOE! WHAT IS IT?!

FORGIVE ME, MY LORD. I SUSPECTED AN INTRUDER.

I WAS **WRONG**.

YOU'RE EVER VIGILANT, TOMOE...

...BUT THERE'S LITTLE CHANCE OF A TRESPASSER.

MY SECURITY HAS **DOUBLED** SINCE THE ASSASSINATION ATTEMPTS BY LORD HIKIJI.

IT WOULD TAKE A REMARKABLY SKILLED PERSON, INDEED, TO GET PAST MY GUARDS!

≥YAWN!≤

THE SWORD IS SAFE ENOUGH IN HERE...NOW PLEASE GET SOME REST.

YOU TOO, LORD NORIYUKI.

I WILL ESCORT YOU TO YOUR SLEEPING QUARTERS.

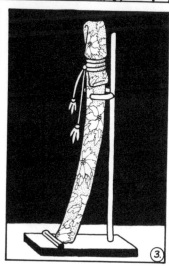

③

UGH! CURSE THIS LEG WOUND! I'LL APPLY SOME HEALING HERBS LATER.

I'VE GOT TO STOP THE BLEEDING BEFORE I LOSE TOO MUCH BLOOD... BUT FIRST THINGS FIRST...

I'VE GOT THE SWORD. NOW TO... EH?

SOMEONE OUTSIDE THE DOOR...

I DON'T KNOW WHY I'M TO GUARD THE MURAMASA BLADE IN THIS ROOM... THERE'S NO WAY A THIEF COULD GET INTO THE CASTLE-- MUCH LESS INTO LORD NORIYUKI'S PRIVATE WING!

THAT'S FUNNY-- I THOUGHT I HEARD SOMEONE MOVING IN HERE...

...MAYBE TOMOE-SAMA ASSIGNED ANOTHER GUARD TO ASSIST ME!

...AS IF I COULDN'T HANDLE A SIMPLE JOB LIKE THIS ALONE! HUH!

WHHHT   WHHHT   THUNK!

YAAAAH

4.

CLOP CLOP CLOP

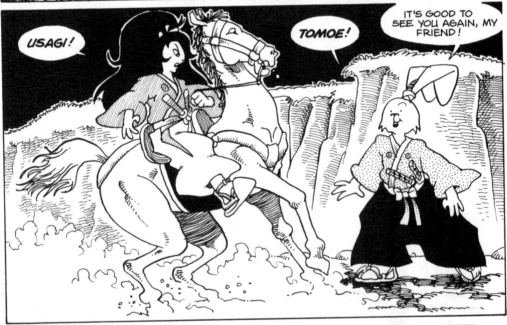

USAGI!

TOMOE!

IT'S GOOD TO SEE YOU AGAIN, MY FRIEND!

HAVE YOU BEEN ON THIS ROAD LONG? DID YOU SEE ANYONE?

NO. IS SOMETHING THE MATTER?

A SWORD THAT WAS TO BE PRESENTED TO THE SHOGUN WAS STOLEN FROM LORD NORIYUKI'S KEEPING TONIGHT!

IT'S NO ORDINARY THIEF!

DO YOU KNOW WHO DID IT?

6.

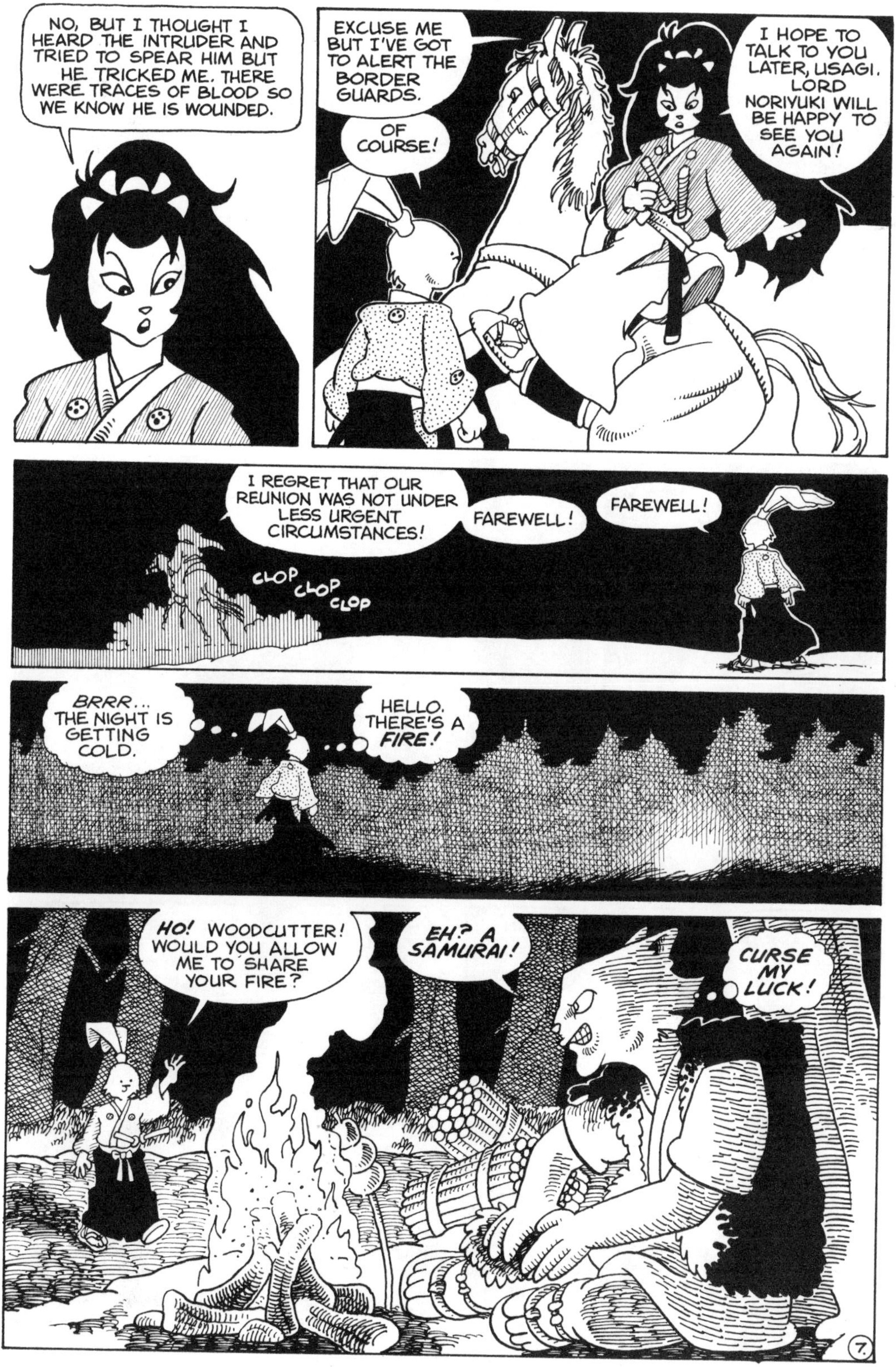
NO, BUT I THOUGHT I HEARD THE INTRUDER AND TRIED TO SPEAR HIM BUT HE TRICKED ME. THERE WERE TRACES OF BLOOD SO WE KNOW HE IS WOUNDED.
EXCUSE ME BUT I'VE GOT TO ALERT THE BORDER GUARDS.
OF COURSE!
I HOPE TO TALK TO YOU LATER, USAGI. LORD NORIYUKI WILL BE HAPPY TO SEE YOU AGAIN!
I REGRET THAT OUR REUNION WAS NOT UNDER LESS URGENT CIRCUMSTANCES!
FAREWELL!
FAREWELL!
CLOP CLOP CLOP
BRRR... THE NIGHT IS GETTING COLD.
HELLO. THERE'S A *FIRE!*
HO! WOODCUTTER! WOULD YOU ALLOW ME TO SHARE YOUR FIRE?
EH? A SAMURAI!
CURSE MY LUCK!
7.

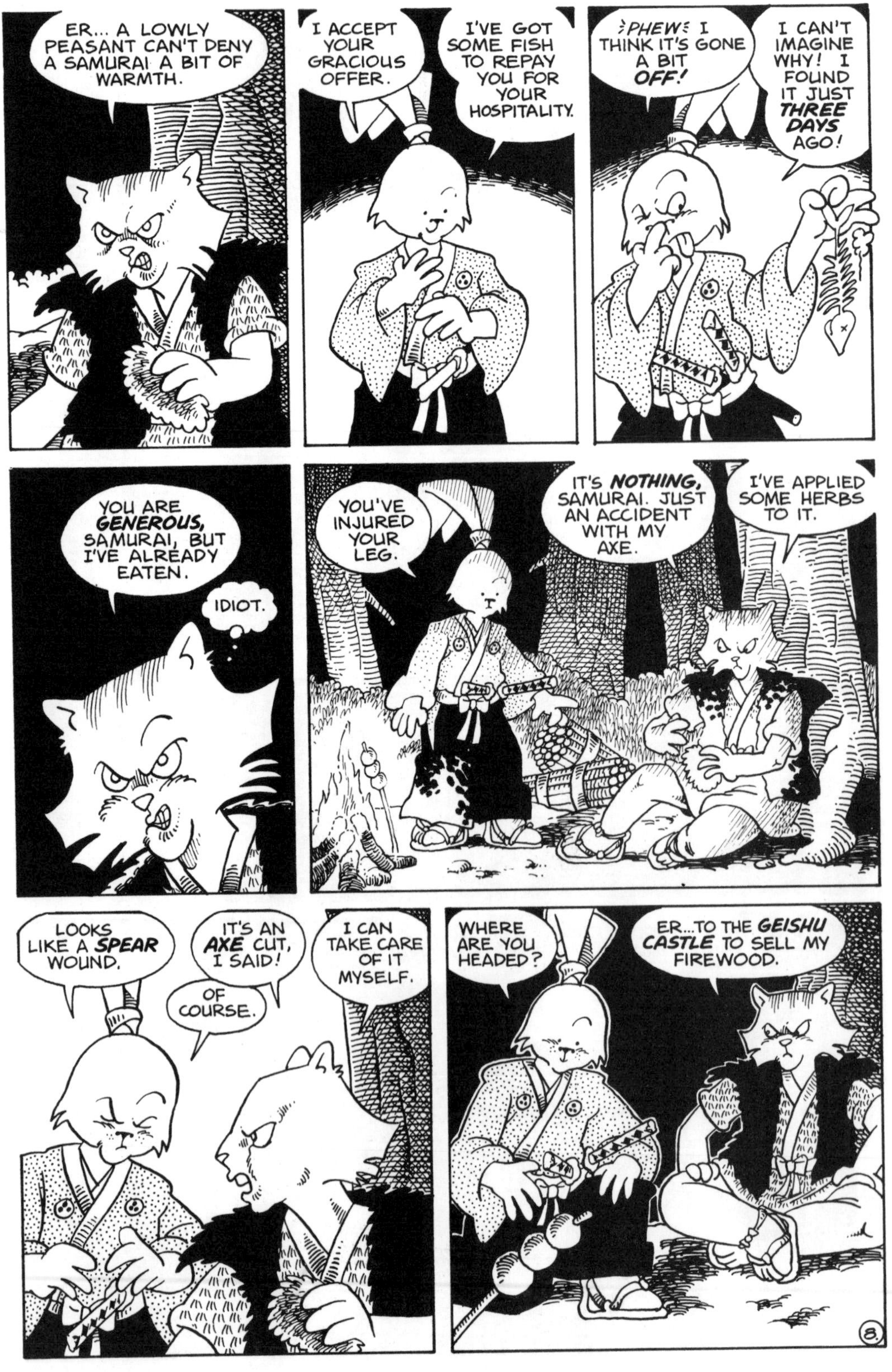
ER... A LOWLY PEASANT CAN'T DENY A SAMURAI A BIT OF WARMTH.
I ACCEPT YOUR GRACIOUS OFFER.
I'VE GOT SOME FISH TO REPAY YOU FOR YOUR HOSPITALITY.
PHEW I THINK IT'S GONE A BIT OFF!
I CAN'T IMAGINE WHY! I FOUND IT JUST THREE DAYS AGO!
YOU ARE GENEROUS, SAMURAI, BUT I'VE ALREADY EATEN.
IDIOT.
YOU'VE INJURED YOUR LEG.
IT'S NOTHING, SAMURAI. JUST AN ACCIDENT WITH MY AXE.
I'VE APPLIED SOME HERBS TO IT.
LOOKS LIKE A SPEAR WOUND.
IT'S AN AXE CUT, I SAID!
OF COURSE.
I CAN TAKE CARE OF IT MYSELF.
WHERE ARE YOU HEADED?
ER...TO THE GEISHU CASTLE TO SELL MY FIREWOOD.
8

121

ARE YOU STAYING AT THIS INN? I *INSIST* ON BUYING YOU A MEAL TO REPAY YOU FOR LAST NIGHT'S HOSPITALITY.

GRRR. I SHOULD HAVE KILLED HIM WHEN I HAD THE CHANCE!

INNKEEPER! GIVE US A TABLE!

I THOUGHT YOU WERE ON YOUR WAY TO THE GEISHU CASTLE, WOODCUTTER.

ER...I WAS... BUT I REMEMBERED I CAN GET A MUCH BETTER PRICE FOR MY FIREWOOD ACROSS THE RIVER.

WHAT ABOUT *YOU*, SAMURAI?

OH, JUST A WHIM. TO A WANDERER, ONE PLACE IS AS GOOD AS ANOTHER!

I WAS FACING THIS DIRECTION WHEN I AWOKE.... SO HERE I AM!

RIDICULOUS! NO ONE LIVES THEIR LIFE LIKE THAT!

EXCUSE US, SIRS, BUT WOULD YOU MIND IF WE SHARED YOUR TABLE?

THE TOWN IS SO CROWDED BECAUSE OF THE ROAD BLOCK THAT THERE'S VERY LITTLE ROOM AND WE NOTICED YOU ARE A FELLOW WOODCUTTER...

WE'RE *BUSY!* FIND ANOTHER--

WELCOME! THERE'S *LOTS* OF ROOM!

GRR...

⑫

124

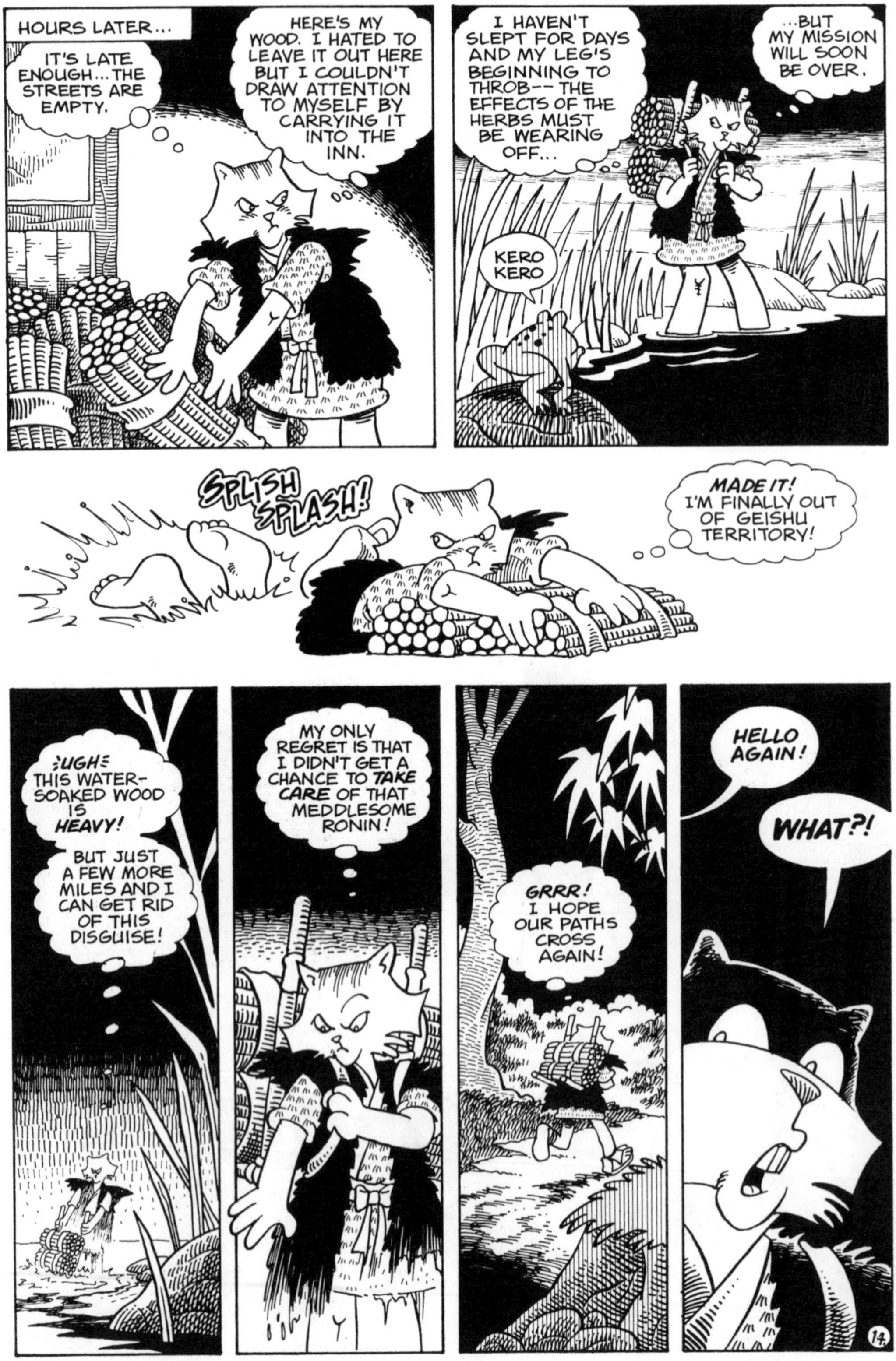
HOURS LATER...
IT'S LATE ENOUGH... THE STREETS ARE EMPTY.
HERE'S MY WOOD. I HATED TO LEAVE IT OUT HERE BUT I COULDN'T DRAW ATTENTION TO MYSELF BY CARRYING IT INTO THE INN.
I HAVEN'T SLEPT FOR DAYS AND MY LEG'S BEGINNING TO THROB-- THE EFFECTS OF THE HERBS MUST BE WEARING OFF...
...BUT MY MISSION WILL SOON BE OVER.
KERO KERO
SPLISH SPLASH!
MADE IT! I'M FINALLY OUT OF GEISHU TERRITORY!
UGH THIS WATER-SOAKED WOOD IS HEAVY!
BUT JUST A FEW MORE MILES AND I CAN GET RID OF THIS DISGUISE!
MY ONLY REGRET IS THAT I DIDN'T GET A CHANCE TO TAKE CARE OF THAT MEDDLESOME RONIN!
GRRR! I HOPE OUR PATHS CROSS AGAIN!
HELLO AGAIN!
WHAT?!
14

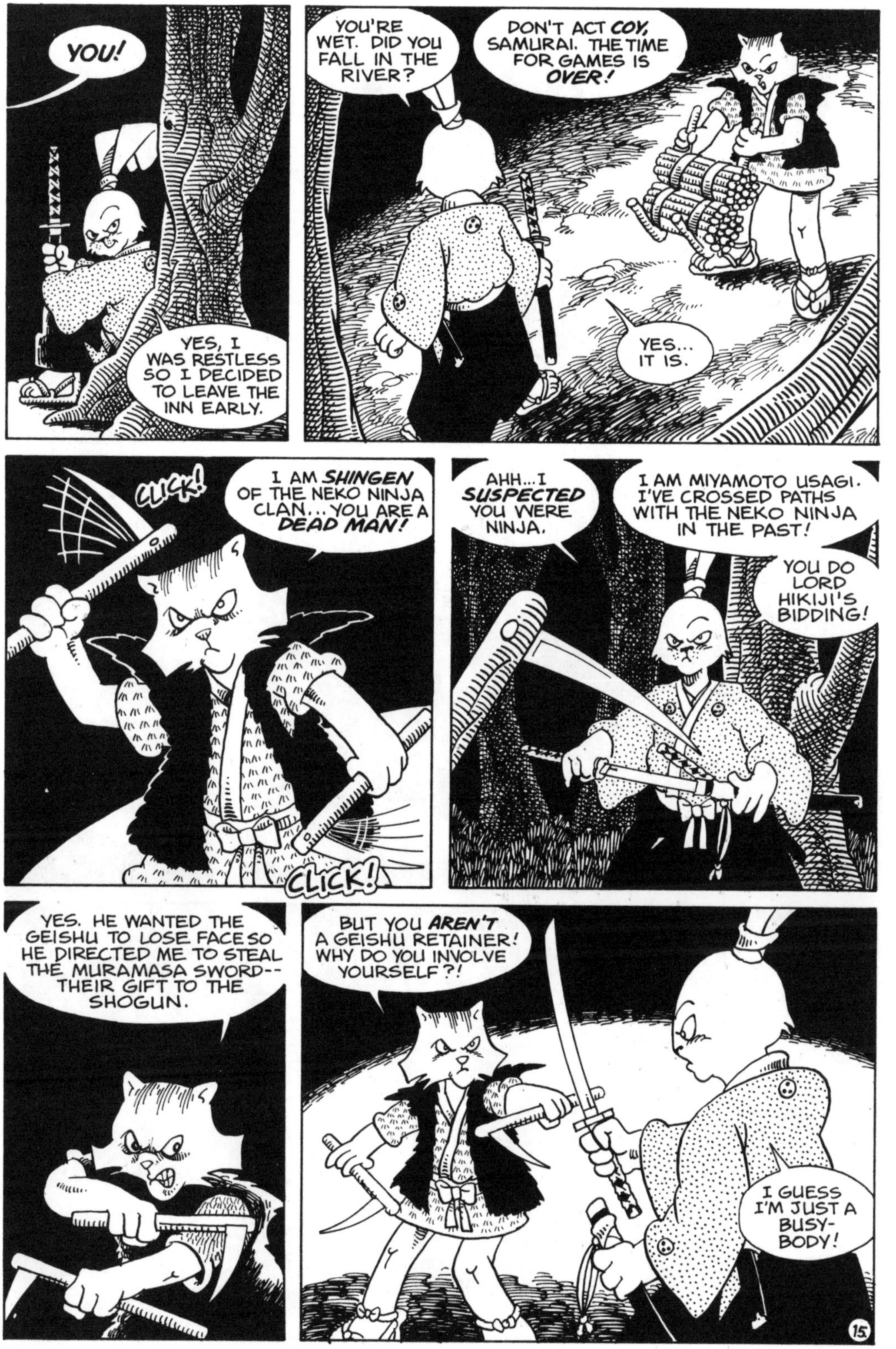
YOU!
YES, I WAS RESTLESS SO I DECIDED TO LEAVE THE INN EARLY.
YOU'RE WET. DID YOU FALL IN THE RIVER?
DON'T ACT COY, SAMURAI. THE TIME FOR GAMES IS OVER!
YES... IT IS.
CLICK!
I AM SHINGEN OF THE NEKO NINJA CLAN... YOU ARE A DEAD MAN!
CLICK!
AHH... I SUSPECTED YOU WERE NINJA.
I AM MIYAMOTO USAGI. I'VE CROSSED PATHS WITH THE NEKO NINJA IN THE PAST!
YOU DO LORD HIKIJI'S BIDDING!
YES. HE WANTED THE GEISHU TO LOSE FACE SO HE DIRECTED ME TO STEAL THE MURAMASA SWORD-- THEIR GIFT TO THE SHOGUN.
BUT YOU AREN'T A GEISHU RETAINER! WHY DO YOU INVOLVE YOURSELF?!
I GUESS I'M JUST A BUSY-BODY!
15

SO, SAMURAI, YOU *AREN'T* THE FOOL I FIRST THOUGHT YOU WERE...

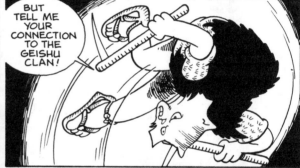

BUT TELL ME YOUR CONNECTION TO THE GEISHU CLAN!

...BUT YOU'RE STILL NO MATCH FOR A *NEKO NINJA!*

I WAS A BODYGUARD TO LORD NORIYUKI WHEN LORD HIKIJI ATTEMPTED TO ASSASSINATE HIM!

I STILL OWE HIM A DEBT OF LOYALTY...

...SO I FOLLOWED YOU TO FIND OUT WHO IS BEHIND THIS NEW PLOT

TANG
TANG
TANG
THOK
THOK
RYAAAA
!
!
SLICE
UHH!
THUD!
18

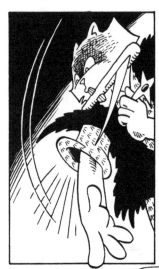

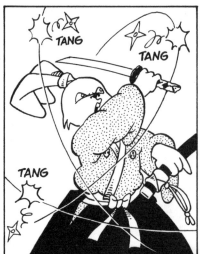

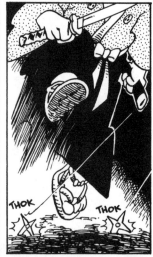

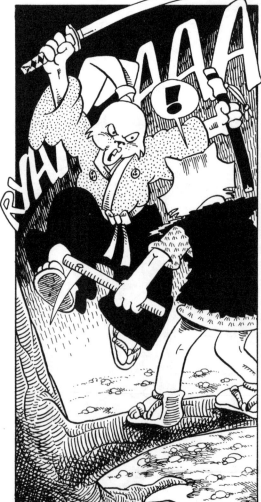

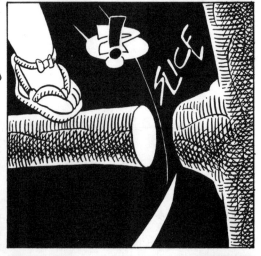

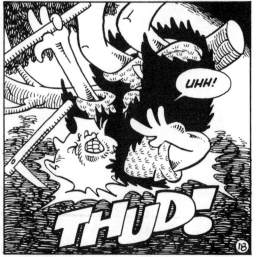

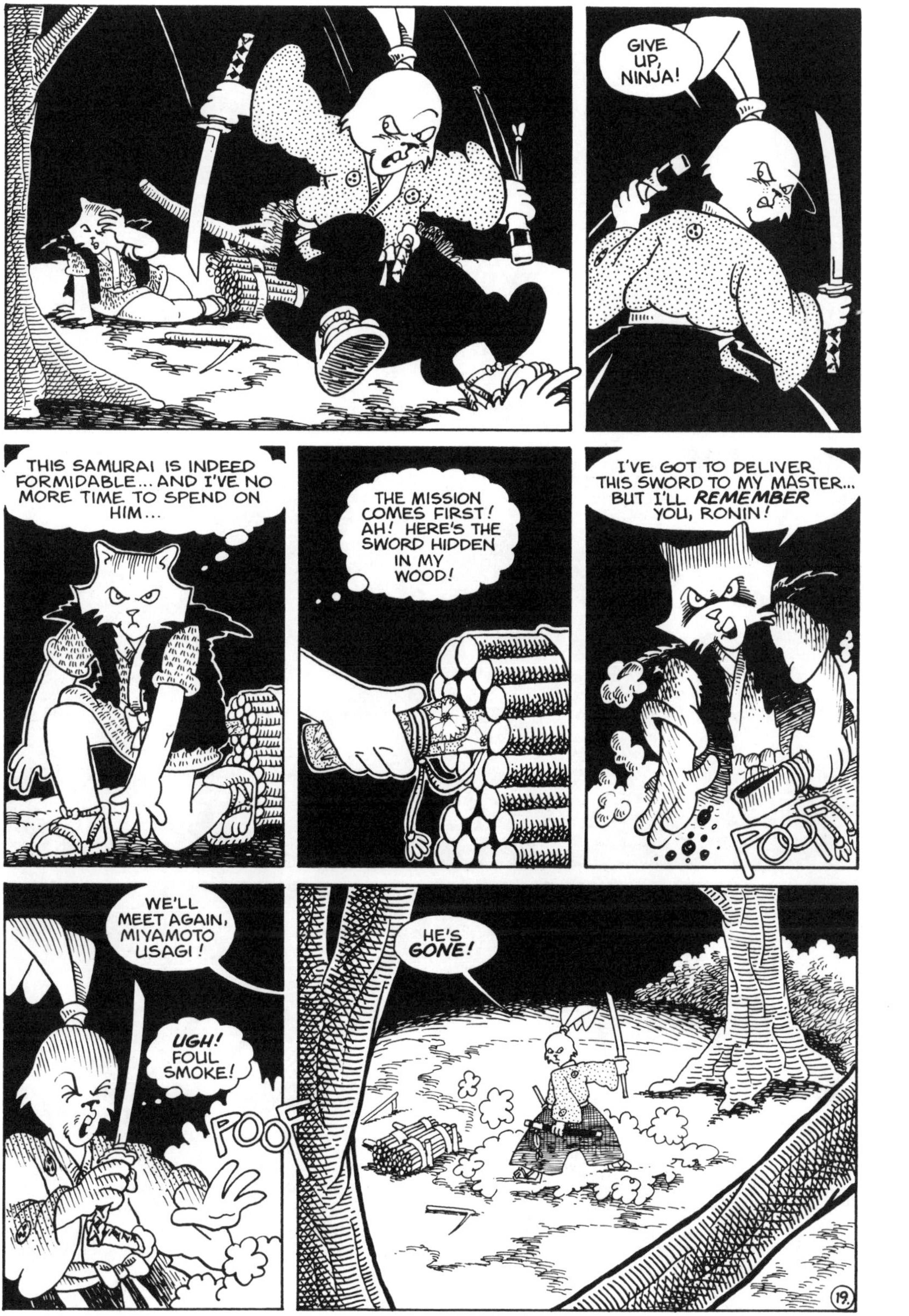
GIVE UP, NINJA!
THIS SAMURAI IS INDEED FORMIDABLE... AND I'VE NO MORE TIME TO SPEND ON HIM...
THE MISSION COMES FIRST! AH! HERE'S THE SWORD HIDDEN IN MY WOOD!
I'VE GOT TO DELIVER THIS SWORD TO MY MASTER... BUT I'LL *REMEMBER* YOU, RONIN!
POOF
WE'LL MEET AGAIN, MIYAMOTO USAGI!
UGH! FOUL SMOKE!
POOF
HE'S *GONE!*
19.

ELSEWHERE...

HA! HE HAS NO IDEA WHICH DIRECTION I'VE GONE!

I'LL TRAVEL A PATH *IMPOSSIBLE* TO FOLLOW!

≥PUFF HUFF≥ I'VE *LOST* HIM NOW!

I'M *SURE* OF IT!

≥CHOFF GAG≥ I'M *EXHAUSTED* BUT I SHOULD BE ABLE TO REST NOW...

MY LEG FEELS LIKE IT'S ON FIRE!

I'D BETTER CHECK ON THE BLADE-- MAKE SURE IT'S UNDAMAGED!

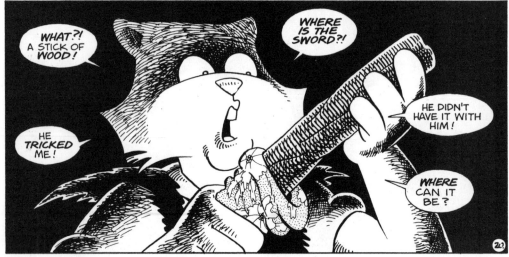

WHAT?! A STICK OF *WOOD!*

WHERE IS THE SWORD?!

HE *TRICKED* ME!

HE DIDN'T HAVE IT WITH HIM!

WHERE CAN IT BE?

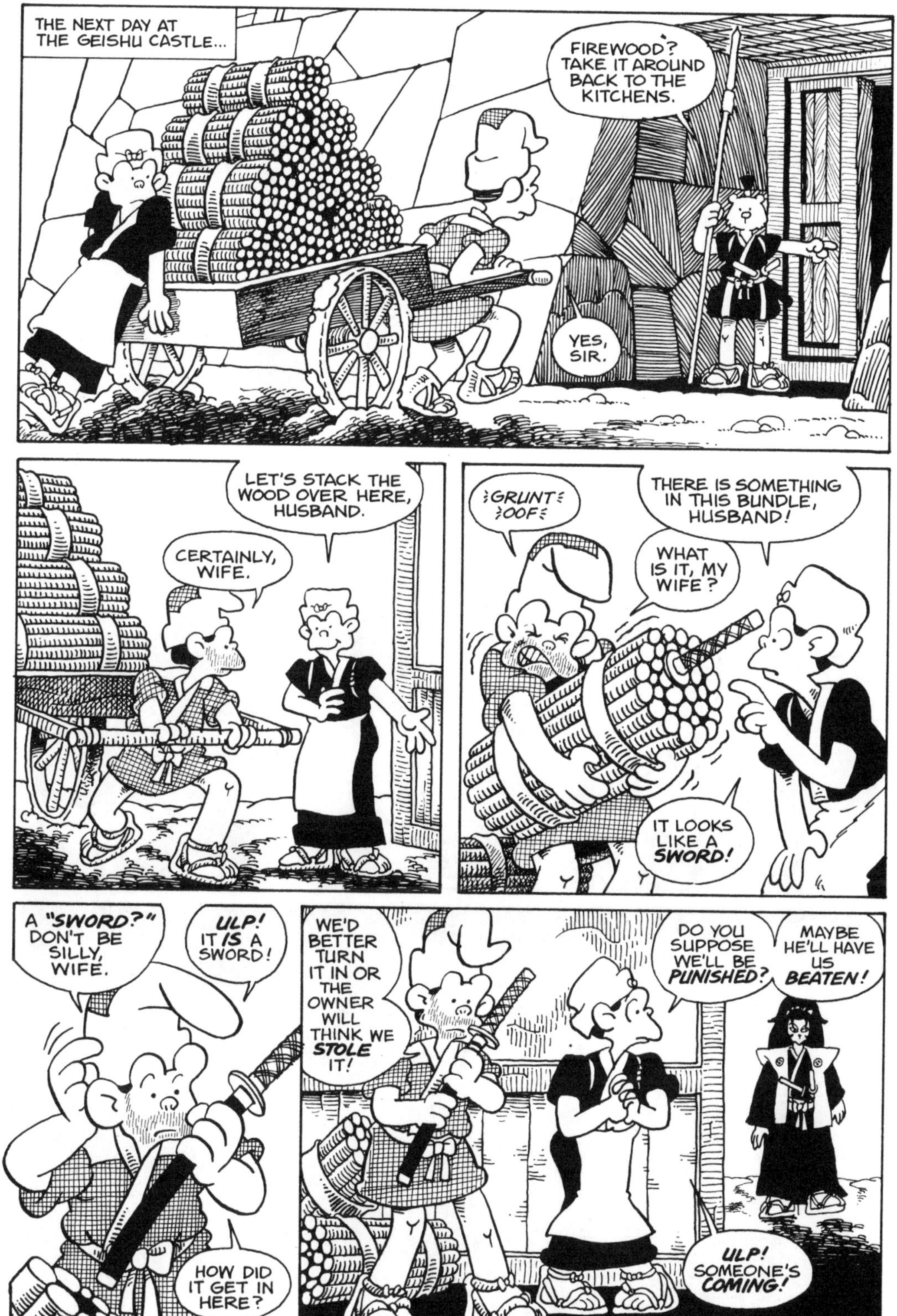
THE NEXT DAY AT THE GEISHU CASTLE...
FIREWOOD? TAKE IT AROUND BACK TO THE KITCHENS.
YES, SIR.
LET'S STACK THE WOOD OVER HERE, HUSBAND.
CERTAINLY, WIFE.
GRUNT OOF
THERE IS SOMETHING IN THIS BUNDLE, HUSBAND!
WHAT IS IT, MY WIFE?
IT LOOKS LIKE A SWORD!
A "SWORD?" DON'T BE SILLY, WIFE.
ULP! IT IS A SWORD!
HOW DID IT GET IN HERE?
WE'D BETTER TURN IT IN OR THE OWNER WILL THINK WE STOLE IT!
DO YOU SUPPOSE WE'LL BE PUNISHED?
MAYBE HE'LL HAVE US BEATEN!
ULP! SOMEONE'S COMING!
21.

BWAAH! DON'T CHASTISE US! WE DIDN'T STEAL IT!

WAHH! WE DON'T KNOW WHOSE IT IS! WE *FOUND* IT IN OUR *WOOD*!

THE *MURAMASA BLADE*! WHERE DID YOU GET THIS?

YOU-YOU MEAN THAT'S THE SWORD EVERBODY IS *LOOKING* FOR?

WE DIDN'T STEAL IT-- *I KNOW*! THAT LONG-EARED RONIN MUST HAVE PUT IT IN OUR BUNDLE! I *KNEW* THERE WAS SOMETHING *FISHY* ABOUT HIM!

"LONG-EARED"? *HA HA HA HA*! YOU MUST MEAN *USAGI*! BUT HOW DID *HE* GET MIXED-UP IN THIS?

HE WAS WITH THAT *UNFRIENDLY* WOOD CUTTER THAT DIDN'T KNOW HIS TRADE!

AH...IT'S BECOMING CLEARER. THAT WOOD CUTTER MUST HAVE BEEN THE THIEF! WE ARE DEEPER IN YOUR DEBT, USAGI. I HOPE WE'LL MEET AGAIN SOON SO THAT I MAY REPAY YOU.

LORD NORIYUKI SHOULD HAVE THE SWORD BY NOW...

HE'S STILL WEAVING HIS WEBS OF INTRIGUE.

...AND I NOW KNOW WHO WAS BEHIND THE THEFT...*LORD HIKIJI*!

I WONDER WHEN OUR PATHS WILL CROSS AGAIN.

END.

134

EPILOGUE

"Turtle Soup and Rabbit Stew"

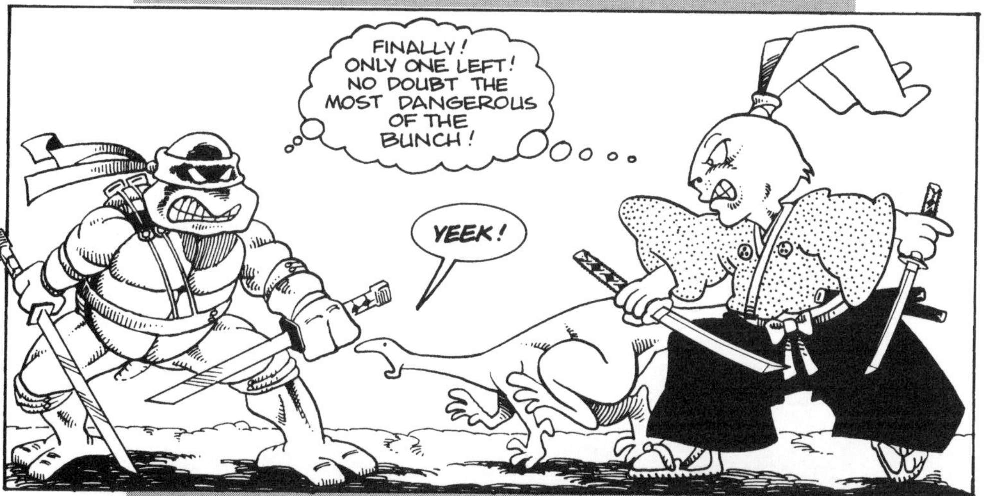

FINALLY! ONLY ONE LEFT! NO DOUBT THE MOST DANGEROUS OF THE BUNCH!
YEEK!

In the Summer of 1986, I was asked by Peter Laird and Kevin Eastman, creators of The Teenage Mutant Ninja Turtles, to participate in a project called *Turtle Soup* in which other artists would try their hands at creating stories featuring their characters.

The story I came up with was "Turtle Soup and Rabbit Stew." This led to a couple of other cross-over stories: Peter's "The Crossing" for *Usagi Yojimbo* #10 and "The Treaty" by myself for Mirage Studios' *Shell Shock*.

A cautionary note to continuity fans: These stories were done just for the fun of it and in no way relate to the Usagi Yojimbo storylines.   —*STAN SAKAI*

LEONARDO™ MEETS USAGI YOJIMBO™ IN TURTLE SOUP AND RABBIT STEW

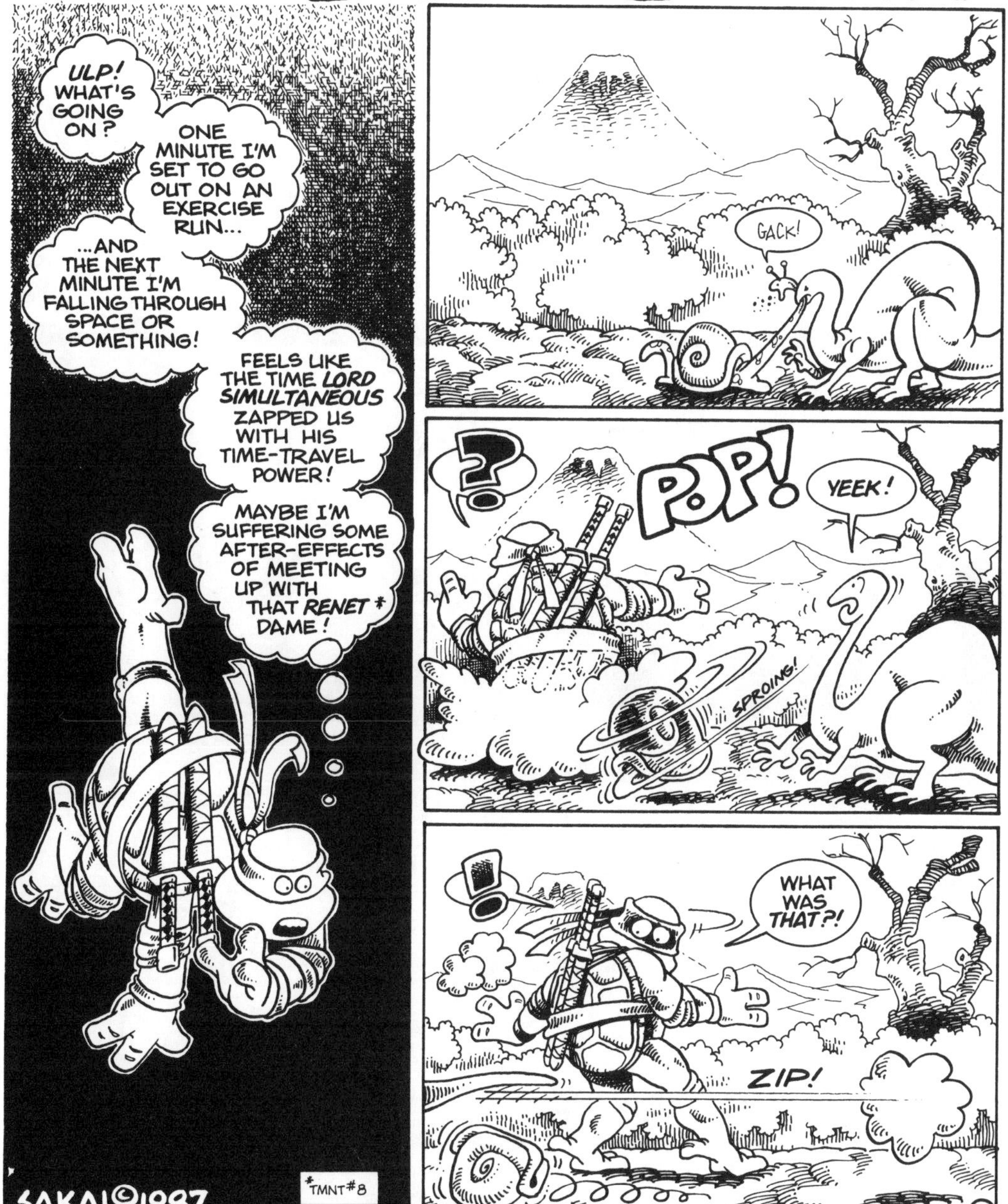

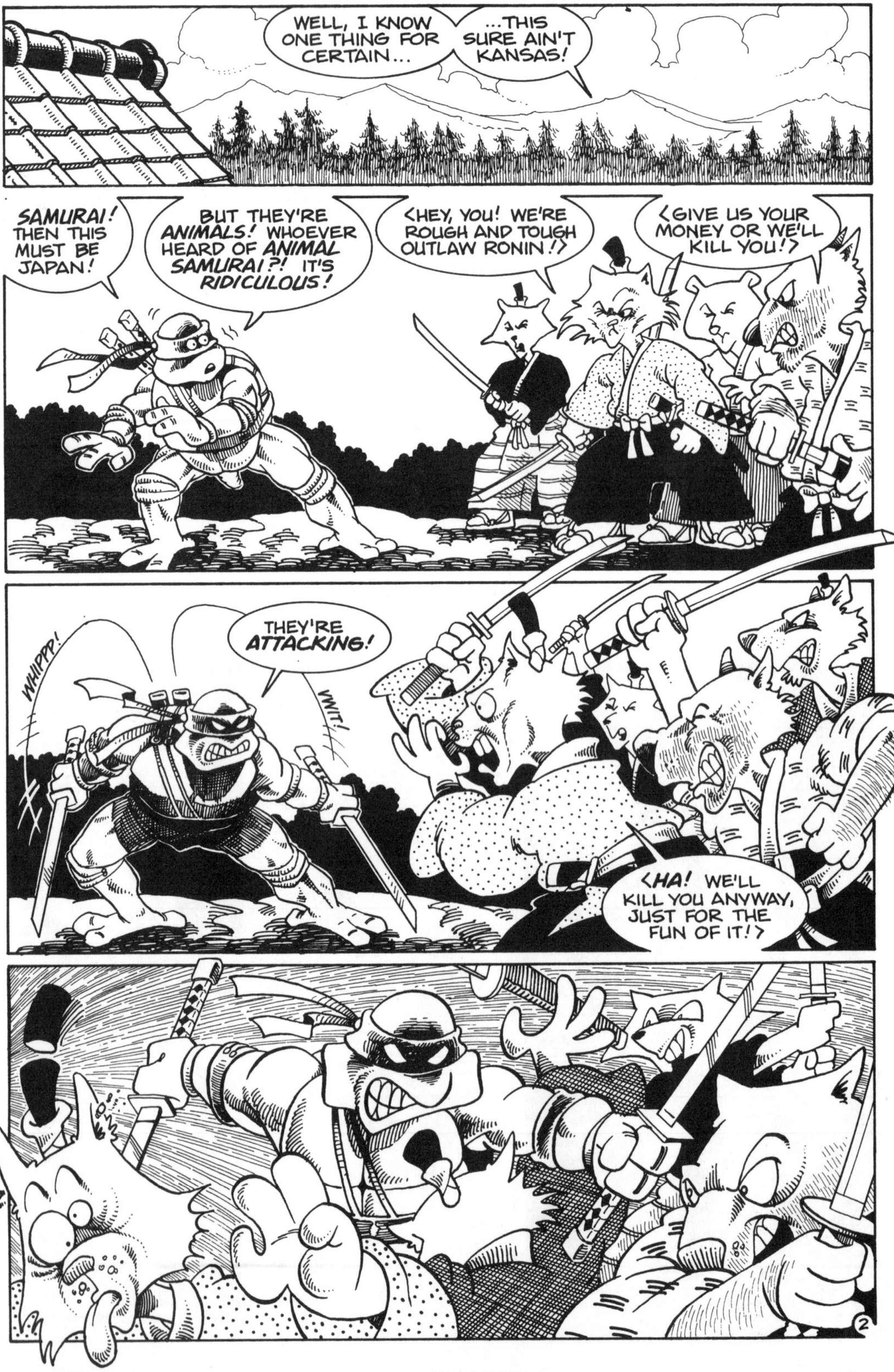
WELL, I KNOW ONE THING FOR CERTAIN...
...THIS SURE AIN'T KANSAS!
SAMURAI! THEN THIS MUST BE JAPAN!
BUT THEY'RE ANIMALS! WHOEVER HEARD OF ANIMAL SAMURAI?! IT'S RIDICULOUS!
<HEY, YOU! WE'RE ROUGH AND TOUGH OUTLAW RONIN!>
<GIVE US YOUR MONEY OR WE'LL KILL YOU!>
WHIPPP!
THEY'RE ATTACKING!
VWIT!
<HA! WE'LL KILL YOU ANYWAY, JUST FOR THE FUN OF IT!>
2

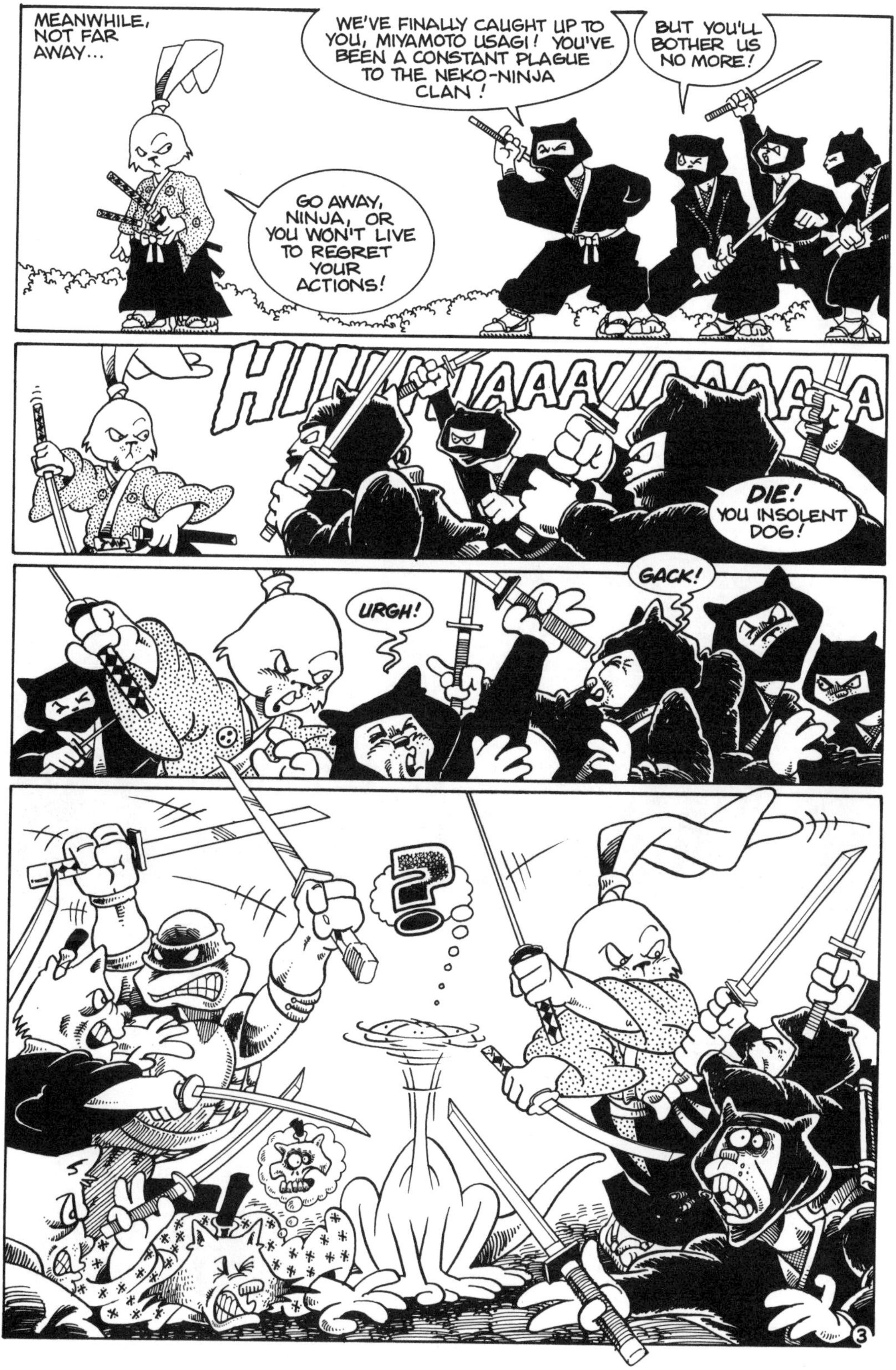

MEANWHILE, NOT FAR AWAY...
WE'VE FINALLY CAUGHT UP TO YOU, MIYAMOTO USAGI! YOU'VE BEEN A CONSTANT PLAGUE TO THE NEKO-NINJA CLAN!
BUT YOU'LL BOTHER US NO MORE!
GO AWAY, NINJA, OR YOU WON'T LIVE TO REGRET YOUR ACTIONS!
HIIIIIAAAAAAAAAAA
DIE! YOU INSOLENT DOG!
URGH!
GACK!
?
!
3

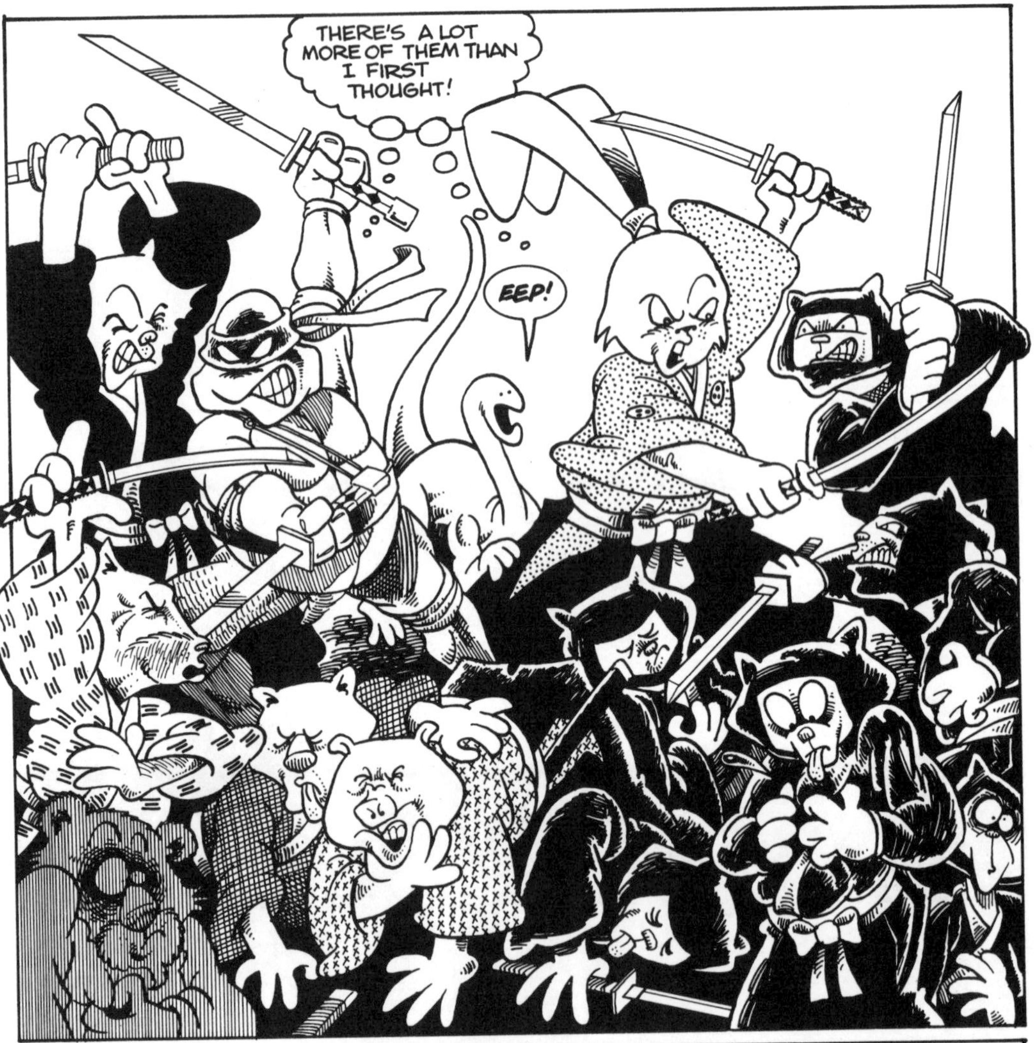
THERE'S A LOT MORE OF THEM THAN I FIRST THOUGHT!
EEP!

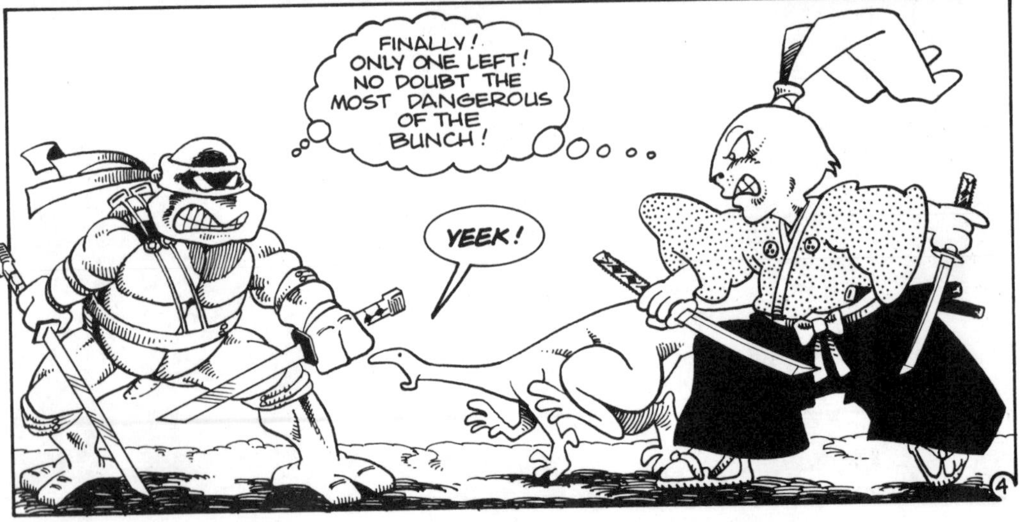
FINALLY! ONLY ONE LEFT! NO DOUBT THE MOST DANGEROUS OF THE BUNCH!
YEEK!
4

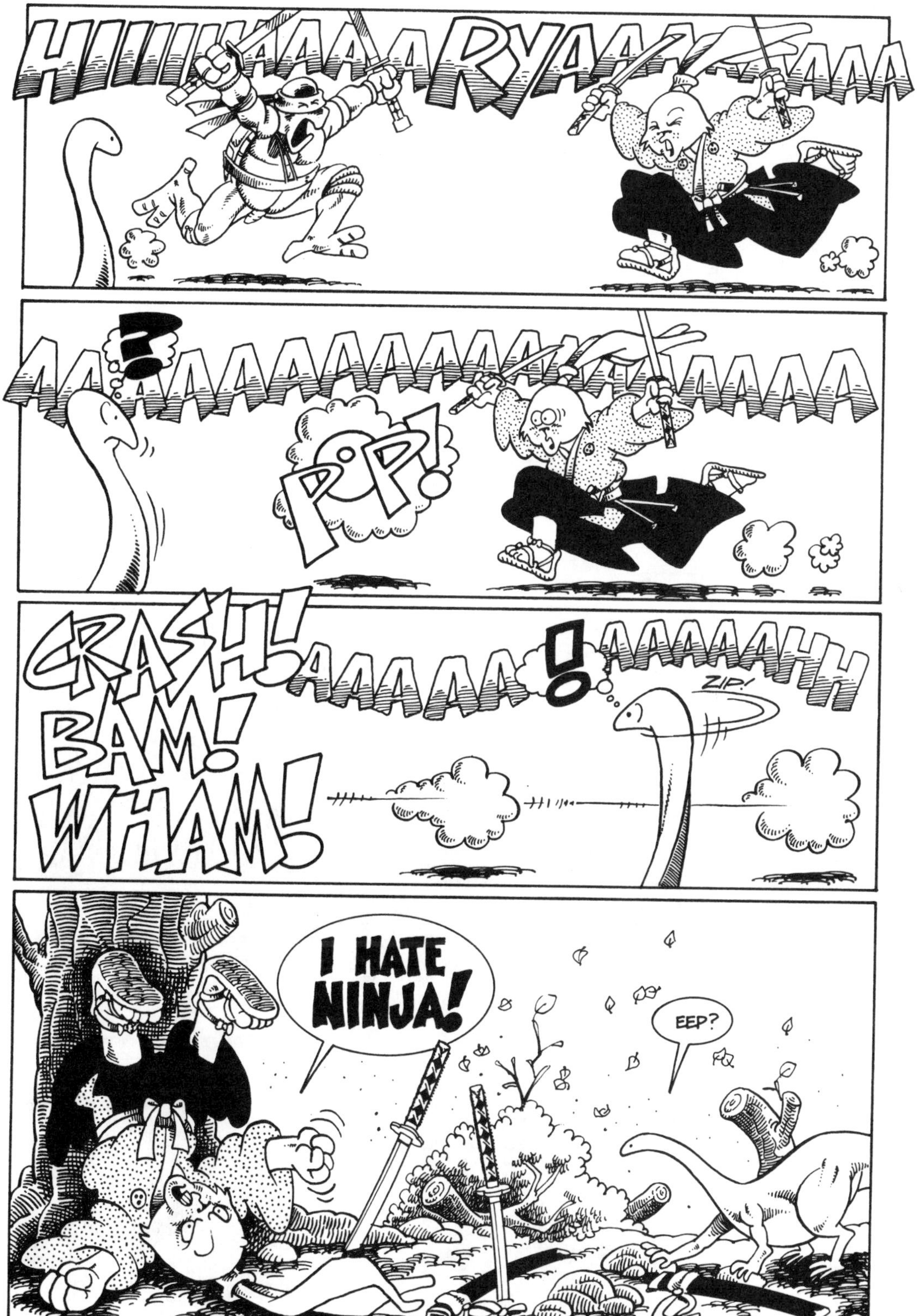
HIIIIAAAARYAAAAAAAAA
AAAAAAAAAAAAAAAAA
?
POP!
CRASH!
AAAAAAA
!
AAAAAAHH
ZIP!
BAM!
WHAM!
I HATE NINJA!
EEP?
5

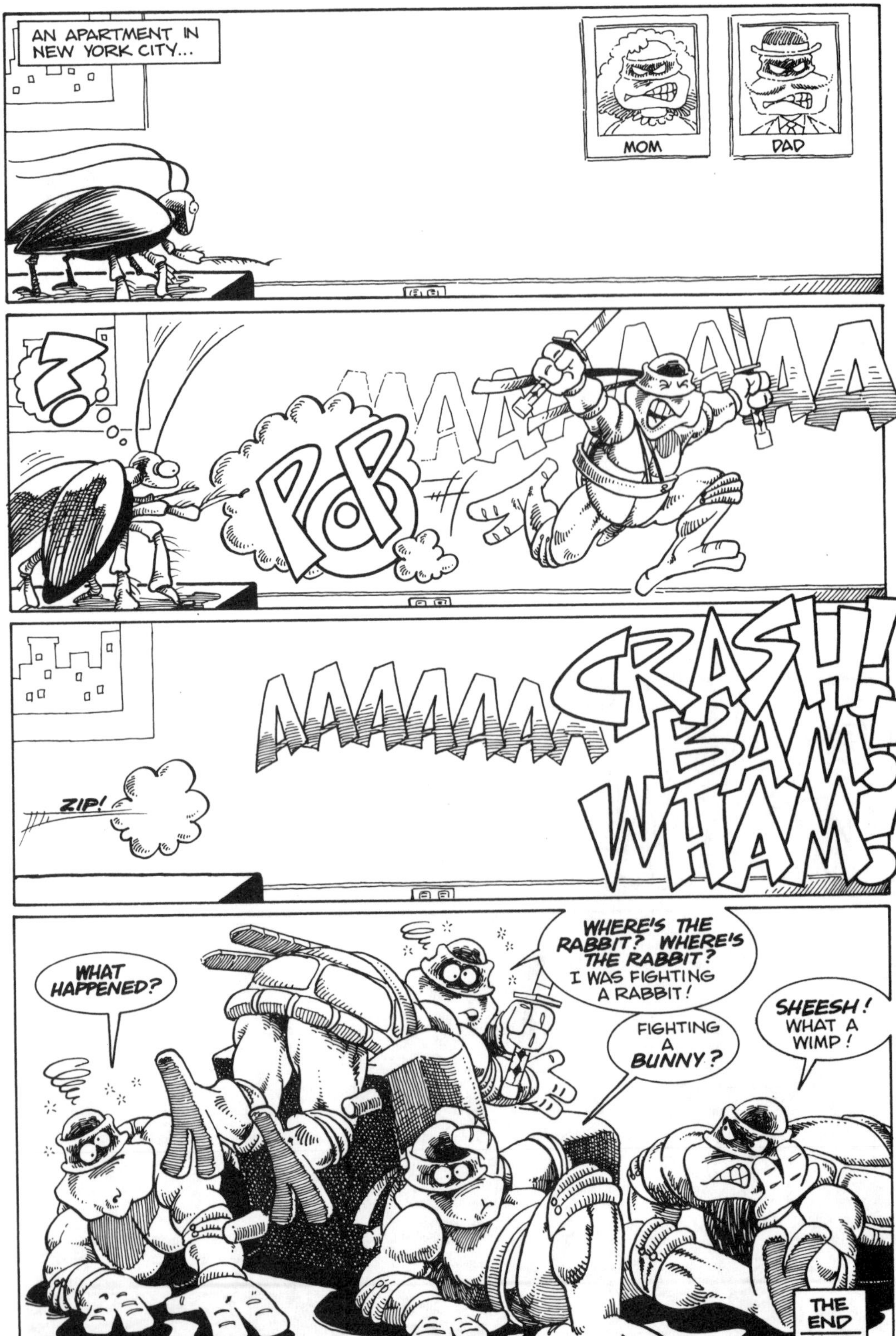
AN APARTMENT IN NEW YORK CITY...
MOM
DAD
Z
POP
AAAAAAAA
AAAAAAAA
CRASH! BAM! WHAM!
ZIP!
WHAT HAPPENED?
WHERE'S THE RABBIT? WHERE'S THE RABBIT? I WAS FIGHTING A RABBIT!
FIGHTING A BUNNY?
SHEESH! WHAT A WIMP!
THE END
SAKAI 2·87

THE USAGI LIBRARY

USAGI YOJIMBO BOOK ONE: "THE RONIN"

Reprints the stories from Critters, Albedo, and the original Usagi Yojimbo Summer Special;
152 pages; $14.95.

(Signed hardcover, including "Early Usagi Sketches," available for $35.00.)

USAGI YOJIMBO BOOK TWO: "SAMURAI"

Reprints the stories from Usagi #1-6; 144 pages; $14.95.

(Signed hardcover, including an original draft of "Samurai," available for $35.00.)

USAGI YOJIMBO BOOK THREE: "THE WANDERER'S ROAD"

Reprints the stories from Usagi # 7-12; 152 pages; $12.95.

(Signed hardcover, including "The Usagi Cover Gallery," available for $39.95.)

USAGI YOJIMBO BOOK FOUR: "THE DRAGON BELLOW CONSPIRACY"

Reprints the stories from Usagi # 13-18; 184 pages; $14.95.

(Signed hardcover sold out)

USAGI YOJIMBO BOOK FIVE: "LONE GOAT AND KID"

Reprints the stories from Usagi #19-24; 144 pages; $10.95.

(Signed hardcover sold out)

USAGI YOJIMBO BOOK SIX: "CIRCLES"

Reprints the stories from Usagi #25-31 and Critters #50; 168 pages; $12.95.

(Signed hardcover, including the Turtles story "The Treaty," available for $39.95.)

USAGI YOJIMBO BOOK SEVEN: "GEN'S STORY"

Reprints the stories from Usagi #32-38 and Critters #38; 192 pages; $16.95.

(Signed hardcover, including the new story "Hebi," available for $39.95.)

All books available from
FANTAGRAPHICS BOOKS, 7563 Lake City Way NE, Seattle, WA, 98115.
Please add $4.00 for shipping and handling to your order. Or call 800-657-1100 to order
with a Visa or MasterCard. We also have classic issues of Usagi Yojimbo available,
including the never-reprinted Usagi Color Special editions!